In memory of my mother,
Brenda Rutherford

MEN'S SILENCES

Predicaments in masculinity

Jonathan Rutherford

Routledge

London and New York

First published 1992
by Routledge
11 New Fetter Lane, London EC4P 4EE

Simultaneously published in the USA and Canada
by Routledge
a division of Routledge, Chapman and Hall, Inc.
29 West 35th Street, New York, NY 10001

© 1992 Jonathan Rutherford

Typeset in Baskerville by Michael Mepham, Frome, Somerset
Printed and bound in Great Britain by
Biddles Ltd, Guildford and King's Lynn

British Library Cataloguing in Publication Data
A catalogue record for this book is available from the British
Library.

Library of Congress Cataloging in Publication Data
Rutherford, Jonathan
Men's silences: predicaments in masculinity / by
Jonathan Rutherford.
p. cm. – (Male Orders)
Includes bibliographical references and index.
1. Men – psychology. 2. Masculinity (Psychology)
3. Sex role.
I. Title. II. Series.
HQ1090.R88 1992

155.3'32 – dc20   92–2801
                                        CIP

ISBN 0–415–07543–2 (hbk)
0–415–07544–0 (pbk)

CONTENTS

Preface   ix

1 LEAVING HOME   1

2 THE THEORY AND PRACTICE OF MEN'S
  SEXUAL POLITICS   27

3 DIFFERENCE COMES TO TOWN   63

4 SILENCE, LANGUAGE AND PSYCHOANALYSIS   87

5 NOSTALGIA   123

6 'THIRDNESS' AND THE FATHER'S LOVE   143

7 VIOLENCE AND MASCULINE IDENTITIES   173

Afterword   195
Notes   199
Bibliography   213
Index   222

PREFACE

During the middle years of the 1980s I worked as a freelance journalist writing on issues concerned with men and masculinity. Much of what I wrote owed itself to my previous involvement in Men Against Sexism. I was, however, increasingly frustrated with the theoretical framework I was using. It felt more and more constrictive, a repetition of certain descriptive terms applied to a singular masculinity. Terms such as 'vulnerable', 'fear of intimacy' and 'emotional inarticulacy' were increasingly used without any wider reference to which specific masculine identities they belonged. And even when they hit the right mark, this newly adopted language of masculinity seemed narrow and increasingly morally prescriptive. Similarly, my involvement in socialist politics and the Communist Party was undergoing a testing as the left, as an imagined cultural entity, fell apart. Around this time I became aware of cultural studies and enrolled at the Middlesex Polytechnic on an undergraduate course. It lasted one year and I continued on to do a Phd. Inevitably this book leans towards the theoretical, but this bias also reflects my desire to try and break out of the theoretical impasse within which men's sexual politics and my own writing had been floundering.

I have taken the classic issue in Men Against Sexism (MAS) of feelings and attempted to address it in a theoretical way. I use the term reflexivity, which means self-comprehension. This 'referring back to the subject one is' was the principal strength of the early men's sexual politics, although I would argue that it gave way to a more morally prescriptive personal politics. Another word I use is historicity, by which I mean a self-consciousness of one's own past. Both of these two processes of self-knowledge are not purely intellectual and rational; they have little meaning without feeling. By feeling I mean the language of affect, the putting into words of instinctual life. The failure to achieve this marks a silence, a gap or absence within an individual subjectivity. Hence men's silences come to represent a partial failure of a reflexive understanding of masculine identities; a difficulty in knowing what one is and the processes that make one.

I have used the theories of psychoanalysis, trying to tread a path between the tangled intellectualism of Lacanian thinking and the tendencies towards functionalism which have beset the employment of object relations theory in social and cultural analysis. Psychoanalysis provides a descriptive framework for analysing the psyche; it cannot encompass or explain every facet of subjectivity. I concentrate on the subject's formative relationship with the figures of the parents and how the gendered ordering of mother–son and father–son relationships produce predicaments in masculine identities. By predicaments I mean a disjunction between instinctual life and the mental processes which constitute thought and language. In other words a subject may know of some element of his or her emotional life, without necessarily being able to either think it or speak of it.

My intention is not to come up with any definitive statement on the nature of masculine identities – I concentrate on my own specific class and ethnic constituency of MAS – but to try and open up ways of thinking about men and male identities. Inevitably I have been bound by the limitations of psychoanalysis itself and the lesson of this work for me is that the ability to think beyond contemporary masculine subjectivities involves developing and moving beyond the theoretical frameworks at our disposal. In such an inquiry there is no actual ending and this book has no neat and tied-up conclusion to it.

In the course of writing this book a number of people have helped me, in particular Peter Middleton. I would also like to thank Claire Pajekowska, Mike Dawney and Frances Angela and last of all, but not least, Keir Rutherford.

1

LEAVING HOME

Hello this is your mother.
Are you there?
Are you coming home?
Hello is anybody home?
Well, you don't know me, but I know you,
And I've got a message to give to you.[1]

'Whereof we cannot speak, thereof we must be silent', wrote the philosopher Wittgenstein in conclusion to his first work the *Tractatus Logico-Philosophicus*.[2] The paradox of his comment is in his own assertion that the matters he is silent about – values and religion, 'what is higher'[3] – are what his work is really about. His comment is a fitting description of men's response to their troubled relations with their heterosexuality, their masculine identities and with women. In another context, time and place, Gayaytri Chakravorty Spivak has addressed this issue of cultural silence. She writes: 'Part of our unlearning project is to articulate that ideological formation – by measuring silences, if necessary – into the objects of investigation.'[4] My purpose in this work is to explore what constitutes men's silences and how they play a significant part in the formation of masculine identities.

In this first chapter I want to provide a historical location and cultural context for this project. My search for a beginning has led me back to the sexual politics of the 1970s and the emergence of Men Against Sexism. This small and often erratic movement was a response to the growing strength of feminism within revolutionary libertarian socialism and within the left more generally. The sexual politics of masculinity was an attempt by groups of mainly heterosexual men to articulate their personal confusions and the

1

social and political dilemmas they found themselves in. I am not looking simply for an empirical account of this emergent discourse and practice. I am interested in grasping a specific concern that was a central feature of MAS's attempt to theorise and think through a reflexive and self-comprehending analysis of their masculine identities and male heterosexuality. This was the nature of men's affective relations; the relationship of men's feelings to the language in which men expressed themselves. In other words what often could not be understood and talked about.

It is the cultural critic Walter Benjamin who provides a clue to unveiling these places of silence when he wrote: 'To articulate the past historically does not mean to recognise it "the way it really was" (Ranke). It means to seize hold of a memory as it flashes up at the moment of danger.'[5] Such silences are not the quiet of nature, they are a negative which are culturally and socially determined and hold the potential for meaning and living social relations. They are known and as such have a determining effect upon masculine identities. They contain those 'flashes of danger'; dilemmas, contradictions, difficulties in the relation of the subject to others, which precede linguistic expression and therefore do not find their way into verbal exchange. These silences are the consequences of predicaments. The purpose of this work is to explore what these predicaments are and define what they mean. Men Against Sexism, from its first group in 1971, expressed, and attempted to give voice to, such predicaments. It was a project beset with internal argument about the priorities of men's sexual politics, a conflict that polarised around the two themes of 'men's liberation' and 'anti-sexist, pro-feminism', inevitably creating uncertainty, doubt and ambivalence amongst men, about each other's intentions.

MEN AGAINST SEXISM

The constituency of Men Against Sexism was composed, in the main, of white middle-class and educated men who formed part of a radical urban intelligentsia. Aged from 18 and into their forties they were a minority within a generation and a half who had experienced the major transformations of family structures and capital accumulation as children growing up in the post-war years. The narratives of masculinity which had belonged to their fathers' generation no longer seemed tenable in the years after 1968.

2

Feminism, gay affirmation and a growing cultural diversity dislocated the cultural and inter-personal authority of masculinity and heterosexuality. MAS was an effort to recover a sense of identity and historicity amongst a specific class fraction of men. It was a struggle to make sense out of the disparity between past lives lived within conventional bourgeois and working-class families and a new milieu of sexual politics and political radicalism. The emergence of a sexual politics of masculinity was a reaction to the partial loss of a male cultural monopoly. Feminism didn't so much remove men's powers and privileges as strip them of their legitimating stories.

It is arguable whether this challenge to masculine authority was a part of or precipitated a wider critique of the values and systems of knowledge that underpinned West European culture. In 1979 Jean François Lyotard had defined the post-modern condition as 'incredulity towards metanarratives'.[6] The Enlightenment vision of history as a progressive linear movement towards justice and emancipation no longer seemed a reliable teleological basis for human society. Reason as the source of truth, and rationality as the legitimator of its claims were being eroded. An unquestioned belief in the universal validity of a civilising ideal had lost much of its appeal with the growth of new oppositional voices. In its place was emerging difference, contingency and polyvalence.

Lyotard's critique and the project of French-structuralism and more recently the debates around post-modernity should not be confused with the disruptive impact of feminism.[7] Lyotard himself makes no reference to gender. Nevertheless the two are coincidental. Rosa Braidotti has argued that historical crises in the West's systems of knowledge have occurred when women have played a more prominent role in periods of change.[8] And certainly the constituency of men who inaugurated MAS were subject to both a cultural and gendered dislocation. Through the expansion of higher education and the changing demands of a service and increasingly information-oriented economy they constituted a class fraction whose social power was derived from the acquisition of knowledge and information; resources that the French sociologist Pierre Bourdieu has defined as cultural capital.[9] In class terms they represented the kernel of a modified middle class, what has been termed the professional and managerial class (PMS).[10] Much of the status and cultural authority of the radical intelligentsia who formed part of the PMS was located within the arts and humanities of higher education. But it was just these institutions and sites of intellectual endeavour that were being challenged by the 1970s.

The legacy of the Enlightenment had placed the ideal of a universal civilising progress as central to European culture. It had ensured the class status and cultural authority of intellectuals. But the proliferation and fragmentation of information and knowledge, coupled with the rise of political oppositional voices, undermined its pretensions. MAS were part of a class fraction removed from the centre of the 'establishment'. They held only the vestiges of a historically redundant cultural authority. The contemporary intellectual was increasingly assuming the role of interpreter and translator of information, confined to a narrow and specialised field whose language held no common, let alone universal currency. His or her status had been stripped to his or her value as a holder of information, a commodity in the market place. The constituency of MAS while belonging to the dominant class formation was, in effect, a dominated fraction within it. It was this displacement and the lack of any perceived meaning in their future economic roles that contributed to political disaffection and militancy.

But revolutionary politics was the relatively easy part. It was neither economic deprivation, nor political or social subordination that prompted MAS and its subsequent theoretical endeavours to make sense of masculinity. In the face of women's new assertiveness and collective anger and in the context of domestic recrimination and broken relationships men were faced with a threat to their psychological order. This problem was not an academic one:

> I recognise that something is terribly wrong but I don't really know what to do about it. I'm shaken by the fury and the bitterness. I find it hard to accept that things can be that bad, though I know that at some level they are. Part of me just wants to flee or withdraw. It is as if all long-term heterosexual relationships in our time are doomed.[11]

The problem was not only to find out what was going wrong, but to figure out what to do about it. If their fathers had managed to sustain some degree of masculine status and psychological order through the subordination of their wives and a commitment to a

4

career and paternal duty, this specific generation had erred from that path and weren't sure where to turn.

This transitory state encouraged a reflexive concern with identity. But if the old stories of masculinity seemed defunct, the disjunction between these apparently redundant vocabularies and men's lived experience, broke the continuity of men's historical sense of themselves. In their place were enigmas, gaps, absences and uncertainties. What was lost and what was struggled for was not simply a gender identity or a reformed set of masculine practices but a sense of self and somewhere to belong. Despite its avowed political intent as a pro-feminist movement, the significant dimension of MAS lay in the realm of inter-personal and subjective life and experience. In consequence its cultural practices were shaped in a significant way by inter-generational conflict and contextualised within the nexus of family and parental relationships. Whatever the grand claims of marxism and revolutionary socialist practice may have been, a significant reason for involvement was men's revolt against their own pasts and a search for reflexivity.

These relations shaped the moods, sensibilities and cultural and political identifications of men's sexual politics. These were not necessarily acknowledged and nor did they always find their way into the everyday parlance of 'making sense'. Zygmunt Bauman has argued that the historical memory of a group does not always surface to the level of verbal communication. Nor is it 'necessarily recognised by a group as a particular concept of the past'.[12] Rather it 'finds its expression in the group's proclivities to some rather than other behavioural responses'.[13] While Bauman was discussing the historical memories of class, his argument applies to those experiences of familial structures and their psychodynamics which produce collective logics of gender identity and subject formation in specific class groups. It is these, I would argue, that hold the key to understanding the processes of change and resistance in masculine identities through a period of historical transition. But, from the beginning of MAS, attempts at self-comprehension which did not directly address the power men wielded in patriarchal relations, were met with suspicion and accusations of self-indulgence.

In the early writings of MAS, as heterosexual men attempted to make sense of women's liberation and gay affirmation, there was a sense of their profound unpreparedness for this new cultural

5

and historic moment. The first response was to disown the masculine sensibilities and languages inherited from their fathers' generation. Writing in *Brothers Against Sexism* (1974), one men's group identified the missing element of emotion from their lives.

> As men in the 'Men's Movement' we recognise that we have to retrace our steps and rediscover in ourselves those traits that we have called 'feminine' . . . passivity, warmth, intuition, love, EMOTION. We have to discover in ourselves that which has lain dormant for hundreds of years, that society has obscured and hidden until we act as robots – stiffly, automatically, coldly.[14]

Such concerns were anathema to other men involved in MAS, reflecting the arguments and disagreements over the value of such self-analysis. The next issue of the magazine was subtitled 'The Pig's Last Grunt'. Produced by a men's group in North London it reported on the November 1974 London Conference of MAS which had witnessed a clash between heterosexual men and gay men. 'The conference was too much about men's lib', they wrote, 'the workshop had little to do with confronting sexism as it oppresses women, nothing to do with how we men oppress women.'[15] The consequence of this internal argument about the purpose and priorities of MAS ensured that discussion and debate tended to polarise around a 'men's liberation' position, concerned with 'men's issues' and a pro-feminist politics that eschewed discussions and activities solely addressing masculine identities and sensibilities.

The reflexive concern with men's sexuality and emotional life remained a central tenet of 1970s men's sexual politics, but it was profoundly shaped by this context of argument over its relationship to feminism and men's 'proper' response to it. Ten years later in *The Sexuality of Men* , the book which came out of the 1970s MAS, Andy Metcalf captures this reflexive preoccupation when he wrote:

> If the majority of men are emotionally illiterate then the social construction of gender, of masculinity, creates an absence, a loss, a silence at the heart of men's social relations. Much of this book is concerned with exploring the consequences of modern man's lack of emotional knowledge and language.[16]

Men were caught between the old masculinities of a previous generation and a new cultural, political and sexual context which their inherited vocabularies of masculinity could not fully make sense of. It was a dilemma which determined the central form of MAS activity; the men's group. Modelled on women's conscious-ness-raising groups, it enabled small numbers of men collectively to explore areas of their lives previously considered taboo subjects in male company. Sexual relations, homophobia, homosexuality, friendship between men, childcare as well as wider political ques-tions relating to sexuality and feminism were common topics. These were subjects reflecting the preoccupation with psychologi-cal well-being and inter-personal relationships. Issues of class and ethnicity and their impact upon masculinity were not significant themes in this practice. The primary concern was a search for an interior realm of feeling in male subjectivity and a language with which to represent it.[17] A concern which itself was determined by the ethnicity and class nature of the MAS constituency.

In the summer of 1978 *Achilles Heel*, 'a magazine of men's politics', made its appearance. Its collective defined themselves as a group of socialist men who had been involved in men's groups and men's politics 'for some time'. The first issue had articles on men's health and sexuality and a long essay on masculinity and fascism. It was the first forum in MAS to provide for theoretical discussion and as such managed to rise above the polarised divi-sion between men's liberation and anti-sexism that had succeeded in establishing a climate of moralism and antagonism. Despite only running to six issues (the last was a double issue 6/7), its themes, the subjects it covered and its priorities drew a disparity of MAS positions and practices into a coherent, if brief, collective identity. Despite opposition to it and claims that it was not representative of anti-sexist politics, it did signify the 'moment' of MAS in the 1970s.

I can recall the appearance of this first issue, when I was 21. It was a moment of excitement and an acknowledgement of many of my own pressing questions about my sexuality and masculine identity. At the time I was involved in running a free school and had a commitment to anarchist politics. But I was very careful to keep separate my own sexual and emotional confusions. I kept these hidden behind a sophisticated political intellect and much deft social manoeuvring. But even these could not ensure the sustaining of my sense of self in an environment where a lot of the rules were being changed or discarded. A time of great excitement was also a time of intense anxiety. In the task of making new cultural forms I was struggling with an identity I sought to erase. While sexual politics was releasing people from old inhibitions, oppressions and denials, it was often heterosexual men who were perceived as the cause of them. There always existed for me an attendant fear of an impending catastrophe of shame and humiliation. It was a time, in retrospect, unequalled in its creative and political activity and unequalled in personal isolation.

Like a sizeable minority of other men who came into contact with it, the women's liberation movement held a great appeal. It had begun to speak a language of private life, making links between our affective relations and the public world of institutions and power. In some indefinable sense it offered us a key to understanding ourselves. It spoke for something that I wanted, too, not in an imperialistic sense, although that of course existed, but a new sense of identity. In a time of radical questioning and the discarding of inherited attitudes and conventions, women's liberation was constituting new identities and a sense of belonging. For many men involved in revolutionary politics during this period, the meteoric and passionate rise of feminism and the heartfelt pleasures women found in its solidarities only served to reinforce feelings of personal isolation. In discarding our own pasts men seemed unable to create new places of belonging. So often it was women who were used, to provide and construct these emotional homes. Women's growing sense of autonomy only reinforced men's feelings of lack and insecurity. To make matters more difficult, its challenge to the conventional practices and definitions of political activity undermined men's one escape route, highlighting our own uneasiness with the version of class politics we espoused. Feminism produced this unenviable ambivalence in its male supporters. What we wanted and supported was what was continually threatening to undermine us. It lent itself to something of a religious moralism tainted by masochism.

While we argued that our socialist political activity and the forms of organisation we undertook should pre-figure the utopian society we wanted, men and masculinity always seemed to be exempt from the process of change. It was always with someone else or somewhere else that the problem or issue was located. This sense of disconnection between men's personal lives and the public world became the central issue in the emergent reflexive politics of masculinity. As one man, involved in the Red Therapy group, commented, 'I became aware that in some way I was missing something . . . that I had lost something. Something emotional. A woman I really depended on left me – saying at one point that she felt that, "there was nothing there".'[18] And Vic Seidler, writing in *Achilles Heel* attempted to conceptualise this idea of emptiness: 'As men we are often brought up to be strangers to ourselves. We experience little connection with our feelings and emotions.'[19] The public world of politics acted as a form of flight from a private life that seemed awkward and uncontrollable. But after the rushing about and the business was over, it was a world experienced as empty and homeless.

The language of affective relations: expressions of comfort, pleasure, pain and vulnerability found little room in our brave new worlds. Instead they were confined to conventional childhoods and suppressed by the moralistic imperative of building a socialist society. If we were in revolt against our parents' generation and the social order they were part of, if we condemned them for their deceitful and hypocritical lives, then the child they had produced had to be destroyed as well. The boys we had been, their pleasures and fantasies as well as their fears and anxieties were suppressed. This form of intra-subjective attack structured the psychodynamic life of masculinity, continually undermining its capacity to change and sustain men emotionally. It was an internal war of attrition that lent a strenuous intensity to men's politics. Feminism undermined this flight from internal reality. It didn't just tug the radical carpet from beneath men – suddenly the struggle had moved elsewhere and we weren't invited – it forced men into some degree of self-reflection. What men discovered was the lack of any vocabulary for making sense of this new reflexive concern with our sexuality and masculine identities. And despite our prominence in the public world, there was a lack of any inter-personal relationships which could have sustained such a project.

This disparity between men's lived relations and their inherited languages of masculinity is described by Andrew Tolson in his account of a men's group:

> We began to discover that we had no language of feeling. We were trapped in public, specialised languages of work, learned in universities or factories, which acted as a shield

against deeper emotional solidarities. When we talked about ourselves and our experiences these would be presented through the public languages in abstract formal ways. The factory manager actually talked about himself as if he functioned like a machine. The student–philosopher spoke about his 'bad faith' and his struggle to be 'authentic'. And the man on the dole, in this context kept silent – and was perceived to be incoherent, swept along by a fluid introspective experience.[20]

While women were struggling to escape the private world of domesticity, childcare and the management of relationships, men were struggling to come to terms with them. This crossing of the threshold betwen inner and outer was addressed by Paul Atkinson, an original member of the *Achilles Heel* collective:

for women feminism has been about recognising the way women have been invisible in, and excluded from, the male order . . . for men there is a complementary problem of how we develop a new relationship with all sides of life which tend to be invisible and unspoken of, to do with the emotional, hidden inner sides of life.[21]

The logic of men's support for feminism took them into the unfamiliar cultural terrain of the private. The primacy of the picket line and the duplicator gave way to looking after children, dealing with personal relationships and confronting men's emotional dependency upon women. It was a transition that undermined the public roles and languages that propped up men's masculine identities. The further men moved into this sphere the greater became their sense of insecurity. And with it, the realisation of just how tenuous men's sense of self was.

While the counter-culture of personal politics and its validation of anti-sexism acted as a safety net, outside its narrow confines, the limited emotional and inter-personal resources of a masculinity without its external structures of support threw many individual men into a crisis. What comes through in MAS writing on role reversal and accounts of men's changing masculine identities is a sense of unease and disturbance which is never quite articulated.[22] 'I am an enraged house husband' wrote one man, 'caught in what is a woman's web of dilemma having to do housework and hating it. My rage is born from frustration and beats angrily in my breast bursting to get out in a scream.'[23] This passionate fury, far from being 'a woman's web of dilemma' is that of a man coming crashing up against himself and without the means to make sense of the impact.

STRUCTURES OF FEELING

It was the late Raymond Williams who provided a framework for the cultural analysis of this disjunction between lived experience and available vocabularies. In his essay 'Structures of Feeling', Williams addressed the emergence of new social groups and cultural identities and their expression through oppositional artistic practice. Williams insisted that the alternative to the hegemonic cultural discourses and language that suppressed them was not a silence of the oppressed and marginalised but, 'a kind of feeling and thinking which is indeed social and material, but each in an embryonic phase before it becomes fully articulate and defined exchange'.[24] Such a structure of feeling exists at 'the very edge of semantic availability'.[25] Williams is describing a pre-formation: 'what is not fully articulated, all that comes through as disturbance, tension, blockage, emotional trouble',[26] which precedes actual cultural practice and identity. Such an analysis can be applied to MAS and the emergence of new masculine identities and sensibilities that had not yet found the means to articulate their lived relations.

This threshold between public and private, the rational and the emotional is historically and culturally determined. Men's 'emotional inarticulacy' represents a specific time and place where changing social relations redefine this threshold and the determining conditions of masculine identities. Men Against Sexism represented the particularly acute experience of a class fraction struggling with its changing economic role and cultural identity. Many men were confronted with their inability to live out these new material, sexual and personal relations. Men's use of language in effect externalised masculine identity; self-descriptions were based on public roles and rational criteria which denied the means for self-comprehension. It was this difficulty that characterised the MAS structure of feeling, creating specific social moods and forms of cultural receptivity that underlay its forms of political and cultural identification. This difficulty in processing men's affective relations became prominent in men's lives because of the new

11

significance attached to the realm of personal and sexual life. In the process it gave rise to a new preoccupation and search for a descriptive language.

Williams's structure of feeling does not attempt to place emotion and actual feelings in a realm above language: 'not feeling against thought, but thought as felt and feeling as thought'.[27] Feelings are a product of language, itself a practice determined by social relations. The task is to identify what social forms and relations produce such structures of feelings. On Williams's own terms, as a marxist and a materialist, his concept remains ungrounded and idealistic. Similar to Baumann's concept of historical memory, it remains without a place in our subjectivity and devoid of its determining effects. Williams does, however, offer a clue as to the originating cultural logic of these structures of feeling, by referring to their specific generational character: 'In spite of substantial and at some levels decisive continuities in grammar and vocabulary, no generation speaks quite the same language as its predecessors'.[28] And, as Peter Middleton points out in his essay 'Why Structure Feeling' (Middleton 1989), Williams is concerned with emotion and not just with cultural representations. Its use as a tool of cultural analysis is dependent upon grounding it within social forms and institutions that mark the reproduction of generations and the changing use of language over time. Williams's work did not address the sphere of reproductive relations, but the logic of his structure of feeling is to locate it within the changing practices and ideologies of the family; in particular within an analysis which encompasses the psychodynamics of language and subject formation. The most significant attempts within MAS at a reflexive analysis of masculinity addressed this site, exploring the disjunction between men's feelings and language and how it effected male subjectivity.

MUM, DAD AND THE FAMILY: STRUCTURING MOODS AND FEELINGS

So the place to begin this reflexive project is our childhood home. And my departure begins in the spirit of June Jordan's comment: 'But everybody needs a home so at least you can have some place to leave which is where most folks will say you must be coming from'.[29] Each one of us holds different memories of our childhood, each has different experiences, but the nexus of gender relations and ideologies of parenting that constituted the middle-class and upper-working-class families of the post-war period produced its own collective experience that has shaped our subjectivity in similar ways. These gave the family its particular socio-psychological form and its attendant processes of socialisation. Men's masculinities are marked by their own private idiosyncrasies, but gender identity is a social and shared set of identifications shaped by class and ethnicity. Men from similar backgrounds share objects of identification as infants and boys. Such objects may be people, aspects of people, even the possibility of a person's presence. They can also be symbols and social processes and values. These are taken in to form our subjectivity and contribute to our sense of who we are and our relationship to others. In this context of the formation of self and gender identity, the primary objects internalised are the processes of parental care and the inter-personal logic of familial relations. These form the preconditions for future social and sexual identifications and determine the idiom of our existence.

It is to this paradigm of the social and psychological relations within the family that we can account for the structures of feeling that preceded the actual cultural practice and political articulation of MAS. Men's attempts to redefine their masculinities were not just the consequence of the synchronic relations they found themselves in, but a history of these relations. Feminism, gay affirmation and the culture of libertarian socialism had a precipitous effect in undermining masculine presumptions, but once in effect they only highlighted the gaps, absences and discontinuities in men's consciousness. This turn to subjectivity and identity demanded a project of historicity; to make a return journey home in order to make sense of the present. It was a journey filled with unease for so much in the present, one's political espousals and moral rhetoric, depended upon the denial of its familiarity. It is the path that I want to follow. And I want to do so through the figures of our parents. It seems a rather narrow opening gambit given the complex determinations of identity, but it will yield a great deal in time.

Our fathers

One man, commenting upon his experience of his parents, in a men's group in 1982, provides a powerful image of the ambivalence of gendered relations in the middle-class family of the 1950s.

> My Dad's very protective of my Mum and acts the man all the time. She does all the cooking, runs the house. She does everything for him and then treats him as though he's fully in control of everything and looks to him to make decisions. He's like a figurehead. It's a very empty role. He always puts his arm about her and comforts her, by telling her his problems.[30]

This image of the father, divested of his authority, but still playing out his role as the head of the household, is a significant figure in men's recollections of family life.[31] Invariably he was a man his son did not know and could not communicate with.

> When I think of my dad I am overwhelmed with questions; about his own life, but also about my own. On the surface our life together seemed like a transitory moment. Like we were passing through the same family on separate journeys. But below the surface he's left me with deep sorrow and a sense of loss.[32]

He was a strange paradox, often distant and preoccupied, he was at once an oppressive presence and an absence that could never be concretely grasped.

> I remember writing an essay when I first started school: 'what do you want to be?' It was everything that he was or had been. Yet I didn't really want that, it was the only model I had. The only model I had was nothing really. When I realised that my dad had nothing to offer me, he wasn't offering me any direction or any particular role, then I really did despise him.[33]

So much ambivalence from sons for their fathers, almost an unrequited love that left its mark in remorse and loathing.

In her survey of men's attitudes to their gender identities, published in 1985, Anna Ford noted: 'The commonest cause of anxiety for many fathers, it seems, is the lack of definition of that role . . . many men told me that they had no proper guidelines to go by and few clues to get it right.'[34] Unlike motherhood, the legacy of ambivalent paternity bequeaths fatherhood with the continual fear of its own redundancy. Masculinity is overly dependent for its coherence upon external public discourses. In consequence, men will experience periods of social and cultural transition as a disturbance to their identities. Changes in the ideology and structure of family life similarly precipitate men into a state of uncertainty in their relationship to the private sphere.

The life of men in the post-war years was overshadowed by the war and National Service. Public representations of masculinity conjured up an image of a resourceful, strong and brave man with the emphasis upon his instrumental role. Expressive feelings were to be repressed. The rugged integrity of the British Army officer was the staple diet of popular fiction during the 1950s. Lynne Segal has noted that: 'The hero is a man untrammelled by the everyday ties and responsibilities of sexual relationships and family'.[35] But such representations made an uneasy pact with peacetime. The duty of war was replaced by a duty to career, and service to the nation became service to the family. This transition into a new domesticity left a significant mark upon men who could no longer live up to the legitimating representations of a soldiering masculinity.

As the family became the new ideological imperative, women and fatherhood were claiming men and they were ill-prepared for the role. Masculinity and paternity became the unspoken theme of many Hollywood Westerns. Alan Ladd as *Shane* (George Stevens 1953) allegorised the decline and death of undomesticated masculinity. And John Ford's Westerns, playing out their oedipal dramas of fathers and sons, addressed a cultural anxiety about the absent father and the power of the mother (*Rio Grande* 1950). In his famous *The Searchers* (1956) Ethan Edwards (John Wayne) a violent and racist enigma, struggles to come to terms with a society no longer organised around war. A search personified in his attempts to regain a sense of home and family through regaining his young niece, abducted by Comanche Indians. War had profoundly shaped men's lives and the move to peace was played out in the awkward struggles around domesticity and fatherhood. In this country the popular success of John Osborne's *Look Back in Anger* (1956) revealed the depth of men's confusion and anger over these new social expectations.

'No there is nothing for it, me boy, but to let yourself be butchered by the women.'[36] Jimmy Porter's misogynistic and venomous monologues attacked every bourgeois convention and value. But it was in his wife Alison that he perceived the fate of the country: soft, passified and feminine. Osborne depicted a masculinity shorn of its empire and devoid of a role, a sharpened intellect that attacked the moral flabbiness of post-war culture. It was a wail of pathos for the lot of men, robbed of their heroic and virile heritage, abandoned to women and without a cause to fight for. Jimmy Porter's unrelenting assaults upon his wife finally succeed in breaking down her impassivity '. . . this is what he wanted from me'. She cries, 'Don't you see! I'm in the mud at last! I'm grovelling! I'm crawling.' But in his moment of victory he is not free. Instead he makes a desperate attempt to clear up the emotional devastation he has caused, scurrying back into the cosy world of bears and squirrels that he fought so hard to be rid of.

The problem wasn't with women and their supposed moral feebleness, it lay in men's own masculinity; a gender identity battling against its own suppressed desires and emotions. Because such feelings were the antithesis of what being a man meant, they were projected onto women. Just as in Ford's Westerns, women came to carry the burden of men's emotional lives. Men needed women to speak that part of themselves that was excluded from representations of masculinity: love, fear, need and intimacy. These were elements of men's lives that were evacuated as masculinity defined itself through its culturally constructed difference from femininity. It was an ambivalence which, though unacknowledged, was played out with great intensity during the post-war years, as society sought to establish a peacetime settlement.[37]

The post-war boom was based upon the emergence of a new service-oriented consumer capitalism and the family was targeted as the prime site for the consumption of goods and services. Women were being encouraged back into the home as new ideologies of femininity and motherhood superseded the war-time image of the independent working woman. The 1950s became an era of reproduction, represented by the growth of the middle-class suburbs; grey-flannelled fathers and mothers busy in the kitchen, attentive to their child-centred family. Yet this solidity was only an appearance. Sexual relationships and marriages were beset with conflicts and problems. 'The divorce rate soared. . . . The solid family that was intent on reproduction was breaking apart.'[38] Public representations of men's role in the family showed a father attentive to his children, aware of his wife and intent upon maintaining the security of his dependants. After a decade of absence, this new paterfamilias was an attempt to reconstruct paternal authority and the social order. Yet men's contribution to family and childcare and to housework remained minimal.[39]

The era had inherited the pre-war ethic of the distant father and housebound mother. But now social expectations in the middle classes supposed him to be involved – he wasn't. The advice books on baby and childcare contributed to this ambivalence about the paternal role. Writing in his widely influential manual *Baby and Child Care* (1958), Benjamin Spock revised his earlier belief that a father's sole function was to support his wife in motherhood.

> Some fathers have been brought up to think that the care of babies and children is the mother's job entirely. But a man can be a warm father and a real man at the same time. . . . The time to begin being a real father is at the start. It is easiest then. The father and mother can learn together.

But this paean to companionate marriage is hastily qualified by Spock. 'Of course, I don't mean that the father has to give just as many bottles or change just as many diapers as the mother. But it is fine to do these things occasionally.' As Osborne's depiction of Jimmy Porter's masculinity revealed, contradictions and ambivalence abound.

While Spock didn't recognise it then, his writing touched upon the effect dominant masculine identities had upon men's relationship to the private sphere of family life. Addressing the father's role in childbirth, Spock paints a poignant picture of a man cut off from his family and very much alone.

> He helps to get his wife to hospital, where there are dozens of people to take care of her. Then he's really alone, with nothing to do outside working hours. He can sit in the waiting room with some old magazines and worry about how labour is going, or he can go to his unbelievably lonely home. It's no wonder that a man may take this occasion to drink in company at a bar.

The promise of masculinity was the relations and solidarities of the world of work. And with them came the relative degrees of privilege and power bestowed by class and race. But even for the white middle-class men who were to become many of our fathers, this alone could not sustain them, however much it validated their masculinities. It served to both separate them from the sphere of domestic, 'feminine' work, but also to cut them off from the world of affective relations, even to separate them from their own bodies. This threshold between inner and outer was a site of intense struggle and friction, for men could not live with work alone, yet nor could they remain for long in the private world of the family without feeling a sense of identity loss and invalidation. The struggle to assert paternal authority, even the attempt to recreate patriarchal sovereign authority, continually floundered in this ambivalence. An ambivalence that only increased with the growth of leisure in the home, and family-centred consumption.

This briefest of sketches suggests something of what these men's sons inherited. The father's authority was no longer enshrined within patriarchal structures. He could not exist outside or above family affective relations. Yet nor could he live within them. It was a contradiction, enhanced by economic and cultural changes that marked a transitional change in men's power over women. A change that shifted authority from the sovereign realm of men's bodies and individual actions and into the realm of culturally constructed meanings, produced through representations, ideologies and discourse. In consequence a father bequeathed to future generations the dread of his own personal redundancy, his desire to be the ideal father figure, frustrated by contemporary social formations. Within the emotional and psychological economy of the household, with his need for his wife to speak for and mediate his affective relations, he could be reduced to an emotional par with the children. A dependant on the mother dressed up as her protector; not unlike his own son. In a poem about his father, Paul Durcan wrote:

> The two little boys at the back of the bus,
> You and I.
> Where would we have been
> Without my mother?[40]

This failure to develop an internal world within familial relations and the relative absence of affective relations in the outside world of work, left many men marooned on the threshold, neither in nor out, undermining both their personal authority and their ability to parent.

Scanning the output of writing from *Men Against Sexism*,[41] there is a preoccupation with this paternal legacy. From about the mid-1980s, it translated itself into the mainstream with numerous books on fatherhood.[42] There are accounts of men's relationships

18

with their fathers and their attempts at new styles of parenting, sharing and role-reversal. There are descriptions of men's relationships with children and the organising of crêches, depicting the desire to get closer to a sphere of life men had been absent from. This legacy of failed paternity coupled with the cultural assertion of women over the previous decade produced a masculinity that shifted its identity further across the threshold into the realm of domesticity. This aspiration for greater involvement in the emotional life of the family, if not in actual house work, characterised middle-class masculinities in the latter part of the 1980s. Its immediate history is to be found in the contradictory and ambivalent struggles around paternity of these men's fathers in the 1950s. But it would be a mistake to explain this trend solely through the father–son relationship. MAS writing has often called up anecdotal evidence to suggest the son's masculinity is solely derived through his father's role and sensibility. Academic research has also concentrated upon the father–son relationship as the primary conveyor of masculinity across generations. Judy Blendis, for example, argues that the father's more instrumental outlook upon life has precipitated the son's expressivity and 'softness'.[43] This approach tends to leave out the relational nature of identity. Masculinity is produced in relation to femininity, it is also determined by race and class, as well as generational and regional variations. But particularly, in this context of inter-personal family relationships, what is startling is the omission within men's sexual politics of the mother. She is passed over in silence.

Our mothers

Men who proclaimed a pro-feminist politics in the 1970s were wary of discussing such a contentious subject as motherhood. The accusation of misogyny was standard armour in the sexual moralism that was becoming a part of men's sexual politics. It created its own policing logic, prohibiting discussion that might reflect badly upon women.

> We didn't want to be thought of as sexist so we watched ourselves very carefully . . . it might have been healthier, if we'd owned up much more to our sexist thoughts and feelings. . . . We would have had to admit all the ways we had been brought up to hate, despise and loathe women.[44]

Men's silence around their mothers was also determined by perceptions of that relationship. Mothers had provided a mediating role within the family, their conflict management often protecting their son from his father. 'I always talked to my mother first to size up the ground. She was always preparing the ground. She'd probably even go and find out what my father thought and do it for me.'[45] Mother was an ally against the unpredictable figure of the father. She provided the comfort for her son's disillusion in him, the confidante who understood the feminised sensibilities of her son. It was this perception of men's closeness to their mothers and their affiliation to her plight as economically powerless, that contributed to her son's revolt against the patriarchy. How many men carried her torch, their anti-sexism an attempt to rescue her love from the crassness and emotional aridity of their father?

This identification with the mother proved to be a far from positive one as men began to explore their psyches. Small numbers of men began to move into groups using psychotherapeutic techniques. This move into therapy seemed a logical progression on from consciousness-raising groups, providing the space for psychological work of an intense nature. The absence of mother from the critical discourse of men's sexual politics ended, often abruptly, with the advent of this practice.

> For me somewhere at the bottom of things living with Ellen brought up a lot of childhood feelings about my mother. They had a similar atmosphere for me, an atmosphere of penetration and control over domestic life. Ellen's being invaded and surrounded me. She seemed to have a similar relationship with her body – her periods, shitting and illness. The same disgust that I'd somehow acquired for my mother's physical presence came up with Ellen.[46]

Far from revealing a companion and ally, psychotherapy began to uncover, 'at the bottom of things' a maternal fantasy that locked men into a contradictory longing for her and a vehement struggle to be free of her. Impingement, control and invasion, the language of men's dread and hatred of the mother reared its head. It's not surprising that descriptive passages, like the previous one, were very rare in MAS literature. Men's silence around their mothers suggested something more than a denial of these unspoken feelings. Men's perception of their mothers was idealised or out of focus for their attachment to this maternal fantasy precluded a real

20

relationship with an actual woman. At an unconscious level, masculinity was organised around sustaining this fantasy of the mother. It maintained an attachment that ensured her presence, but it ensured a dependency upon her that fuelled an intense hatred. Whether idealised or hated, mothers were an extremely uncomfortable subject to grapple with – particularly for a group of men supposedly opposed to misogyny and the everyday sexism that denigrated women.

Men's preoccupation with the legacy of the absent father complemented the cultural discourses that associated men's masculinity with the inherited sensibilities and languages of their fathers. The experience of partial loss and transition inaugurated by economic and cultural change inevitably invoked an attempt to reconstruct masculine identities in relation to the father. MAS tended towards an overevaluation of the father, a concern which was played out in the numerous personal accounts of being and becoming a father. In this MAS was part of a wider social redefinition of fatherhood which sought to re-establish a paternal authority within the family, albeit different to previous historical models. In this respect, it remained within the cultural logic of patriarchal relations, intent upon inventing masculine identities appropriate to the social changes. But where MAS broke with this logic was in the recognition, by a small but growing number of men, of the significance of the mother in the formation of masculine identities. The belief that the psychodynamics of masculinity was determined by the figure of the father was reversed by arguing that he was a defensive figure, protecting masculinity from the threat of the mother and her symbolic equivalents. The silence that surrounded her presence institutionalised the logic of patriarchal relations. It maintained the myth that the male subject is ontologically for himself and his masculinity derived from his own being and authority. The psychotherapeutic practices of small groups in MAS revealed that men's historicity began with women, with the mother. And this fact was a profound influence upon the formation of men's subjectivity and masculine identities.

The cultural redefining of paternal power and masculine authority in the post-war period could be witnessed in the intensification of ideologies of motherhood. The post-war era produced a growing institutionalisation of women and children into a dyadic bond in service to the child's psychic well-being.

Barbera Ehrenreich and Deirdre English remark, with irony, on the experts' advice to mothers in this period. 'She instinctively needed her child as much as her child needed her. She would avoid outside commitments so as not to "miss" a fascinating stage of development, or "deprive" herself of a rewarding phase of motherhood.'[47]

Women became the objects of a new discourse of child psychological development that served to bind together women and children, further privatising childcare and placing a heavy burden of isolation on women. While the figure of the father was enhanced through appeals to authority, order and structure, motherhood was being regulated through a psychological discourse. Cultural commentary on the role of women as mothers mobilised the psychoanalytic theories of the British school of object relations. D.W. Winnicott, in a series of broadcasts during 1944 and in popular books, introduced his British audience to the work of Melanie Klein. The Kleinian child was dependent upon the mother for his or her psychological development and well-being. The Freudian emphasis on innate libidinal drives moving the infant through various stages of psychological development implied that, left to his or her own devices, the infant would achieve maturation. Object relations stressed the centrality of the environmental set-up in the well-being of the infant and childhood. And particularly, in Winnicott's phrase, 'good enough' mothering.

This new popular discourse on child rearing emphasised a child-centred, need-oriented approach that placed a new emphasis upon women's propensity to mother. John Bowlby was propounding his theory of human attachment in which infants' and children's experiences of loss and separation from the mother was central to their psychological health. His work with children in institutions during the 1940s led him to postulate his idea of maternal deprivation. After the war his concept began to play a significant role justifying the Government initiative to push women out of work and woo them back into the home. The popularising of this psychoanalytic work on the mother–child relationship in the ideological conjuncture of the post-war reconstitution of the family, effectively mobilised it into endorsing a woman's role as mother and housewife. In such a climate psychoanalytic theory served to psychopathologise motherhood, providing new grounds for the condemnation of 'bad mothers'. To neglect her child could lead to its permanent psychological damage; a suitable yardstick for the regulation of women in motherhood. No longer was motherhood a task of managing resources and running a household. The new discourse of child development, enshrined in the early welfare state, argued that children had psyches and that demanded something extra from women. Motherhood now expected women to provide empathy and primary identification with their infants, experiencing them as continuations of their own selves.

This era of reproduction fixed women as mothers, freezing them into domesticity.[48] Maternal deprivation became the cause of every conceivable social problem and personality disorder. It was an obsessive concern with the mother–child relationship that inevitably produced its own moral panics. Research in the United States began to claim that mothers were overprotecting their children and failing to allow them to separate.[49] The image of the doting, smothering mother increased masculine anxiety, already beset by the ambivalence of its paternal role. And with the rise of middle-class youthful rebellion at the end of the 1950s, this image merged with the icon of the dutiful mother to produce a motif of social conformity; the warped and stifling world of bourgeois domesticity.

The figure of the mother in the nuclear family was its significant psychological principle. Such an element in a developing cultural formation was not fixed; women mothered in a disparity of ways under a diversity of conditions. Nevertheless, it constituted a social and institutional fact. Its cultural significance was born out in the revolt of its own children. In the words of R.D. Laing, writing in 1967, the bourgeois family existed: 'to create one-dimensional man: to promote respect, conformity and obedience: to con children out of play: to induce a fear of failure: to promote a respect for work; to promote a respect for respectability'.[50] It wasn't the father's ambivalence which became the main target of this youthful revolt. It was women's failings as mothers, their own pain and relational difficulties; too warm or too cold, too cloying or too restrictive, her petty tyranny or her ineffective platitudes. These drip out of the prison house of motherhood to epitomise the corrupt and hypocritical bourgeois conformity of the post-war years. Misogyny fuelled the angry young man of the 1950s and a decade later it had a determining effect upon the language of revolt in the counter-culture of the 1960s. Repressed, silenced, long suffering, the mother of the 1950s emerged as a figure of blame and contempt.

MAS came out of a counter-culture schooled in such anti-family rhetoric. Criticism or analysis of the institution of motherhood was almost impossible without a misogynistic reception. Within feminism discussion of motherhood was subject to its own cautious parameters, which excluded recognition of women's power over children and the violence and mental cruelty that mothers were capable of handing out to their offspring.

> Questioning the maternal function at times touches upon heresy for me . . . I can't tolerate hatred of the mother; nevertheless, I find it vital to attack the maternal function. But I am distrustful because I suspect the vast apparatus of hatred of the Mother of being one of the most prodigious and effective bastions of misogyny.[51]

Here was a key to understanding the formation of masculine identities. But it had been placed out of bounds through a mixture of political caution and internal moral policing.

This brief sketch of the ideologies of parenting and familial relations depicts the centrality of a mother/child culture within the middle-class home. It was a culture that determined affective relations. In contrast the father was a relatively peripheral figure. What is significant in the psychodynamic formation of masculinity is less the public world and language of the father, but the communications between the mother and child. Communications that originate in the pre-verbal period of life and are defined by the idiom of touch, gesture and gaze. It is from this realm of the pre-oedipal period of life that the fantasy of the mother emerges into MAS's critical discourse of masculinity. It is a fantasy of an ontological longing for home and equally a measure of men's failure to achieve independence and a sense of their own belonging. The mother–son relationship plays a central role shaping the oedipus complex and the male infant's entry into speech, language and the embodiment of his gendered identity. It is a relationship which creates the space in which the external processes of language and cultural representations meet the internal instinctual processes which do not belong to speech. The father may come to symbolise the external world of culture, gender identity and language, as its patriarchal representative, but the process of individuation and becoming a separate human being belongs in

24

the pre-linguistic world of the mother. It is in this process that the idiom of subjectivity is determined in the gendered acquisition of language.

LEAVING HOME

Raymond Williams's 'Structure of Feeling' (1977) enables us to locate the origins of a men's silence in the psychodynamics of family life and the pre-oedipal mother–child relationship. It is here that the relationship between inner psychic life and the external world is formed creating the foundation for the relationship between feeling and language. MAS's initial expression of the disjunction between men's use of words and their feelings produced an attempt to contest the vocabularies of hegemonic masculinities. Silence around the mother was the point at which reflexivity found its limit. It is the place which marks the edge of semantic formation in self-descriptions of masculinity. This limit is to be found in the communicative relations of the mother–child culture and the way it is retrospectively structured into masculinity through the function of the father in the oedipus complex. There is nothing historically new or unique to this process. But it became enhanced by the post-war reconstituting of the privatised nuclear family, and took on a cultural significance that came into social effect in the 1970s and later, in different ways, in the 1980s.

Williams's concept of a structure of feeling enables us to give it an historical context, showing how psychodynamic processes, excluded from linguistic representation, play a determining role in cultural formation and identities. Because Williams insists on the cognitive nature of these forms of feeling and mood – 'We are talking about . . . affective elements of consciousness and relationships: not feeling against thought, but thought as felt and feeling as thought . . .' [52] – he enables us to address the social effect of a space which marks the relationship between the interior psychic realm and the external world of objects and language. A space which is individual but which is determined by wider structures of gender relations and so a social form.

MAS's recognition of the disjunction between language and feeling created an opening for the exploration of male subjectivity. It is a disjunction that emerges into the social as a structure of feeling, a non-linguistic, though cognitive effect that precedes the semantic articulation of a new cultural formation. MAS and its various crises of masculinity represented this transition from a structure of feeling into a cultural practice of reflexivity. While its political character, rooted in its relations with feminism and gay liberation, was shaped by men's arguing the case for women's liberation and gay affirmation, its reflexive element attempted to evaluate men's own lived experiences by tracing them through men's consciousness of their own pasts. Such a project drew upon feminism and its new languages and practices but these alone could only highlight the gaps and silences, not bring them into signification. That demanded something more, something of men's own creating and it was to this end that numbers of men began turning to therapy. It was the beginning of a recognition that to leave behind the vestiges of an old way of life one had to be able to make a new one. Such a process was not about severing the past from the present, but knowing it and so being able to move beyond it.

In the next chapter I want to examine how MAS made theoretical sense of its reflexive project and how it attempted to develop a description of this arena of silence that was marking out the limits of change in masculine identities.

2

THE THEORY AND PRACTICE
OF MEN'S SEXUAL POLITICS

INTRODUCTION: THERAPY AND POLITICS

The turn to therapy was not simply a part of the post-1968 revolutionary politics. It was a response to the failure of its utopian visions.[1] I have already argued that it was neither economic deprivation nor political subordination that prompted MAS into a reflexive exploration of men's masculine identities. It was precipitated by men who faced a threat to their psychological order. This personal dimension led a significant minority of men involved in MAS into therapy. This move had its own historical precursors in the work of Wilhelm Reich, Herbert Marcuse and Erich Fromm, as well as R.D. Laing's more contemporary attempts to bring together politics and psychoanalysis.[2] They provided a theoretical basis and a legitimation for introspection and self-analysis: 'We were open to the insights of psychoanalysis but also felt the significance of the breaks with the Freudian patriarchal and intellectualist tradition being made in what was loosely called the "growth movement"'.[3] It was a fairly pragmatic and non-dogmatic attempt to link men's political practice with a psychotherapeutic analysis of their subjectivities. 'Therapy is for fighting internalized capitalist ideology', wrote the Red Therapy collective in their pamphlet (*Red Therapy* 1978). It was a recognition of the complex ways individuals are held within unproductive and often destructive social relations. In this view, sheer masculine will and the odd barricade, far from heralding a new dawn, was only going to continue contributing to hierarchies of oppression.

It seemed, however, much easier to provide intellectual blueprints of political strategies and practices than to carry them out. That is the nature of politics. But in this context the blueprints

27

applied to personal relationships and modes of living, not just detached analyses of objective class forces.

> Some of us had been active in libertarian politics and the Women's Movement and had had experiences of conscious-ness-raising groups, collective living, personal politics – trying to change our lives.
> We wanted to work together politically in non-hierarchical ways, find some kind of sexual freedom and non-oppressive relationships between men and women and adults and children, etc.
> I think we found it was ALL HARDER THAN WE THOUGHT – that we couldn't somehow will ourselves to be liberated and wake-up the next morning feeling wonderfully collective, non-jealous, confident, non-competitive etc. We couldn't suddenly change the patterns of a lifetime which we had been forced to conform to in this society.
> The changes had to take place at a deeper level than just intellectual and political understanding. We had to go back into our pasts, unlearn our conditioning, break out of the blocks that had been instilled in us since childhood.[4]

The relationship between therapy and politics proved a hard one to reconcile: 'At the time it was manic politics and manic therapy with little connection between the two.'[5] The attempt to bring together the public and the private and explore the interactions between the psychodynamics of men's lives and their public roles began to founder on the divide. Consequently, a number of those involved in Red Therapy withdrew from the revolutionary organisations they had been active in. Therapy was challenging the puritanism and self-sacrifice, the moralism and self-denial that fuelled much of the political activism of the time. Combined with the feminist challenge to their practices and cultures, the organisations of the far left were becoming anachronisms in the light of their own rhetoric of liberation and equality.[6]

THE TURN TO PSYCHOANALYSIS

By the mid-1970s working-class militancy was in decline and the left was entering a political crisis. The forebodings of a major economic recession, a growing swing to the right in the country and its own internal contradictions, marked the beginning of the end of the libertarian left. As a response to this downturn a significant number of the intellectual left had made a 'linguistic turn'. The attempt of the French marxist Althusser to wrest marxism from its humanist adherents introduced many to French Structuralism and its theoretical roots in the linguistic theory of Ferdinand de Saussure (see his *Course in General Linguistics*, published in 1916). Althusser's theory of ideology developed a sophisticated description of the determination of individual subjectivity by social relations. He analysed the way individuals were 'interpellated' or, literally, hailed, by what he termed ideological state apparatuses, into an identification with the ideologies of the dominant class.[7]

Althusser's use of Freud and psychoanalysis introduced the work of Jacques Lacan. Lacan reinterpreted Freud's writing in the light of structural linguistics and the structuralist anthropology of Lévi-Strauss.[8] Both Althusser and Lacan shifted the meaning of an individual's utterance away from the myth of an inner truth. They argued that the subject is constituted in language, reversing the common idea that language and hence meaning derive from some inner realm of being.

> Only since Freud have we begun to suspect what listening and hence what speaking (and keeping silent) *means*; that this *'meaning'* of speaking and listening reveals beneath the innocence of speech and hearing the culpable depth of a second *quite different* discourse, the discourse of the unconscious.[9]

The implications of this statement challenge the idea that individuals can make conscious choices based upon a perceived truth of a situation. Similarly, it suggests that a person's identity is precarious because it doesn't form an essence, but is rather the result of a contingent set of processes and determinations of language and meaning. For Lacan, the unconscious is not some sealed heuristic sanctum, but the product of language, its meaning derived from the external social organisation of symbols and representation.[10]

This seemed an attractive proposition for those arguing that femininity and masculinity were neither determined by biology nor an ahistorical essence of subjectivity. However, its deft removal of the historical agency of the subject left the individual all but divorced from the political process. As a result critical or oppositional voices, lacking an ethical basis, could be as easily deconstructed as a vociferous support for social subordination or oppression might be. But this intrinsic political pessimism of structuralism was offset by its capacity for complexity, abstraction and theoretical sophistication. With the appearance of post-structuralism and the engagement of French feminists with Lacanian psychoanalysis, it began to play a central and referencing role in the critical discourse of sexual politics.

Despite its similar concerns with gender and sexuality, MAS writings did not engage with structural linguistics and post-structuralist theories.[11] Writing in retrospect of this moment, Vic Seidler associated the changing intellectual climate to the failure to realise the political possibilities of May 1968. Arguing that it marked a new and deep pessimism in the prospects for political change, he wrote:

> Structuralism and the post-structuralist theory that followed a partial reaction against the writing of Althusser, Lévi-Strauss and the psychoanalytic work of Lacan, marked a profound shift in our sense of place of individuality and subjectivity. We have lost a sense that we could shape our own lives, even if not in the circumstances of our own choosing.[12]

The antipathy to the political conservatism of structuralism was shared by other contributors to *Achilles Heel*. Paul Atkinson wrote:

> This structuralism often makes it difficult to bring real people as conscious subjects into theory. Yet paradoxically many of the areas with which recent theory has been concerned are directly related to individual subjectivity. . . . This raises a fundamental issue. How do you allow in your theories of society for people to be active, self-conscious subjects affected by the structuring of society into which they are born yet willing and able to assert themselves against that structuring.[13]

It was the adherence of those involved in MAS and Red Therapy to a practical political project that led to their distance from an increasingly influential academic discourse. Again it was a praxis which determined their approach to psychoanalysis. The emphasis was upon expressive therapies using groupwork and not on psychoanalytic theory. It was bioenergetics, Gestalt, guided fantasy, psychodrama, regression, encounter and co-counselling that informed these men's sexual politics. The kind of abstract intellectual theories that characterised Lacanian psychoanalysis seemed of little relevance to the practical application of these therapies.

But it was something more than a simple difference of intellectual discourse that was dividing sexual politics in the late 1970s. Within the academy the humanities were in decline as the cutting edge of critical theory. In its place cultural studies was seeking a *rapprochement* across disciplines, creating a new intellectual approach to the study and analysis of culture and political processes. The constituency involved in MAS, Red Therapy and men's consciousness-raising groups had looked to the humanistic social sciences, to sociology, psychology and the early Marx, for the language and theoretical constructs of their analysis. As such the idea of experience as a central and valid focus of inquiry held predominance. Contrary to this position, a new generation, working their way through universities and polytechnics were picking up on the new sites of critical discourse and beginning to speak a different language of oppositional culture and politics.[14] This division defined a specific 1970s sensibility in both feminism and men's sexual politics which was counterposed to the new cultural studies of the 1980s. Unfortunately, it was a division that, over time, reinforced itself, creating mutual antagonism between the two intellectual formations.

The growing predominance of structuralist accounts of language and subjectivity in intellectual circles, was matched by a growing political hostility within MAS to them. The result was the exclusion of linguistic theory from the analysis of the relationship between men to their feelings. Instead, it relied upon the disciplines of sociology and humanistic psychotherapy. This commitment to the practical application of group therapy and consciousness-raising mitigated against the influence of psychoanalysis.

NANCY CHODOROW AND OBJECT RELATIONS THEORY

While I don't want to underestimate the disparate and often antagonistic positions and practices within MAS, it is *Achilles Heel* which represents the political and cultural moment of MAS in the 1970s. Its collective spanned the divide between therapy and politics, and between the libertarian left and consciousness-raising groups. Its content reflected the liberal sexual politics of 'men's liberation' and anti-sexism. It also attracted its share of criticism for self-indulgence, copping out and political feebleness from men and feminist women alike.[15] All in all it provides, in retrospect, an authoritative representation of MAS politics. It wasn't until 1985 that this moment of MAS was given a theoretical summation, with the publication of *The Sexuality of Men*. It was edited by two members of the *Achilles Heel* collective, Andy Metcalf and Martin Humphries, and it provides an exposition of the magazine's analyses of masculinity.

Many of the essays in the book seek to explain the contradiction between the outward self-assurance of masculine identities and the inner doubt and insecurity that many men involved in MAS felt. In his introduction, Andy Metcalf describes the two broad themes of the book:

> One is that much of male sexuality can be understood only if the family constellation around the infant is brought into the picture, and the psychoanalytic approaches discussed. The other theme concerns the changes that have occurred over the last thirty years in women's place in the world.[16]

Jennifer Somerville has pointed out in her review of the book, that the textual emphasis is on the relationship between the two themes; the psyche and the gendered sphere of the social (Somerville 1989). This relationship is a central concern of the post-Freudians in psychoanalysis, particularly in the theories and practice of the British school of object relations.[17] Object relations theory underpins many of the psychoanalytic statements to be found in the book, but its theories are not developed nor are they explored in any depth. Instead *The Sexuality of Men* draws heavily on the feminist reworking of object relations (Chodorow 1978; Dinnerstein 1976; Eichenbaum and Orbach 1982, 1984).

In particular the work of Nancy Chodorow forms a central reference in the MAS characterisations of masculinity. Her book *The Reproduction of Mothering* (1978) has gained the status of a seminal text of feminist object relations theory. It sought, as did the other feminist texts, to displace the centrality of the father and the oedipus complex as the ontological source of gender identity and subjectivity. Instead it describes the formation of gender identity in the infant's pre-oedipal differentiation from the mother, arguing that masculinity is defined through its defensive relation to the feminine. It is this analysis which provided MAS with a particular lexicon for their masculine gender personalities; fragile, fearful and insecure. Words that conjured up an emotionally impoverished and psychologically unstable gender identity.

Nancy Chodorow opposed the new feminist interest in Freud and Lacanian psychoanalysis.[18] She argued that Freud and his antecedents such as Melanie Klein, Ernest Jones and Karen Horney, despite their differences, 'remain bound to a theory of development and an account of the oedipus complex which stress libidinal and instinctual shifts and biology even while emphasizing difficulties in the attainment of biological destiny.'[19] Because these theories rely upon an innate libidinal energy that precedes the infant's relationship to objects they inevitably collapse the acquisition of gender identity into a biologically determined realm. She argues that Freud's is a 'one-person psychology' of 'libidinal determinism', which cannot address the relational and social construction of gendered subjectivity.

In his earlier writing, up to his essay, 'On Narcissism: An Introduction' (Freud 1914c), Freud had argued that individual psychology consists of innate and unorganised drives that seek gratification according to 'the pleasure principle'. These drives are defined by their location in specific 'erotogenic zones'. These zones stand for a place: the mouth, anus and genitals and a practice: oral sucking and ingestion, anal withholding or releasing, genital arousal or orgasm. They provide both a source of gratification and a means to achieve it. As an infant grows, the erotogenic zones through which the libidinal instincts seek gratification change. Libidinal energy moves from mouth to anus to genitals. It is a movement shaped by repressions, fixations and gratifications, organising the character of individual sexuality; an outward-oriented, instinctual search for pleasure. In other words, relations with others play only a minimal part in human development.

In contrast to Freud's early writing, object relations theorists downplayed libidinal economy. Although object relations is itself an open description and its adherents hold different ideas, its project can be, if rather crudely, summarised as the attempt to understand the individual as a product of social relations with other real persons (objects) in interaction with the unfolding development of his or her unique 'psyche-soma'. Psyche-soma is a term which expresses the interactive and dynamic relationship between an individual's organic, biological life and the formation of mental representations in the psyche which derive from its impulses. These mental representations are called instincts. Object relations addresses the way that external objects enact instinctual life and enable it to develop. This is achieved through the creation of an internal object world which enables the formation of the infant's ego and its sense of self in relation to others. The objects that form this internal world are determined by the infant's relationship to real external objects. But they are not simply objective perceptions. They are formed in the process of the infant's apprehension of them, that is in his or her subjective conception of them.

The notion of an object comes originally from Freud's early theory where he describes it as something impersonal upon which impulses of energy are discharged. The object is only recognised for the purposes of the subject's pleasure seeking and relief. It was Melanie Klein who began to use the word extensively in her work. Nevertheless her adherence to 'libidinal determinism' places her outside the object relations school, despite the formative, groundbreaking influence of her ideas upon it. The object relations school emerged out of the British Psychoanalytical Society and contained a number of well-known figures including D.W. Winnicott, R.D. Fairbairn and M. Balint. Fairbairn occupied the most uncompromising position in his insistence that outer reality wholly shapes internal reality and that innate instincts play no part in stimulating psychic activity. Psychical activity is not governed by the pleasure principle but is aimed at seeking objects. The pleasures involved in object relations have a selective and formative function, but are not the primary aim of the activity. 'It follows,' he writes, 'that behaviour must be oriented towards outer reality and thus determined by the reality principle from the first.'[20] It is a position challenged by Balint (Balint 1956) and certainly not held by many other object relations theorists who maintain, as Freud himself did, an open mind as to the actual role of the instinctual economy in the maturational development and the life of human beings. Fairbairn's distance from Freudian psychoanalysis has proved seductive to sociologists who have wanted to utilise object relations theory.

Within the social sciences, object relations has been used to explain the relationship of the individual to society.[21] This relationship is Chodorow's main intellectual consideration; the socio-psychological reproduction of familial and gender relations.

34

Chodorow uses an amalgam of object relations theories and synthesises them to classical Weberian sociology. The theoretical heritage of this model predates Chodorow's own work, owing much to the American sociologist Talcott Parsons. His theory of sex roles has provided an analytic framework that dominated the sociological work on gender in the 1960s and 1970s (see Carrigan *et al*. 1985). His investigation of the mother–son relationship in the American middle-class family drew a correspondence between the acquisition of masculinity, the psychodynamics of family life and the organisational demands of capitalism (see Parsons and Bales 1953). This perspective and his emphasis upon socialisation and the generational transmission of culturally dominant gender personalities resonated with the more political and radical work of the Frankfurt Institute of Social Research. Chodorow also uses their work in the writing of Alexander Mitscherlich (Mitscherlich 1963) and Max Horkheimer (Horkheimer 1972).

Like their better-known contemporary Herbert Marcuse, both these men sought a synthesis of Freudian psychoanalysis and marxism. Unlike Marcuse's emphasis upon libidinal repression, they focused upon the way capitalism structures the family and in particular the function and authority of the father. They argued that the increasingly bureaucratic nature of society undermines his patriarchal authority. This diminishes his children's internalisation of his figure, effecting the strength of their super-ego. In consequence individuals grow up with a reduced capacity to assert their rational critical faculty of conscience against oppressive authority. The result is a decline in individual rationality and a new mass conformity in populations of Northern Europe and North America. Chodorow is indebted to this intellectual legacy, but her feminism ensures that her engagement with it is critical. The same may be said of her use of Parsons's sociological model of gender acquisition. Neverthless, in occupying this intellectual discourse and its dependency upon a mixture of marxism and classical sociology, her theoretical paradigm describing the relation between the psyche and the social is susceptible to their reductionism.

Briefly stated, Chodorow's thesis is that capitalism has structured women into a mothering role that is increasingly concerned with personal relations and psychological stability. The archetypal family unit in Western industrialised societies is characterised by the father's relative absence and the woman's exclusive mothering.

It is an arrangement that structures the maturational development of infants, predisposing them to inherit gender personalities
that mirror the inequalities between men and women. They reproduce men's dominance and women's propensity to nurture and
mother. Chodorow argues that it is this exclusive parenting of the
mother that initiates gender differences in her children. Her
downplaying of the significance of the oedipus complex reflects
her commitment to object relations theory. However, she is not
without criticism of this legacy and its failure to address sexual and
gender difference: 'Object relations theorists . . . have hardly
begun to address questions concerning differences in male and
female ego development, gender differences in object relational
experiences, and the effect these have on the differential constitution of mental structure and psychic life.'[22] Chodorow sets herself
the task of providing a description of the pre-oedipal object
relations and processes that constitute gendered difference and at
the same time to link these with the sociological structuring of
women's place and function within the family.

Chodorow argues that a mother's identification with her
daughter prolongs the pre-oedipal period, ensuring that the little
girl's future attachments will retain a significant element of this
pre-oedipal phase and its sensibilities. This serves to explain
women's capacities for empathy and intuition and a primary
identification with their own children. These are all qualities that
originate in the undifferentiated state of the pre-oedipal period,
when boundaries between self and other are blurred and porous.
In this time, communication exists on a pre-verbal level passing
out of and into the infant's unformed ego through the processes
of touch, feel, sound and body. As a consequence, women tend to
define themselves in relation to others and retain a need to be
incorporated in a relationship.

In contrast the male infant's pre-oedipal relationship is curtailed and sexualised by the mother. The absence of the father as
an emotionally responsive and supportive spouse, social isolation
and women's own ambivalence to the male sex shapes mothers'
contradictory responses to their sons. A son may become a surrogate spouse, but he is always an unfamiliar object. It is in this
positioning of the male infant as other to herself, that the mother
figures his gendered difference. The mother provokes a premature separation with her infant son. The process of his
individuation remains incomplete and this failure to fully achieve

differentiation forms a central element in masculine identities. In Freudian psychoanalysis, gendered subjectivity is the product of the oedipus complex, a process that is determined by the figure of the father. Chodorow reverses its logic by implying that the boy's biological difference (i.e. his penis) far from asserting his birthright, represents the moment of his ontological loss and displacement.

From the first weeks of birth the infant's future masculinity is constituted upon its otherness from the maternal body. Men's primary sense of self is engendered and sexualised through its separateness from its maternal origins. Premature separation is marked by a sense of abandonment in which the unintegrated ego of the infant is subject to stress and anxiety. Unlike women's more expressive gender personalities this fear of disintegration inhibits men's relational capacities, encouraging the development of strong ego boundaries and a propensity towards aggression in their defence. Chodorow's account strips masculinity of any positive referents of its own. The significance of this pre-oedipal, maternal relationship is enhanced by the ambivalent presence of the father. His partial absence from familial affective relations reduces the phenomenological effect of the masculine third place of the oedipus complex contributing to the boy's struggle to assert a sense of himself within a gendered identity. What emerges is a masculinity constructed out of its own ambivalence towards women and intimacy, both needing emotional sustenance but eschewing closeness for the threat it poses to the male subject's sense of separateness. From this psychic constitution arises men's individualistic rationalism and an internal compulsion to seek psychological order through the domination and control of others.

SOCIOLOGY AND PSYCHOANALYSIS

Chodorow's thesis offers a convincing picture of contemporary gender personalities and relations. But there are a number of problems and these come to light in applying her work to a reflexive analysis of masculine identity. In providing this detailed and sophisticated model of a masculine personality she assumes its unitary nature. It doesn't account for differences between men and the effects of class and race upon the formation of masculine sensibilities. There is also a danger in explaining the sociological character of masculinities exclusively in the psychodynamics of the domestic division of labour. For whatever compelling descriptions it produces it is reductionist and will omit other significant determinations.

Her description of the psychodynamics of men's gender acquisition has much in common with Talcott Parsons's own account: 'relative to the total culture as a whole, the masculine personality tends more to the predominance of instrumental interests, needs and functions . . . while the feminine personality tends to the primacy of expressive interests, needs and functions.'[23] This argument for the existence of clearly definable sex roles and gender personalities presumes a direct correspondence between these and the needs of the social order; if bureaucratic corporate capitalism needs men with specific instrumental skills and internalised attitudes towards authority and hierarchy, then that is what the psychodynamics of family life will produce and perpetuate. This is a functionalist account, the explanation of a phenonemon is defined by its apparent use value. As Carrigan *et al.* have argued, Parsons's account offered a persuasive solution to the problem of how to link person to society, the psyche to the social (Carrigan *et al.* 1985). By employing Freud's theory of the oedipus complex, Parsons argued that sex-roles become part of the psychic constitution of the individual through their internalisation. In other words if a mother is soft-spoken, house-bound and deferential to her husband, such traits will serve in constructing the femininity of her daughter. While there is some truth in this, it is patently less than half the story as the revolt of the daughters in women's liberation proved. Its inadequacy lies in the simplifying of Freud's psychoanalytic theory, for it ignores the significance of the psyche-soma which is partially autonomous from actual human relations.

The socio-psychological accounts of gender that emerged out of and in response to Parsons's work have struggled to marry together sociology and psychoanalysis. Each deals in a realm of human experience that has a highly complex relationship to the other. There has been a tendency to describe the internal psychic life of the subject and his or her outer reality as a simple two-way exchange. The various defence mechanisms employed by the psyche to mediate this relation and, in the process, transform it, are left out of the equation. For example, there is a tendency to describe external objects as taken into the unconscious to become mental figures directly corresponding to their external value and character. It is a misconception that suits the interests of sociological inquiry. Object relations theory is reduced to a form of social psychology. The psyche becomes a mere adjunct of the social, a conduit through which socially appropriate gender characteristics are channelled. Even those who have sought to evade a simple causal explanation have fallen foul of this interrelationship between psyche and social. For example, Iain Craib argues for the relationship between gender personality and social structure being based on the notion of 'elective affinities'.[24] But in struggling to introduce an element of human autonomy into the equation he lands up entirely removing the relationship between the psychodynamic acquisition of gender identity and the sphere of social relations. They cease to have any sort of mutually determining interrelationship.

For Freud in his later writings, for Klein and for the school of object relations theorists, object relations as a psychoanalysis is concerned with the interrelationship of the subject with his or her own subjectively conceived objects and in the way these relate to objectively perceived objects in the external world. There is no simple causal relationship between the two spheres of life. It is not simply real relationships, real roles, real functions and values which determine a subject's life and gender identity, it is in the specific ways that the subject apprehends his or her objects. This poses a huge obstacle for sociologists who wish to explain in total the psycho-sociological formation of subjectivity within an historical framework.

For Parsons, phrases like 'masculine personality' imply that his argument is based upon a standard model of masculinity, an ideal type whose description will unveil the underlying causes of its existence. It emerges as a singular and normative identity that is a function of the general economic and social relationships of a 'total culture as a whole'. There is a real dilemma here for Chodorow, for her description of gender acquisition teeters on the edge of just this ahistorical functionalism. Her reduction of the determinations of masculine identities to the sexual division of labour produces a standard model. As a result she is unable to explain what does not conform to her model of development, not only on a sociological level, but in psychoanalytic terms, too, for there is a little bit of everybody that does not conform to the project of their own identity, let alone to the functions and representations of dominant gender identities. Individual, cultural, sexual and ethnic identities can only be explained in terms of their deviancy or psychopathology. And while Parsons was willing to do this, Chodorow is not, which leaves those processes of cultural negotiation, translation and difference, which produce changing meanings and definitions of masculinity and femininity, out of the thesis.

Chodorow's work was an attempt to provide a total explanation for the reproduction of gender identity. The result was a static model which could not cope with changing identities and changing social processes. The insights of its psychoanalytic descriptions were undermined by grounding them in a functionalist sociological account of family relations. Yet I want to leave her text open. It has been subject to a great deal of scrutiny and criticism (see for example Craib 1987; Flax 1990; Segal 1987, 1990; Seidler 1985; Somerville 1989) and is frequently presented as the paradigm of a feminist object relations developmental model. But it has not been developed. Either rejected or accepted uncritically it has remained a curiously static text locked into a particular cultural and political discourse associated with the sexual politics of the 1970s. I don't propose to seal it off, but to explore how it came to determine the theoretical language of MAS's account of the acquisition of men's gendered identity, and later in Chapter 4 to re-address its findings.

THE SEXUALITY OF MEN

A similar psychoanalytic account of masculinity can be found in the writings of Louise Eichenbaum and Susie Orbach (Eichenbaum and Orbach 1982, 1984). In 1976 they opened the Women's Therapy Centre, providing an institutional base for the emergence of feminist therapy. They represented a strand of feminist thinking and practice closely aligned to those practising therapy within MAS. Unlike Chodorow, Eichenbaum and Orbach argue that the mother–son relationship can facilitate an appropriate separation. But the nature of society perpetuates men's physical and emotional dependence upon women. It is in the nature of masculinity to deny this dependency. Men repress this need for women by sublimating it into the pursuit of archetypal male behaviour. By pursuing cultural stereotypes, men can enhance a sense of masculine selfhood that is constantly threatened by this unacknowledged dependency. While their psychoanalytic account is not burdened by Chodorow's functionalist sociology, they still produce a normative model of development which presumes a singular masculinity existing within a homogeneous culture.

The troubles inherent in these feminist appropriations of object relations theory and the added burden of a functionalist and reductive sociology offer a rather inauspicious basis upon which to build an analysis of masculinity. While not all the essays in *The Sexuality of Men* conform to the thematics laid out in Andy Metcalf's introduction, there is a characteristic interest in the object relations analysis of the mother–son dyad and its significance in the formation of masculinity. Tom Ryan, in the opening essay, 'The Roots of Masculinity', writes: 'There is reason to believe that the intersexed nature of the mother–son relationship is the key to the understanding of men's fragile gender identity and the related problems of fear of commitment and intimacy.'[25] Ryan, himself a practising therapist, addresses the fears men have of being suffocated, swallowed up or dominated by women. He suggests that these feelings are not simply concerns with the loss of freedom or autonomy within a relationship but, 'a more basic fear about disintegration or loss of their sense of maleness. Behind this fear appears to be a wish to surrender to the woman, to be like her, to be in union with her.'[26] This wish touches upon a central dilemma of heterosexual men; the paradoxical desire for women and the need to be separate from them. It is a struggle which centres on the threshold between subject and object, and the way that the relation between inner and outer is formed in the process of individuation. It is this threshold, translated into the dichotomy between psyche and social, which is addressed in the chapter on pornography. It is through this chapter by Andy Moye that I want to explore the consequences and problems that emerged out of MAS's use of theory and its reliance upon a sociologically influenced reading of object relations psychoanalysis.

In his essay Andy Moye deploys similar models of masculine and feminine gender personality to the Chodorow/Parsons binary of instrumental and expressive.

The contradictions inherent in masculine authority have been traditionally sustained in this way, with women as the 'natural' bearers of the nurturing, comforting role bringing understanding and support to the knotted tensions and

41

insecurities lying beneath the surface of men's public persona.[27]

Moye argues that men's use of soft pornography is a direct result of the changing economic, political and sexual shifts in relationships with women. Men can no longer rely on the security of the private realm to prop up their public personas. In consequence, male heterosexuality is increasingly denied a complementary, subordinate, female sexuality. One which will be complicit with men's denial of their needs and willing to give sustenance to their emotional insecurity. Pornography offers men a place in the phallic brotherhood reassuring their masculine authority and control.

Moye bases his description of male heterosexuality on the work of Wendy Hollway, a feminist psychologist. In her essay 'Heterosexual Sex: Power and Desire for the Other' she analyses the results of a survey she conducted amongst male friends and colleagues. She describes men's paradoxical need and fear of sexual intimacy with women.

> Sex is the most powerful expression of this desire [desire for the mother] – the site where men want and need most and therefore feel most vulnerable. . . . Men 'enter' women when they make love. There is a metaphorical slippage between the womb of the mother (the ultimate in protection and security and the antithesis of separation) and the vagina, wherein they can feel engulfed in the love of the Other/Mother. Women's vaginas can thus be dangerous places – dangerous because men's identity depends on separation from the mother; a maintenance of fragile ego boundaries which are most vulnerable . . . when attraction to the woman heralds desire for the Other/Mother.[28]

In Hollway's account of male sexuality, men's sexual desire is the analogue of the mother, the primary object in men's lives. Sexual desire and maternal object love come to be one libidinal force. Sexuality is reduced to relations of dependence and independence, desire is determined by an object relation rather than the determinant of an object choice. Hollway's account confronts us with the status of sexuality in the use of object relations theory, where the object relation precedes and determines libidinal economy.

I have already mentioned Fairbairn's object relations theory. His contention that libido is object seeking and not pleasure seeking leaves unresolved the place of sexual desire in the central paradigm of processes of differentiation and individuation. If only by default, sexuality remains within both Kleinian and object relations theory a relatively autonomous, often socially incongruent force, but, nevertheless relatively untheorised. Its presence here in an analysis of pornography highlights that central dilemma of the relationship between the sphere of the inner psyche and external social relations. In his essay Moye makes a direct comparison between the state of social relations and men's sexual expressivity, suggesting that the latter is a product of the former. Again the psyche threatens to become a simple receptacle for the internalisation of external relations.

Moye's argument implies that men turn to sexual fantasies when changing social relations create a disjunction between their sexual desire and its object. But this social transition doesn't produce the sexual fantasies in the first place. Pornography gives a representation to men's sexual fantasies, but it doesn't explain their formation, unless one is to argue that the representations themselves produce psychical mimics. The answer to what determines sexual fantasy lies in the processes of subjective conception and objective perception which through a mutual process of transformation produce instinctual representations which are neither purely external object, nor solely instinctual, but a product of the two which becomes a third term. These are symbols. They give rise to images and words which express sexual feeling. But a recognition of this complexity and the struggle to balance inner and outer is missing from Moye's analysis. His account suggests a fairly straightforward and unproblematic relationship between object love of the mother and sexual desire for women. Desire is reduced to a simple metaphorical slippage, a correlation of object love. This reduces the complex determinations of sexuality to a single cause, the vicissitudes of the internalised object of the mother. Moye applies this account to a sociology of men's use of pornography and the result is similar to Talcott Parsons's, a functionalist account of subjectivity.

The origins of Hollway's analysis can be found in Freud's essay 'On the Universal Tendency to Debasement in the Sphere of Love' (1912d) in which Freud argues that heterosexual desire is constituted through two libidinal currents; one affectionate, the other sensual. The first 'corresponds to the child's primary object choice',[29] the mother. Later a second 'affectionate' current develops out of this first, whose principle is the sexual desire of another woman. This second cannot but follow the model of the first. Male heterosexual expression is constituted out of the necessity to keep the two apart. Failure to achieve this separation fixates sexual desire on the forbidden incestuous figure of the mother. The result, argues Freud, is impotence. The degree to which this is experienced is relative yet, according to Freud, it is a universal fact of male heterosexuality. Men seek objects that do not recall the figure of the mother: 'Where they love they do not desire and where they desire they cannot love. They seek objects they do not need to love, in order to keep their sensuality away from the objects they love.'[30] Freud's description asserts the autonomy of sexuality and the pleasure principle yet it simultaneously acknowledges its interdependency with the preceding object love of the mother.

What is at stake in Freud's account is the way that culturally specific experiences of gender and familial relations affect the interrelation between the two libidinal currents in male heterosexuality. Hollway is aware of this and she provides the possibilities of a more culturally specific analysis of male heterosexuality than Moye's wider claims. Hollway was intrigued by the growing number of men she knew who were eschewing sexual relationships with women. She wanted to find out why. Far from offering a general model of male heterosexuality, it is these men's cultural specificity which provides clues to the nature of their heterosexuality. They belong to a culture and generation intimately bound up with the post-war family and the rise of feminism in the 1970s. Consequently, the power of the maternal, sensual current in relation to the affectionate current in men's psyche can be accounted for historically. The particularly acute experience of feminism and women's new assertiveness in these men's adult lives produced a much greater ambivalence about sexual relationships. The combination was indeed a form of cultural and sexual impotence in which celibacy seemed the safest option. Moye seeks to extrapolate Hollway's analysis to include all men under a single masculinity. By generalising her analysis its reflexive dimension is lost and the possibilities of her work left undeveloped.

While Moye addresses the nature of male heterosexual desire, eroticism, pleasure and fantasy, the confusion over exactly what

44

sexuality is continually gives it a reductive social character. Holl-way's work leaves its psychoanalytic element too simplistic. Moye embeds it in the social further by arguing that changing social relations have a direct correlation with men's heterosexual desire. Parsons's functionalism looms large and the picture that is painted remains a general one, made with broad brush strokes that obscures what doesn't conform to the general pattern. While Moye's essay cannot stand in for the rest of the essays in *The Sexuality of Men*, it does grapple with that complex relationship between inner and outer and demonstrates how the theoretical tools used by MAS were not up to the task of analysing the complexity of male subjectivity. The emphasis on the social sciences meant that any reflexive element in the work was turned into a broader and more generalised account of a singular masculinity. And likewise, the use of psychoanalytic concepts remained relatively undeveloped in the face of a reductionist sociology. There was also another and more far-reaching consequence, to which I now want to turn.

MAS AND THE POLITICS OF EXPERIENCE

It is an irony that it was MAS's commitment to a political praxis that undermined its psychoanalytic and reflexive exploration of male subjectivities. I agree with Jennifer Somerville when she wrote of *The Sexuality of Men*:

> The exploration of the boundaries of social relations and the psychical domain, the identification of points of intersection, of mutual conditions of existence are displaced by the imperative of finding strategies for changing institutions in ways that will liberate men and women from the social and emotional straitjackets deriving from the current division of labour.[31]

It is probably true to say that this commitment made many involved in MAS highly suspicious of using Freudian theory at all. The turn to group work and the growth movement philosophies in Red Therapy highlighted this suspicion with psychoanalysis. However, when *The Sexuality of Men* came to be written, the place of psychoanalytic concepts was central to that project, as Andy Metcalf makes clear in his introduction. Nevertheless, this engagement with the intellectual constructs of psychoanalytic theory tended to bring them to the level of phenomenological experience. As Vic Seidler comments this was often in reaction to the structuralist terms in which the relationship of psychoanalysis to feminism and marxism was being set.[32]

One of the major problems with MAS's turn away from structuralism and linguistic theory was the reliance upon a phenomenology of experience. It tended to an assumption that the subject contained a totality of meaning, whose expression was frustrated by the inadequate medium of language. It is the seductive idea of a totalising theory that underlies such a phenomenology. A theory which can explain and encapsulate the relation of the psyche to the social in one neat model. There has been a long tradition in Western marxism and radical socialist politics for a theoretical construct that will explain and describe the totality of social relationships (see Jay 1984). During the 1970s the emerging political constituencies organised around feminism, race and homosexuality confronted the left and marxism with new subjectivities, disrupting its totalising picture. These new reflexive politics proved more than the left could cope with. Marxism's insistence on Big Pictures and the practice of reading off the objective relations of class forces couldn't address the new antagonisms, nor account for the presence of these new political subjects. Its epics of 'history, class and party' had no language to address that myriad of struggles around dignity, sexuality, relationships and personal confidence.

In shifting the parameters of politics to include personal and private life these new constituencies undermined the left's rhetorical commitment to equality and personal autonomy. The classical marxism which predominated subsumed the antagonisms of sexuality, race and gender beneath the primacy of class. What still mattered was the singular subject, the worker. At the same moment that the left provided a birth place for new constituencies of politics it attempted to deny their difference, reducing them to the determinations of class. This classical conception of classical marxism believed that it could address the totality of social relationships. Any non-marxist theory was simply rendered redundant and its concerns secondary. The emergence of a new libertarian left, of which MAS was a part, was a reaction to this sectarian and narrow approach. But despite its heterogeneous nature and the diversity of its activities, its theoretical legacy still lay within a conception of classical marxism. It was unable to theorise the new subjects of the social movements and their different determinations into an overall analysis.

This impasse has a history in the epistemologies of marxism and the influence of Hegel and the German Romantics. Hegel's philosophy was an attempt to find unity and wholeness with the collapse of divine order and monarchical absolutism in the seventeenth century (see Taylor 1975). It was a period that marked the transition from the pre-modern age of the collective to the modernist era of the individual. The concern of the German Romantics was to try and articulate the fragments back into a whole and so recreate a sense of intelligibility and history. Hegel sought to explain the totality and complexity of differences and contingencies by an appeal to their underlying unity. Relations and identities for Hegel were no longer governed by divine providence, but they nevertheless were governed by a single process of self-unfolding. In other words history and the march towards Enlightenment replaced God as the rationale of humanity. Hegel enabled Marx to develop his theory of historical materialism and provided the intellectual and philosophical legitimation for marxism's economic determinism. The radical political discourses of the 1970s were dominated by this belief in the underlying unity of differences. It wasn't simply a case of narrow sectarianism but an inability to get outside of the history of thought and knowledge which had fashioned it. Somerville's comment that it was the political commitment of MAS which undermined its reflexive psychoanalytic inquiry gains meaning in the light of this heritage. The phenomenology of experience contained and moderated psychoanalytic theory.

The assumption of an underlying totality to human relations and identities existing prior to their cultural articulation and linguistic representation informed MAS's political reception of psychoanalysis. The appeal of Melanie Klein and object relations lay in an apparent endorsement of this position. Their emphasis upon the necessity of human relations for the formation of the human psyche, could be translated into human beings having a shared nature; an innate social morality eschewing conflict and aggression. To retain its legitimacy, such a position must argue that it is the imperfections of language and culture that distort the innate goodness and co-operativeness of individuals. The task of a sexual politics of masculinity in this context is to find a subjective position which will remove men from the distorting effects of

47

language and culture. The exploration of experience in consciousness raising groups can be interpreted as an attempt to find a
pre-existing but repressed and damaged emotional inner world
which is the truth of the subject. Andy Moye completes his critique
of men's use of pornography with the comment: 'In shoring up
the structures of traditional masculine authority soft pornography
serves to reproduce the grounds of our continued alienation.'[33]
While his essay suggests the possibilities for a complex understanding of the construction of male heterosexuality, he ends it by
implying that men have an authentic, essentially moral nature
which patriarchal language and representation has divorced them
from.

The emphasis upon feelings in *The Sexuality of Men* and the
critique of Freud's intellectualism (see Seidler 1985) leans to the
view that men have an innate moral propensity to undermine the
social relations that privilege them. This possibility is denied men,
because masculinity is constructed around the suppression of the
human sensibilities of relatedness and human solidarity. Masculinity splits men from themselves, accentuating language over
feeling and so cutting men off from their pre-existing inner world
of feeling. If language cannot be trusted to represent feeling,
subjective meaning must be located in a concept of experience, a
site where unmediated feeling is communicated both to the subject
and to others. Intimacy, empathy, intuition, become the pass-
words to a new masculinity for they cast a light upon men's
repressed inner realm of emotions. They exist as a kind of pre-cog-
nitive truth of one's self that makes its appearance through somatic
experience. The logical end of this approach is to turn one's back
upon rationality and reason and privilege feeling as the font of
truth.

PSYCHOANALYSIS AND MORALITY

The political reception of Kleinian and object relations psychoanalysis comes out of this concept of experience and it points to the
fate of the MAS project of reflexivity. In an article in *New Left
Review*, Michael Rustin puts forward the argument that these
theories of human development ascribe moral and altruistic capacities to human beings as part of their essential nature. He writes:

Individuality is shown to be not the starting point, but the emergent result of a prolonged and delicate process of dependency. Innate concern for the well-being of the other, at a very deep level, appears to arise in this conception from the earliest lack of differentiation between self and other, and from the process whereby this differentiation comes about. Pleasure and pain are only slowly located in space and time, and in relation to the whole persons. This intense experience of pain, as given and received, and this deep involvement with the caring person as the source of all well- and ill-being, gives rise to the capacity to experience the pains and pleasures of the other with an intensity comparable to the pains and pleasures of the self.[34]

Rustin's aim is to incorporate Kleinian psychoanalysis into the realm of social morality to use it for a socialist analysis of subjectivity. He is attempting something very similar to MAS's own efforts to synthesise psychoanalytic concepts with political praxis. Rustin's main claim for this incorporation is that the process of the infant's separation from its mother both invokes and lays the foundations for human solidarity. I want briefly to turn to Klein and her theories of infant maturation and see if this claim can stand.

In 1910 Melanie Klein had gone to live in Budapest with her husband and children. Here she discovered psychoanalysis and received her analytic training under the tutelage of Sandor Ferenczi. In 1921 she moved to Berlin. Under the supervision of Karl Abraham she developed her work on infant and child analysis. It was a practice Freud had avoided. His one child analysis of the boy Little Hans (Freud 1909b) had been conducted through the boy's father. Language and the mental processes of representation were central to Freud's first topography of the mind (Freud 1915e) and his therapeutic practice of free association. Infants and small children, without a grasp of language, were beyond the bounds of Freudian practice. Similarly psychosis, in which the disturbed subject loses a coherent relationship to language and external reality, was an area that Freud felt uncertain in treating. His famous analysis of paranoia in the case of the Judge, Dr Daniel Schreber, was undertaken from the man's autobiography. He notes at the beginning of this case study: 'We cannot accept patients suffering from this complaint [paranoia], or, at all events, we cannot keep them for long, since we cannot offer treatment unless there is some prospect of therapeutic success'[35] (Freud

1911c (1910)). It was to be Klein's analytic work with children that enabled psychoanalysis to address both the stage of pre-verbal psychic development and psychosis.

Klein's first essay to be published in the English language, 'The Psychological Principles of Infant Analysis' (Klein 1926) gave no hint of any break with Freudian metapsychology. But from this time on her clinical work with disturbed children led her both to reformulate many of Freud's propositions and to develop her own. This challenge to Freudian orthodoxy was to culminate in the 'Controversial Discussions' of the British Psychoanalytic Society that took place between January 1943 and May 1944 (see Kohon 1988).

Like Freud, Klein believed that infants were born with innate instinctual drives. She accepted Freud's belief in 'Beyond the Pleasure Principle' (Freud 1920g) that there are two conflicting drives, the sexual instinct and the death instinct. She parted company with him over the central role she gave this latter instinct. For Klein anxiety is the motor of maturational development. 'I hold that anxiety arises from the operation of the death instinct within the organism, is felt as a fear of annihilation (death) and takes the form of a fear of persecution.'[36] This isn't as outlandish as it sounds. She accepted D.W. Winnicott's description of the infant's immature ego as 'unintegrated'. Its lack of cohesion gives it a tendency to disintegrate and fall apart in a state of anxiety. In effect the infant experiences a form of psychotic breakdown, a fundamental rupture with the psychic preconditions of living. The central task of the infant ego is to protect itself from this potential catastrophe. But it is a catastrophe that is an inevitable consequence of its dependency upon an outside object for its conditions of existence. Central to Klein's description of maturational development are the primitive defence mechanisms employed by the infant ego to defend itself against excessive anxiety. It is the motive behind growth and development.

The last essay in Freud's published work addresses the ego's defence mechanisms of splitting and projection. He locates their operation in the oedipus complex (Freud 1940e (1938)), where the ego splits off a dangerous wish or anxiety and projects it out into an external object which takes on the character of that wish or anxiety. Klein developed the theory of splitting and projection. She described how a sadistic rage is precipitated in the infant by an external failure to satisfy its needs. It is an aggression that threatens to destroy the fragile cohesion of the infant's ego and is projected out onto an object. The infant then perceives this object as the source of its own sadistic rage and it becomes a persecutory object which threatens to destroy the infant.

> I have often expressed my view that object relations exist from the beginning of life, the first object being the mother's breast which to the child becomes split into a good (gratifying) and bad (frustrating) breast; this splitting results in a severance of love and hate.[37]

At the same time as the infant is projecting out its sadistic impulses it is taking in or introjecting the good object which is constituted through feeding and the comfort and touch of the mother. In the infant's mind there exist two separate objects, the good and the bad, which in reality belong to the same object of the mother.

The two-way non-verbal communication of introjection and projection is a phase of development that Klein has termed the paranoid-schizoid position (Klein 1946). This is a period during the first 4 or 5 months of life, during which the infant is dominated by its aggression and the anxiety this produces. Gradually, however, the introjection of the good object produces a counterweight to this splitting. It creates a framework or container which holds the infant's internal objects. This is the formation of the ego, an 'I' which marks the growing individuation of the infant from his or her mother. The infant begins to perceive that the mother incorporates both the good and the bad object. This process of introjection provides the infant's developing ego with cohesion and unity. The defensive mechanism of splitting diminishes and the infant begins to develop an appropriate relationship with the external world of objects. While persecutory fears continue, the infant senses the damage that it has caused its object through splitting and projection and begins to fear its destruction and loss. This process of mourning marks the depressive position, which in Kleinian metapsychology takes on the same significance as Freud's oedipus complex.

The depressive position establishes a relationship between internal reality and the outside world which enables the development of language and communication. The defence mechanisms of splitting and projection in the paranoid-schizoid position obscure the boundaries between self and other as reality is coloured by internal fantasies and made threatening by projected aggression. These positions are not discrete and clearly definable stages, they need to be worked through. Most individuals carry aspects of splitting and projection into their adult lives where they create problems in communication and relations with others. Klein argued that the development of language and an appropriate relationship between internal and external worlds is dependent upon the psychic formation of symbols. These mental representations of objects are like metaphors and form the preconditions for verbal communication and the establishment of the depressive position. A continuing existence of intense anxiety will disrupt symbol formation allowing for the continuation of splitting and projection and psychotic or autistic elements in individuals.

Symbols are formed when anxiety about sadistic impulses and the fear of retaliation from an object which has been attacked, drives the infant to take on another object that will stand in for the feared one. In this way the child can escape the dangers he or she bestowed on the original. Thus objects and events in the world will be invested with displaced meanings; they become symbolic representations of the child's inner world and form the basis of play and communication. Symbolism marks the relation between inner and outer; 'upon it is built the subject's relation to the outside world and to reality in general.'[38] Klein's work places the figure of the mother at the centre of theories of psychoanalysis. Not only in relation to the child's maturational development, but to the precursorial mental processes that constitute thought and language.

To incorporate maturational development into the language of social morality, as Rustin would do, is to risk mixing cultural and discursive concepts with a process that is not governed by linguistic exchange nor has recourse to constructs of value. Klein's description is of a nascent ego structure struggling to develop its potential as a complete entity against the threat of internal and external persecutory objects. Even in the introjection of the whole good object and mourning for the fear of its loss, the infant has no sense of moral indebtedness. In Klein's view there is a feeling of love and gratitude for the object, but to translate this into a moral intersubjectivity belies its very specific nature. The depressive position is not just a product of the infant's guilt at its sadistic rage, but also a self-interested fear that without the good object there will be a hole, a nothingness where there was once sustenance. The processes of introjection and projection and the establishment of object relations, make for the profoundly intersubjective nature of human life and development. But there can be no assumption made of an *a priori* moral dimension to this intersubjectivity.

Rustin's reception of Kleinian theory reveals a central dilemma. His description of psychological processes suggest an inner psychic world which is a container of untransformed external objects. Inner and outer are a simple correspondence that enables the infant to begin formulating a language cotermineous to both. It is an assumption that is a consequence of Klein's own ambivalent reworking of Freud's theory of the unconscious, which she called phantasy.

In her clinical work with children she noted the very narrow demarcation between conscious and unconscious. She describes the relation between inner and outer as made through the complex interaction of projection and introjection excluding the idea of a primary and secondary level of mental processes (see Freud 1915e). Instead, her description offers a more direct relationship between inner and outer. Klein's phantasy is formed by the mental representations that constitute symbol formation. 'Thus an inner world is being built up in the child's unconscious mind, corresponding to his actual experiences and the impression he gains from people and the external world, and yet altered by his own phantasies and impulses.'[39] Her description doesn't contain the Freudian concepts of condensation and displacement (see Freud 1916), and is less complex than his topography of the mind. It is too easy to dismiss phantasy and symbol formation as simply a container full of contents (see Mitchell 1988). However, Freud's own accusation that this 'psychology of consciousness'[40] is incapable of solving the problems of dreams and so, implicitly, the problem of the unconscious, has some justification. The status of the psyche and its autonomy in relation to external reality is left ambivalent in Kleinian metapsychology. In the context of Rustin's reception of Kleinian theory, this ambivalent status *vis à vis* the descriptive languages of material philosophies and social morality can lead to its conflation into social relations and a dismissal of its relative autonomy and its structural uniqueness.

I have dwelt at some length on this theme because it illuminates the problems of MAS's theoretical exposition of male subjectivity. There is an assumption at work that has little to do with psychoanalysis and much more to do with the Romantic notion of the divine inwardness of human beings. With the destruction of the divine order and the age of Enlightenment, meaning was relocated in the realm of history and reason. It was also sought for in the interior life of individuals. Feelings and imagination take on the meaning of truth. External facts become mere symbols of a moral law within each individual. But such a moral self takes on a transcendence without history, neither a product of nature, time or chance. This illimitable moral self underlay the Romantics' notion of the poetic imagination of inner truth. Rustin sails as close to this tradition as he does to psychoanalysis.

Freud's essay 'Narcissism: An Introduction' (1914c) clearly refutes the idea that an individual's attachment to others has a foundation in concern for their well-being. In narcissistic object choice an individual comes to love 'what he himself is'. In anaclitic attachment one may love 'the woman who tends' or 'the man who protects.'[41] The philosopher Richard Rorty cites Freud's comment on 'the narcissistic origin of compassion'. He goes on to say that this, 'gives us a way of thinking of the sense of pity not as an identification with the common human core which we share with all other members of our species, but as channelled in very specific ways towards very specific sorts of people and very particular vicissitudes'.[42] But as Jane Flax has shown, Freud's writing that dates from his essay on narcissism begins to show a much greater concern with object relations and the way that the self is partially determined by the quality of its relations with others (see Flax 1990). Rorty's claim which places psychoanalysis outside the realm of social morality is but one reading of Freud. But Freud remains ambivalent about the exact relationship between his theory of libidinal determinism and his recognition of the significance of object relations. And as Flax writes, he remained committed to both and unhappy at the tension and contradiction these different models created. 'Despite the claims of the later object relations theorists, Freud seems driven to incorporate object relations material *within* an economic model.'[43] To settle these contradictory readings of his work, the last word should go to Freud. Writing in conclusion to his essay on Leonardo da Vinci, he argues against the idea of a paradigm human being with an intrinsic nature:

> we are all too ready to forget that in fact everything to do with our life is chance, from our origin out of the meeting of spermatozoon and ovum onwards – chance which nevertheless has a share in the law and necessity of nature, and which merely lacks any connection with our wishes and illu-

sions. . . . We all still show too little respect for Nature which
(in the obscure words of Leonardo which recall Hamlet's
lines) 'is full of countless causes ['*ragioni*'] that never enter
experience'.

Every one of us human beings corresponds to one of the
countless experiments in which these '*ragioni*' of nature force
their way into experience.[44]

If a particular reception of psychoanalysis presumes a model of
human development founded upon its propensity for moral
identification with humanity, its value as a critical and reflexive
discourse is undermined. In place of self-comprehension it will
dispense moral judgement on its universal criteria for goodness
and rightness. Such a turn to a universal and totalising descriptive
language cannot sustain a reflexive analysis of subjectivity. Its
morality lays down a specific criteria of ethics that define the
parameters of investigation. What was to be descriptive can quickly
turn into a new language of prescription. I would argue that this
is what Rustin's reception of psychoanalysis is in danger of doing.
It is also the fate that the MAS project of reflexivity succumbed to.

The emphasis in *The Sexuality of Men* is not upon the contingencies that produce male subjectivity but upon the presumption of a
paradigmatic model of masculinity. The consequence is a subtle
shift in the text from a reflexive investigation into the relationship
between feeling and language to a more personalised account of
what it means to be a man. An account that is grounded in the
primacy of experience. It is here, I would argue that the reflexive
project of MAS runs aground. In its use of theory and psychoanalytic concepts, the task undergoes a metamorphosis. It is no longer
a search for new descriptions and vocabularies of masculinity. In
place of this task of self-creation, of understanding and moving
beyond the past, there emerges a more conservative concern with
finding oneself and with it the necessity to try and live up to certain
moral standards. Moral standards conceived out of a belief in the
underlying unity of all identities and social formations. It would
be grossly unfair to argue that all the essays in the book perpetuate
this approach. They do not (see, for example, Dyer 1985) and
some actively attempt to evade any fall into a prescriptive politics.
But from within the theoretical frameworks employed this is
self-defeating for the languages employed carry with them value-

laden assumptions about what are good and what are bad masculine sensibilities.

One of the problems is that in working and writing from within a praxis of anti-sexist politics there is no clear understanding of what produced the phenomena of MAS in the first place. It is ironic that the vocabulary employed in some of the pieces produces a description of masculinity that cannot account for the processes of change that brought the writer and MAS more generally, into existence. Chodorow's conclusion that a mother-dominated family produces a masculine personality that conforms to the needs of bureaucratic capitalism negates the existence of MAS, whose constituency is derived from the very conditions she describes. The predominance of this descriptive paradigm of a singular normative masculinity inevitably leads to a functionalist account. It happens that MAS writers don't share this model in its entirety and they certainly wish to be rid of many of its characteristics they may hold. But the reason why they feel this way remains unexplained.

The way around this dilemma is through an appeal to an underlying, common moral character. By doing this *The Sexuality of Men* (Seidler 1985) is able to sidestep any conclusion that its presence is a mere historical deviance which, in time, will be ironed out. The attempt to make sense of the contradiction between the assured public facade of masculinity and men's inner doubts mark out the parameters of this project. The truth of men lies in the inner doubt, in the damaged human capacities for relating and intimacy. The political nature of therapy, in dislodging 'internalised capitalist ideology', is in the healing of pain and the restoration of men to a truly human moral propensity that will overcome the discord imposed upon them by culture. In this context language is a snare and the search for an interior realm of feeling is the struggle to find a truth that will counterpose representation. We are back again to this idea of a somatic experience which transcends language and within which men can truly speak of themselves, not in the act of redescription or creation but in the representation of a hidden truth.

MAS's initial articulation of the disjunction between men's use of words and their feelings produced an attempt to contest the vocabularies of hegemonic masculinities. The silence that I referred to in the first chapter represented the failure of reflexivity, the incapacity of old vocabularies to speak of new cultural and historical relations. By concentrating upon this disjunction, through therapy, consciousness-raising groups and in writing, MAS provided an opening for the exploration of relations between the psyche and the social in the formation of subjectivity and gender identity. But it was in MAS's use of theory that it muted its insights and analysis. Instead of a reflexive politics, MAS adopted the language of the personal. The emphasis on the personal and the implication of the truth of personal experience, prioritised the phenomenological and immanent over language and representation. This was part of the political culture MAS was an element of and it was further emphasised by the intellectual tools of humanities and social sciences which continually downplayed the elements of contingency in both psychoanalysis and marxism. In accepting a paradigmatic model of masculinity, MAS remained caught in the old vocabularies, trying to argue them better, by calling upon a moral position which could justify the necessity of men to change. I want to conclude this chapter by looking at some of the consequences of this impasse in which MAS found itself.

SEXUAL MORALISM

The publication of *The Sexuality of Men* in 1985 was the representative moment of MAS's theoretical endeavours. It also marked the effective closure of the collective MAS project of reflexivity. The problems encountered in theorising a description of masculine identities and heterosexuality meant that no new languages and descriptions were forthcoming which could challenge the development of a narrow 'men's movement' perspective. Three years earlier in 1982 *Achilles Heel* had ceased publication. It had had one foot in the counter-culture and one in the revolutionary left. As both began to wane at the beginning of the decade with the rise of Thatcherism and the onset of economic recession, the original political and cultural context of MAS was pulled apart. An era of revolutionary socialism and oppositional politics was at an end and *Achilles Heel* went with it.[45]

MAS had always been beset by the tension between its reflexive concerns and its character as a political, pro-feminist movement. The great strength of *Achilles Heel* had been its refusal to see them as mutually exclusive. It had been out of this tension that *The Sexuality of Men* (Seidler 1985) had been written. Much of the cause for its relative failure can be ascribed to the inevitable ambivalence created by the contradictory components of MAS. *Achilles Heel*'s disappearance as a public theoretical forum, revealed MAS split into two distinctive groups; the liberal or men's liberation wing and the pro-radical feminist wing. Despite having a decade in which to accentuate their differences from one another, they shared certain tendencies; an emphasis upon anecdotal evidence to the exclusion of critical theory and a trend towards a moralistic and prescriptive politics. While *The Sexuality of Men* could not be reduced to either camp it was unable to establish a third position that could counter these trends.

The public focus for the political differences fell by default to the longstanding, but irregular *Anti-Sexist Men's Newsletter*. Never able to sustain a polemical discussion about men's sexual politics and produced by a rota of different men's groups, it relied upon unsolicited, often anecdotal contributions. Reading it was a frustrating experience, each issue seemed a repetition of its predecessor, giving the impression of a sexual politics stuck in an intellectual rut. It did nevertheless serve as an indicator of the political and personal concerns of those involved in men's sexual politics. Issue number 18, published by a group of men from Brixton, South London, was the first to be both polemical and thematic.

The issue was devoted to the question of men's accountability to the Women's Liberation Movement. In their introduction, the group challenged the prevailing tendency of 'men's liberation'.

> For some years now, 'anti-sexism' among men in Britain has been dominated by the ideas of 'men's liberation' . . . men against sexism have tended to see sexism and patriarchy as a 'sex-role system' which oppresses both women and men equally, rather than an ideology of male supremacy and the practical expression of men's power over women and children. As a result they have stressed the 'problems of masculinity'. . . . We believe those men who most strongly identify with 'men's liberation' at best run the risk of creating new demands on women's time and energy in the guise of 'freedom of expression'.[46]

The reflexive element within MAS is conflated with sexual liberalism and seen as a simple reassertion of men's patriarchal interests. Men, instead of being concerned about themselves and their own sexual identities should be listening to, understanding and taking account of women's demands. It meant; 'developing an anti-sexist practice not on our terms and in men's interests but on women's terms.'[47] In effect such a politics rendered masculinity invisible, erasing men from the question of gender relations and sexual differences. In practice it depended upon men denying their own emotional needs, feelings and personal interests. These were to be negated rather than negotiated.

Inevitably such a politics demanded a high degree of self-denial and moral masochism which fed into the sexual and moral puritanism of men's bourgeois upbringings. This *mea culpa* politics was only exacerbated by the moribund state of men's sexual politics and the virtual disappearance of the oppositional culture that had existed during the 1970s. For those of us who embraced the radical feminist assumptions that men were the agents of a universal, ahistorical and monolithic system of male supremacy, reflexivity was akin to pitiable self-indulgence. We embraced radical feminism like a crusade against our own subjectivities, its simplicity of analysis only fuelled our determination to believe in it.[48] It was a curious and deeply unproductive period for men's sexual politics, best summed up by the comment, 'I have seen the enemy and he is us.'[49] By 1983, the economic recession and Thatcherism had wiped away the last traces of the 1970s counterculture and after those heady days anti-sexist men were left only with themselves and the uncertainty about who they were and what they wanted.

In contrast to this position there emerged a reaction against this culture of despair. The legacy of therapy within MAS ensured the growth of co-counselling. But while Red Therapy, grounded in a revolutionary political culture, had maintained an eclectic approach to its practice, co-counselling, cut off from any political culture produced a narrow and deeply reductionist language of sexual politics. Its technique of one-to-one mutual counselling provided a democratic environment in which men could explore feelings and personal conflicts. But its emphasis upon praising men's innate goodness in order to reinforce a sense of self-worth, only reinforced the moralistic and essentialist dimension of MAS's excursion into the growth movement. This celebration of masculinity and men reduced politics entirely to the realm of the personal. In the end, all oppressive structures of power could be explained in terms of individual 'distress'. It was a tendency that erased politics.

In 1986, issue number 23 of the now renamed *Anti-Sexist Men's Newsletter* epitomised this position. Its editorial, written by a group of men in Bristol stated:

> We want to build a new non-violent masculinity. As a result of this we decided not to print any material that abuses or ridicules men . . . wallowing in images of how awful we are does not help us change. In fact it makes us powerless.[50]

Here, then, was the language of reflexivity, but devoid of any critical theory or wider sexual political reference. The almost desperate repetition of the positive qualities of men ('It is a wonderful group – we have made enormous strides in trust, love and affection together';[51] 'I am very good at making friends. I am also a very good friend.'[52]) were a litany that kept at bay some dreadful self-disgust. As a discourse of sexual politics it was almost entirely meaningless for each invocation seemed designed to ward off these inner doubts and the external negativities of feminists who didn't like men and anti-sexist men, who also didn't like men.

While co-counselling's embracing of men differed from its counterpart's rejection of them, it shared with pro-radical feminist men a simplicity of analysis. Any theoretical or political development was stymied. By the mid-1980s, the 'men's movement' was in a political and cultural backwater. It had the quality of the last vestiges of a social formation, hanging on to the coat-tails of what had preceded it. Devoid of its excitement, stripped of its cultural and political context it seemed an anachronism in an era of great change. Yet despite this, it did not detract from the growth of men's groups around the country. Even in 1982 *Achilles Heel*, in its final editorial, acknowledged the growing interest in the issue of masculinity. 'From being the only public forum for discussion about masculinity in this country, we have begun to see an increasing range of popular magazines beginning to write about "men" as an issue.'[53] And Jeff Hearn, writing in 1987 confirmed this popularising trend: 'In Britain in 1975 there were between twenty and thirty groups and five national conferences had taken place. By the mid-1980s, most medium sized and some small towns and rural areas, have at least one group'.[54] It was a growth reflecting the impact of feminism upon sections of the middle class and the subsequent challenge to individual men.

GOODBYE TO MAS

The issues that had begun to emerge out of the MAS reflexivity of the 1970s represented the precursor of a less intense, more widely dispersed cultural and political contestation over the meanings of masculinity. Feminism had confronted men with themselves, at once challenging them and offering new concepts that could begin to explain the sense of unease many men felt in a culture which was primarily organised to privilege and service them. Feminism impelled a search for new vocabularies of identity and self-description and expression. It was this search that brought men to the limit of their reflexivity, to a silence. It was this silence that formed a structure of feeling. MAS marked its precipitation into the first vestiges of a cultural practice, as, through consciousness-raising groups and in different therapeutic practices men attempted to explore their subjectivities. The concern for the relation of feeling to language defined the parameters of this silence but it never managed to explore it and bring it into words, for in its theoretical endeavours MAS sheered away from its reflexive analysis.

The search for an interior realm of male subjectivity constantly threatened to pitch MAS into a new romanticism in search of men's truth of themselves. But its commitment to feminism and forms of revolutionary politics gave it a critical edge. It was with the collapse of that world in the 1980s that co-counselling took men's sexual politics into a romanticism, while pro-radical feminist men led it up another cul-de-sac. MAS theory recognised the centrality of the mother in the formation of male subjectivity and combined with its critique of patriarchal relations it was moving in the right direction to invent new definitions of male subjectivity. But its conflation of the psyche with the social and the emergence of a sexual moralism brought its reflexive project to a halt.

The demise of MAS politics was also brought about by the changing cultural and political sensibilities of the 1980s. Its emphasis upon a singular masculinity gave it a class and ethnic exclusivity at a time when the politics of difference was becoming a significant issue in radical and socialist milieux. The project initiated by MAS in the 1970s was left to founder in its own cultural exclusivity and its universalist language, an embarrassing *faux pas* in the era of difference. It was as if the displacements effected by feminism, gay affirmation and the new politics of ethnicity excluded any consideration amongst white heterosexual men of a reflexive analysis of their hegemonic masculinities. By the mid-1980s, the 1970s seemed a staid and conservative decade dominated by a moral puritanism and an allergy to pleasure. MAS and men's sexual politics suffered a similar image. Yet the intellectual project started by MAS had only just begun. Its attempts at a totalising theory prematurely derailed what its specificity had to offer; a definition of the parameters of a cultural silence in the relationship between men's feelings and language. What this silence is and what it contains and the effect it plays upon masculine identities are subjects to be investigated. But they were issues that were buried during the 1980s as the mounting rejection of the sexual politics of the 1970s condemned all its insights to the scrapheap.

3

DIFFERENCE COMES TO TOWN

THE CULTURAL POLITICS OF MASCULINITY

The 1980s created its own sexual and political agenda out of the historic defeat of the left and the regeneration of the capitalist market economy. It was consumerism and the market, rather than political struggle and therapy that was providing a language for changing masculine identities. The trend was identified by Frank Mort in an article in 1986 on men and style. 'Flat tops, rappers and razor partings dancing late into the night. Something is definitely happening to men's wear and young men.'[1] The argument that consumption, fashion and pleasure were contributing to changing definitions of gender identity led to a hostile response from many active in 1970s sexual politics. But Mort was anticipating this generational antagonism. 'It may be that young men and women are already renegotiating their personal and sexual relations, negotiations which have been made on the back of the gains of feminism, but which 1970s men and women are too frightened to accept as possible.'[2] In a similar vein younger women were becoming critical of feminism: 'What I'm asking for is less bloody reverence all round.'[3] The growing interest in what was happening within popular culture rather than the concerns of a politically conscious vanguard reflected the shift in the leading edge of critical theory from the social sciences to cultural politics. With it came a broadening of feminist and sexual political analysis as they began to address differences of class and ethnicity.

The 1980s was the decade of Thatcherism and it spawned a contradiction of images and metaphors of masculine identity: toy boy, new man, new father, lager lout, the yuppie. In this mixture of sexual, familial and economic identities existed the contradictory structural changes that characterised the decade. In 1987 men found their way into the pages of the Mothercare catalogue. In the Summer catalogue the new Mothercare man was on the front cover, in his late twenties, he seemed a far cry from his own dad of the 1950s. Sally Olliver, the Mothercare spokeswoman at the time commented: 'Men aren't ashamed to come into our shops anymore. We're reflecting what's happening in the family.'[4] The decision to put in images of fathers had been the chairman's; an intuitive feel that times were changing. Indeed there were an increasing number of men pushing buggies down high streets on Saturdays. There was a dramatic leap in the numbers of fathers attending the births of their children. Yet any attempt to actually quantify and gauge the changing trends of masculine identities and practices was a notoriously difficult occupation.

With the lack of any comprehensive statistical data, commentary focused on the new representations of masculinity and on simple anecdote and conjecture. There was a feeling that changes were in the air, yet no one could actually put their finger on what these were. In consequence it was a decade that bred a good deal of scepticism. Writing at its close, Angela Phillips had little good to say of it. 'The 1980s was the decade in which the New Man gave up trying. He swapped his jeans for a designer suit, stopped pretending to share the childcare and got heavily into the new culture of cash.'[5] Yet despite this scepticism, men and masculinity were regular subjects of media analysis.[6] Introducing a special section for fathers in *Practical Parenting*, the editor Davina Lloyd reflected the confusion by arguing that the new father was a myth. Drawing upon unpublished research by the sociologist Ann Oakley she wrote: 'Men are as little involved in day to day care of their children as they were twenty years ago.'[7] What small amount of research existed backed up this assertion. The Family Policy Studies Centre published an Occasional Paper, *Inside the Family*, which drew on evidence to suggest that the division of domestic work within the family was broadly unchanged. The rise of the two-income family within the middle class led to the employment of domestic help and nannies. And in working-class families, the increased participation of women in the workforce led to their doing two jobs as worker and as housewife and mother. The greater equality of opportunity for middle-class women led to the transfer of some of their domestic responsibilities to working-class women rather than to their husbands.

Research in advertising revealed a far more cautious attitude towards the changing expressions of masculinity than many of its new images suggested.[8] Advertising agencies were loath to figure the New Man in food- and shopping-related adverts.[9] Even in fashion, where the new sexual expressivity of men was initiated, there was caution. Murray Partridge of Yellowhammer, an agency with a profile that was youthful and progressive commented: 'The male sex symbol is the mid-Atlantic stereotype. A 1950s/1980s person, good looking, clean cut and healthy. We still operate within conventional masculine stereotypes.' And he added, 'I think this country would still prefer to see more realistic violence in the media than male nudity.'[10] This note of caution and pessimism wasn't shared by women working in the media. Kitty O'Hagen, then Planning Director of the advertising company GGK, produced market research to show women's dissatisfaction with the images of men in advertising.

Women are dissatisfied with the images of men. . . . Where are the men doing household chores? More men do them now, but it's like a closet activity they don't admit to. Women want to be represented as independent and resourceful individuals. Men must want something different too![11]

It was women's aspirations that seemed to be fuelling this media concern with issues of masculinity. Nowhere was this more in evidence than in women's magazines. Commenting on *Cosmopolitan*'s attempt to launch *Cosmo Man* in the late 1970s, editor Linda Kelsey said:

It was a kind of missionary zeal that prompted us to do it. We thought that men had changed as quickly as women and that the time was right to offer them a magazine which would discuss sex, relationships, emotions, clothes and grooming without embarrassment, but we were wrong.[12]

Cosmo Man retreated from the market place and continued as a quarterly supplement, firmly bound to its big sister, catering for an estimated 500,000 men who read the magazine, but would never buy it. The idea of a mass market magazine had been mooted in publishing circles for years. The failure of *Cosmo Man* suggested that the British male was too conservative to buy such a product.

The new upsurge in men's fashion consciousness spurred many

of the women's magazines to cash in on the advertising revenue and produce their own supplements for men. There was a recognition of men's covert interest in 'women's issues'. This new move put magazines like *Elle* onto the leading edge of the new market-led masculine sensibilities. Contradicting the scepticism of his elders, Marcus Van Ackerman, the editor of *Elle Pour Homme* said: 'This is the generation of the baby boom. Younger men aren't scared to look at themselves. They're less likely to follow the crowd.'[13] And it was just this combination of individualism and a loosening of the homophobic refusal to take pleasure in the looks of other men that provided an opening for a new-style men's magazine.

In 1986, the publishers of the highly successful magazine *The Face* produced the first non-pornographic, self-conscious magazine for men, since the collapse of *Cosmo Man*. It survived. *Arena* represented a curious mix of traditionalist prose and homoerotic visual imagery. Men had the pleasure of looking at other men's bodies, but the message of the feature writing was that the conventional male concerns with money, power and status remained, albeit through the lens of a new male interest in consumption. Despite this similarity with *Playboy*, it carried a sensibility of masculine self-consciousness that gave it a greater critical edge. Steve Taylor was an original member of the editorial staff. He comments on this difference between image and text and the lack of any overt sexual politics in the magazine.

> Sexual politics doesn't appeal to any of us. For our generation – I'm thirty-five – that discussion was blown. It was no fun. We don't want to go back to it. I think it would be really yuck to have a *Cosmo Man* style; talking to other men about their feelings would be a commercial death wish.[14]

By the end of the decade the era's fashionable individualism was crumbling in the face of new economic recession and a credit squeeze. An emergent green consciousness had begun to reshape masculine acquisitiveness. Traditional masculine products like cars were being sold on the basis of their safety, their environmentalism and the protection they offered child passengers. If the New Man of the mid-1980s had been identified by the clothes he wore, his presence by the end of the decade was marked by a baby and a new social responsibility. Men's emotions and relationships were subject to increasing scrutiny. The 1970s with its image of a prescriptive moral and sexual politics was no longer *passé* as the economy blew a hole in itself and began to sink towards a new recession. In 1989 *Cosmo Man* conducted a telephone survey of 500 men. Lacking any scientific rigour it came up with a reasonably accurate impression of male sensibilities.

> our survey indicates that, in general, younger men especially have a greater respect for women's equality. They're more aware of women's sexuality than expected, and feel less threatened by it. They display a positive attitude towards working women. They are romantic, want to fall in love, and most say they want to marry and have children – when the time is right.[15]

The fashionable snubbing of the 1970s was giving way to a concern with relationships. Marriage and children were desirable motifs of a successful masculinity.

'Let me welcome you to the thirty-something Utopia', wrote Geoff Deane in *Options* magazine in February 1990. 'For many the nineties will herald an emotional Armageddon. Divorced, defunct and unfashionable to boot.'[16]

While he was writing for a women's magazine, it was men he was talking about. In April's issue of *Elle* magazine in the same year, Alex Morgan was reiterating the original MAS concern with reflexivity, albeit in a different context. 'I'm a man, no worries in that department – . . . but not macho and not sexist. No, a modern man. A real . . . a real . . . in fact that's the whole problem – a real what?' He concluded his article with the comment, 'what we need now is to find a new masculinity.'[17] It was full circle and back to the beginning of MAS. This convergence between the market-led identities and the earlier concerns of MAS offered a new beginning. If the 1980s and the 1970s met, perhaps there could be a *rapprochement* and a new more popular exposition of a men's sexual politics.

It was this attempt to revive a sexual politics out of the widespread interest in men and masculinity that a group in North London, under the auspices of *Marxism Today*, organised a day event; 'Breaking Out. Men's Sexual Politics for the Nineties', in June, 1987. The mix of concerns – workshops on fatherhood, gay and straight men, fashion, politics and race, covered the new and older sensibilities of men's sexual politics. But the final plenary session revealed that a divide still existed between the language of the men's movement and the newer cultural politics of masculinity. A *rapprochement* didn't seem impending.[18] Meanwhile a new moralism was emerging from within the men's movement in response to the debates on pornography.

MALE HETEROSEXUALITY, PORNOGRAPHY AND THE NEW MORALISM

During 1989 a 'Campaign Against Pornography', initiated by the Labour MP Clare Short, was launched. At the same time a number of those involved, concerned about the implications of censorship, formed a separate campaigning body called the 'Campaign Against Pornography and Censorship'. Clare Short had attempted to pass a Bill through the House of Parliament, outlawing the *Sun*'s Page 3. This had drawn up the battle lines. Pilloried by Conservatives and the popular press and supported by thousands of letters from around the country, the issue of pornography was on the political agenda. Much of the analysis of the role, function and definition of pornography was drawn from radical feminist writings of Susan Brownmiller (1976), Andrea Dworkin (1981) and Susan Griffin (1982). This discourse on pornography reduced the issue to a moral level. If an individual was not opposed to pornography or did not actively seek its erasure, then he (sic) was against women. 'Pornography is . . . a hate campaign to humiliate and brutalize all females, women and children. . . . This is not a pretty time. If my assessment is correct, it is a time of war.'[19] The contemporary history of feminist campaigns against pornography had always been shrouded in a reductive moral language. (For an alternative position see Rogerson and Wilson 1991.) My interest is not with the polemic of feminist debate, so much as the effect it had upon men's mobilisation in the anti-pornography movement. For the moral language resonated with the men's movement's own tendency to prescriptive politics. Through the lack of any other position, the languages of pro-radical feminism and co-counselling formed an uneasy amalgam which dominated the discourse of men's anti-pornography politics and attempted to both analyse male heterosexuality and redescribe it within a moral framework.

'Pornography', writes John Stoltenburg, 'tells lies about women. But pornography tells the truth about men.'[20] Stoltenburg was aligned to the US radical feminist anti-porn campaign led by Andrea Dworkin and Catherine MacKinnon (see Everywoman 1988). He was invited to speak at a London-based event in September 1990. 'Opposing Pornography: A One-Day Conference for Men', was organised by the 'Campaign Against Pornography and Censorship'. Stoltenburg told his audience that, 'Pornography . . . keeps sex between people an experience of hierarchy and objectification rather than intimacy, mutuality and profound partnership.'[21] In his book *Refusing to be a Man*, Stoltenburg argues that pornography is a direct representation of male supremacy.

> Your penis is a weapon, her body is your target. And pornography says about that sexuality, 'Here's why': Because men are masters and women are slaves; men are superior, women are subordinate; men are real, women are objects, men are sex machines, women are sluts.[22]

The unrelenting logic of this demagoguery offers men no room to manoeuvre. And while it is rhetoric rather than analysis, the very lack of theoretical analysis within the men's movement gave it both credence and legitimacy. Its implications suggest that theory is simply a product of male supremacist thinking and rationality is a form of thought that perpetuates male dominance. The only strategy in such a context is a fundamentalist moral one. The only meaning of male sexuality is the radical feminist analysis that men's use of pornography indicates a male heterosexuality in unremitting and violent assault upon women.

The logic of this moral fundamentalism has an effect upon the politics of experience predominating in men's sexual politics. It extends the authoritative discourse of personal experience into a place where men can find a site of opposition to this seamless totality of male supremacy and potential brutality.

> If pornography is the way that war is being waged to this juncture in the history of male supremacy, and it sure as hell seems so, then count me out, I defect, and count on me as a conscientious objector.[23]

The dilemma is, how can one refuse to be a man? It is possible to struggle to change aspects of masculine identity that are oppressive and damaging to others. But there can be nowhere in language or culture where it would be possible to refute one's biological existence. The only place to turn is to that 'inner realm' of feeling. This is what MAS addressed in the 1970s and found it had no vocabulary to address and represent it.

Here then, in this silence, it might be possible to turn one's subjectivity inside out and construct an identity whose sole legitimation is derived from what the old one repressed and failed to speak. Such 'soft' feelings as empathy, gentleness, nurture have been culturally defined as feminine attributes. Dominant ideals of masculinity have been constructed in contradistinction to them. It is possible, then, that men could establish a common identification with women through these repressed 'feminine' sensibilities. At the same time they would be able to avoid the totality of social and linguistic relationships that bestow upon them supremacy and a potential brutality. Such a manoeuvre represents a parody of the original reflexive concern with the relationship of men's feeling to language. What cannot be spoken of in dominant discourses of masculinity assumes the place of an oppositional font of moral truth. It is romanticism and fundamentalism combined. The attempt to redefine masculinity and to explore male heterosexuality is turned into an assumption that what is silent within male subjectivity is feminine and consequently what women have and want and therefore the basis for a new masculinity. One that is wholly defined by an essentialist binary logic.

The consequences of this perspective reduces the psychodynamic formation of male heterosexuality to the realm of feeling. It refutes the idea of a psychic sphere in subjectivity, providing an attempt to define it in moral terms. The result is a language and analysis that cannot begin to get to grips with the fantasies, desire and pleasures of male heterosexuality. Peter Baker, a central figure in the Campaign Against Pornography and Censorship has called for a new model of male heterosexuality to replace the aggression and emotional failings of the old.

> Tender men . . . are more interested in closeness and cuddles than in copulation. They prefer to kiss and pet for hours, rather than come in minutes. Tender men may go for days or weeks without desiring sex, and when they make love, they want to take their time and not be obsessed about how well they perform. For them the expression of intimacy and tenderness is more important than creating orgasms which last for hours.[24]

Baker's notion of 'good sex' assumes that the 'soft' feelings men deny in themselves are more authentic than feelings of, for example, erotic aggression and that they constitute the psychodynamics of sexual desire. There is also the assumption that these 'soft' feelings are congruent with female sexuality and what women want, both in their feminine identities and from relationships with men.

In this congruence of feelings, differences between men and women are erased. Not just differences of gender, but the separateness of self from an other. 'Good sex' is defined in opposition to the fantasies and objectifications of pornography. Representation is itself pornographic so that whatever cannot be experienced as immanent – the pure presence of two individual consciousnesses – is part of the cultural and linguistic realm of male supremacy. The new morality of male heterosexual practice is born of this desire for an unmediated union, to completely know and experience the other individual. The insights of psychoanalysis that suggest the impossibility of such a union, are dismissed along with the knotty problem of sexual fantasies which refuse to fit into the new regime. Eroticism is reduced to its 'nice' components. Aggression, sadism, masochism, objectifying lust, the 'dirty' elements of sexuality are erased through an act of will. It is a longing for a sexuality that replays an idealised mother–infant relationship. The desire for such an undifferentiated state of being is a part of sexual desire, but it is only a part. By promoting it as the true and authentic expression of selfhood in communion with an other, it closes down the analysis of men's heterosexuality

The conservative nature of this moralism is not only its presumption about the nature of sexuality but also the form its discourse takes. To overcome men's alienation from this inner realm they must disclose their feelings. This practice of self-disclosure was central to consciousness-raising groups and psychotherapeutic groups within MAS. But now it was in danger of becoming the source of all truth and meaning.

> It's time men opened up about how they feel and what they think . . . men just need to find trusted friends or partners who will listen while they talk openly and honestly about the difficulties in their lives, and who will be sympathetic should they start crying or feeling frightened. This is the key to men being more loving and intimate, more expressive about their feelings and consequently less domineering.[25]

The problem with the discourse of self-disclosure is its similarity to the Catholic notion of confession. It is the absolution of sin. Its concern is with the production of a new truth and not with the exploration of one's subjectivity.

Michel Foucault has written about the role of such self-disclosure in the establishment of relations of power and meanings of sexuality; 'one's sins, one's thoughts and desires, one's illnesses and troubles; one goes about telling, with the greatest precision, whatever is most difficult to tell.'[26] It is this confession which establishes the interlocutor into a new discourse of sexuality, regulated through his relationship with what he is telling:

> the agency of domination does not reside in the one who speaks (for it is he who is constrained), but in the one who listens and says nothing; not in the one who knows and answers, but in the one who questions and is not supposed to know.[27]

Its task is a regulation of the subject rather than a search for knowledge. Disclosure of men's 'feminine' inner world enables the banishment of the bad old male ways. In other words to 'open up' is morally good. It is a discourse of self-disclosure based on the moral evaluation of specific sexual feelings and emotions. It was a genuine attempt to challenge prevailing ideologies of masculinity and to move out of the impasse in which the men's movement had buried itself. But its lack of any theoretical analysis gave it the character of a moral fundamentalism. Instead of pursuing an analysis of the relationship of men's feelings to language it sought to construct certain moral truths out of its engagement with radical feminism and the anti-pornography campaign. In the end it was not romanticism it offered, but a narrow, authoritarian prescription for masculinity and male heterosexuality.

DIFFERENCE COMES TO TOWN

In the light of the increasing narrowness of the men's movement, it isn't surprising that the first significant analysis of masculinity since the publication of *The Sexuality of Men*, came from outside its borders. In a critical essay on the book, Kobena Mercer addressed the ethnic exclusivity of MAS and its failure to recognise the racial differences of masculine identities (Mercer 1986). The preoccupation with a psychological account of the formation of male subjectivity was, he argued, at the expense of a sociological consideration of men's differences. White sexual politics, 'is an interpretation of the radical slogan "the personal is political" which is made in an individualistic manner and thus excludes questions of race and ethnicity because it is preoccupied with the "self" at the expense of the "social".'[28] In consequence he asks, 'What happens to the political if it goes no further than the purely personal?'[29] Mercer replies to his rhetorical question by citing the organisational form and the language of MAS; the men's consciousness-raising group, a cultural practice which demands specific class and cultural skills and vocabularies. Similarly, he argues, the description of masculinity as emotionally inarticulate is particular to the class and ethnic constituency of MAS and cannot be extrapolated beyond its own cultural borders. The concern with 'inner feelings' and the failure to relate them to the external factors such as class and ethnicity produces a psychological inquiry which, 'abstracts the psyche from its specific cultural, social and historical formation.'[30]

It had been the theoretical tools available to MAS that made an analysis of the determinations of cultural difference upon masculine identities next to impossible. By default, *The Sexuality of Men* had produced the description of a singular and normative model of masculinity. But this failure reflected the subtle shift that took place within much of its text, moving from a reflexive concern with the authors' own masculine identities to a broader extrapolation of these to include all other men. The advocacy of personal experience as the font of meaning was translated into the definitive practice of sexual politics and its central priority. The simple point of Mercer's critique was to argue that this wasn't true, that men with different histories, different ethnicities and different sexualities had different priorities and strategies, and sought different means of expressing them.

The failure to recognise the actual plurality of masculine identities lay in the assumption that masculinity was an internally undifferentiated category. R.W. Connell has termed this 'categorical theory' (Connell 1987). It amounts to a sexual politics that is unable to theorise the formation of people and their identities within a number of relationships, e.g. class and race, simultaneously. The social order is portrayed in terms of two major categories that tend to subordinate all other antagonisms to their conflict of interest and power relation. The consequence is an appreciation of power and conflict of interest between categories, but a failure to cope with the complexities of difference both within and between them. The debates and polemics within *Achilles Heel* were never able to make these links, but it was with its demise, and the predominance of the two counterpoising strands with their moral language, that this simplifying picture is most marked. A metaphysical solidarity between 'all women' is pitted against an all-pervasive, trans-historical male supremacy. Differences of class, race and culture are subordinate to this universal structure of male domination and female subordination. Such a debilitating and pessimistic scenario provides fertile soil for forms of political and moral fundamentalism.

While the 'men's movement' was caught in its political impasse, the problems of the differential relations of class, sexuality and race were tearing the women's movement into fragments. Difference was becoming an increasing preoccupation amongst feminist intellectuals (see Segal 1987). Cynthia Cockburn, in her study of working-class men employed in the old newspaper print rooms, addressed the way gender and class interacted in masculine identities (Cockburn 1985). She argued that it was the tendency to try to mesh together two static structures; the marxist theory of class and the feminist analysis of patriarchy, that undermined bringing class and gender into a single focus.

> (In my study) . . . I was paying attention to processes, the detail of historical events and changes, and in this way it was easier to detect the connections between the power systems of class and gender. What we are seeing is a struggle that contributes to the formation of people within both their class and gender simultaneously.[31]

It was this emphasis upon the processes constituting identity, rather than identity itself, which had led so many to turn to theories of structural linguistics and post-structuralism. For while they had little to offer political agency, their employment in the field of textual and cultural analysis enabled the theorising of complex determinations.

DIFFERENCE AND THE FRONTIERS OF IDENTITY

Ernesto Laclau and Chantal Mouffe sought to produce a theoretical framework which could address the proliferation of social and

political antagonisms and identities in society, moving beyond
Connell's description of 'categorical theory'. Their beginning was
the 'break' with orthodox marxism, made by Louis Althusser.[32] In
his essay 'Contradiction and Overdetermination' (Althusser 1971)
Althusser challenges the idea that the economy is the sole determining factor of social relations. Overdetermination, a word taken
from Freud, means that an effect is not the consequence of a single
cause but the result of several. It assumes the presence of contradiction – an outcome is determined by the relation of contradiction
to determinations. Althusser's use of the term implies that society
has no fixed boundaries that define it. Its meaning and its form
are constituted within its own practices. What constitutes the social
sphere is potentially open-ended, closed only by its structural
logics, themselves overdetermined. Althusser challenged the prevailing marxist assumption that the superstructure was a reflection
of underlying economic relations. But he drew back from the
possibility that overdetermination challenged the central concept
of historical materialism which defined human progress in terms
of changing class relations. Instead he ended his essay with the
assertion that in 'the last instance', the economy does determine.

Laclau and Mouffe argue that the implications of Althusser's
theory undermine his rather desperate last-minute return to
orthodoxy. There can be no underlying totality to social relations
and identities, either economic or metaphysical. They argue that
his essay is, a 'critique of every type of fixity, through an affirmation of the incomplete, open and politically negotiable character
of every identity.'[33] To accept this description is to agree that
individuals have no essential core or essence that gives rise to their
identity. Identity and subjectivity are products of discourse, made
out of the linguistic descriptions and the practices which define
them. These configurations of different elements of class, race and
gender, individual and collective histories and personal and familial experiences, make our identities. They are relations and
elements constantly in the process of being articulated into an
identity, which can never be fixed for all time. Laclau and Mouffe
describe this articulation as, 'any practice establishing a relation
among elements such that their identity is modified as a result of
the articulatory practice'.[34]

Laclau and Mouffe use Saussure's structural linguistics to
underline the notion that there is no principle fixing or constituting of the field of difference. All values and all differences are

values and differences in opposition and defined, not by some organising principle, but by their difference from one another. This theory of linguistics implies that our class, ethnic or gender identities only have meaning in relation to other identities. On their own they mean nothing. For example, masculinity is given meaning through its culturally constructed difference from femininity. There is a danger that such a theory offers only an endless series of identities and social forms in a state of infinite dispersal. But Laclau and Mouffe argue that the articulation of identities produces equivalences of difference that constitute a social space organised around an antagonism. It is this space that marks the limit of the social, where the emergence of new identities and subjectivities are forced up against the limit of the dominant social discourses. Such frontiers cut across and re-arrange previous social relations. For example, the emergence of antagonisms around sex, race and gender in the social movements of the 1970s did not exist parallel to class antagonism, they intersected it and in those multiple conjunctures transformed the theory, practice and descriptions of class politics. These equivalences that constitute such frontier effects within the social are an articulation of a multiplicity of individual identifications with a shared interest or oppression. They are both contingent and temporary in their character. The political and cultural identities they constitute will change as the forces determining them change.

These frontiers are not simply signifying and ideological structures. They are organised by affective relations of emotion, pleasure and mood. The formation of identities occur through the production of these frontier effects, masculine/feminine, heterosexual/homosexual, one ethnicity in opposition to others. They mirror the binary distinction of self and other. As social effects they give rise to political and social relations of domination and subordination. The frontier between the dominant term and the subordinate term becomes an unbridgeable gap between the liveable and unliveable.[35] The philosopher and post-structuralist Jacques Derrida addressed such an exclusionary, binary system of differences with his concept of logocentrism.[36] This is the belief that an individual can utter the essence of meaning. A system of knowledge which depends upon such an originating moment of truth, some unquestionable and absolute guarantee on which to build hierarchies of value and meaning, sets up a system based upon an exclusion of what it is not. Structures of linguistic exchange are determined by this binary distinction. Gender differences, for example, are constructed through a seriality of dichotomies; active/passive, culture/nature, rational/emotional, hard/soft, masculine/feminine. It's a seemingly endless list and it shows how this binary operation of language and meaning, naturalises relations of discrimination and injustice.

Alice Jardine, an American, feminist intellectual has critically engaged with this binarism in an attempt to rethink what 'woman' means in Western society. She argues that the 'otherness' of 'woman' has been the defining binary of modernist cultural knowledge (Jardine 1985). For the past 150 years, in the period of modernity, what has been symbolically uncontainable within structures of thought and knowledge has been connoted with 'the feminine'. This binarism suggests the terms; centre and margin. The dominant term in its discursive and material operations marginalises and subordinates the other term. By assembling the heterogeneous possibilities of language and meaning into frontier effects, identities are reduced to polar opposites. Hegemonic political relations achieve their authority and leading position by producing a sense of what is liveable and what is not. In this way the emergence of new subjectivities is regulated and oppositional identities are marginalised. For Jardine, feminism marks the intensive exploration of the margins, putting the binary term into a state of uncertainty. It is when the other speaks back, when the marginalised term begins to wrestle with language to represent itself and cease being defined by the dominant term that the 'master narratives' (Lyotard 1987), what Jardine has reinterpreted as the 'paternal fiction', are called into question.

The conception of a frontier as a margin marking the limit of the centred, dominant term is not a simple boundary. It acts like a supplement. It is the antithesis of the centre in that it is excluded from it, but it is also a necessary part of it. Without the supplement to it the centred term remains incomplete. It's an operation which can be translated into gendered terms. Woman-as-supplement disturbs the boundaries of masculine/patriarchal authority for it both makes up for what is missing and exposes its lack.

When a number of years ago, *Cosmopolitan* magazine asked Jeffrey Archer who his sex symbol was, he replied; 'Dame Edna Everage. She's everything a woman should be.'[37] His quip illustrates 'woman' as a supplement of 'man'. She is a negative, a reflection of man's shadow. But this raises the question of what is 'man'? Masculinity can only define itself through its difference to femininity. But if it is no more than what masculinity is not, meanings of gender disappear into the ether. The question suggests that a complex interrelationship exists between the two terms. Femininity is 'unliveable' for men because its definition is based upon its containment of elements that have been rejected by masculine identities. There is a psychodynamic effect to the frontiers of binary differences in which the defensive mechanisms of splitting and projection play a prominent part. Masculinity is defined in its dividing off of the elements it must disavow and projecting them into the subordinate term of femininity, filling it with the antithesis of its own identity. The female body in its very alienness is both idealised and loathed by men. It represents the good maternal object men have lost and still long for, but it also mirrors and represents the bad, persecutory elements of the mother, which threaten to overwhelm men's boundaries of self. To maintain the fiction of its own identity, the masculine must maintain the binary distinction. Splitting and projection illustrate how psychic processes are mobilised in defence of frontiers. Blackness and ethnic difference, femininity and homosexuality have, historically, formed the threatening 'others' of the hegemonic white masculinities of our culture. Yet these masculine identities are integrally linked to these others through processes of psychical and cultural disavowal.

On the frontier effects lie the fears of difference: the racial fear of swamping, sexual pollution and aversion; the male taboo on sexual passivity, masochism, effeminacy and homosexuality; and the threat of female sexuality. 'The obscenity of the feminine sex', wrote Sartre, 'is that of everything which gapes open.'[38] This is the hole that threatens men with nothingness and the loss of self, waiting to suck men in and rob them of the integrity of their separateness from the maternal body. Masculine identities are articulated within these relations. The psychodynamics of relations between differences plays a significant role in constructing the 'unliveability' of the other. And psychoanalysis shows how seemingly antithetical identities, such as masculinity and femininity, are actually products of an individual history of a complex and antagonistic interrelationship, which has emerged out of an original synthesis of the terms in the individual unconscious.

Psychoanalysis cannot account for identity. But it can address a significant and central element in its articulation. It can describe the way that emotions, moods and fantasies serve to construct and maintain individual political and cultural identifications with specific social relations, institutions and values. And it can explain the way individuals cathect with these relations, making a deep emotional investment in them. This is to give it a different relation to the social implicit in Chodorow's thesis where the structuring of social relations serves to structure the psyche. In such a context, the character of masculinity is literal, pragmatic and practical; a necessity derived from the demands of the social order. Masculinity and men's heterosexuality are, in consequence described as functional, closed and complete. But the idea of articulation is that identity is both open-ended and contingent. Its closure around fixed meaning is a result of overdetermined equivalences and the construction of frontiers.

By concentrating upon the assumed functional necessity of masculinity, the disjunctions between the psyche and the social, between feeling and language are missed. This is why *The Sexuality of Men* (Seidler 1985) was able to describe the parameters of men's silence, but was unable to enter its space. It is the threads at the edge, rather than the fabric in the middle, the frontier effects and the margin, which will provide an understanding and analysis of how masculinities are constructed as cultural identities and how men come to live and speak within them. This is as Freud argued, when he wrote that apparent slips of the tongue, discrepancies, memories, fantasies and dreams have a social character (see Freud 1900a, 1905c). Despite their apparent peripheral relation to the subject they unveil its literal nature and apparent functional necessity. In other words necessity is not literal but a product of contingency. It is an attempt to fix the differences of a relational system into clearly defined frontiers. Laclau and Mouffe address this relation of contingency to necessity.

> This presence of the contingent in the necessary is what we earlier called *subversion*, and it manifests itself as symbolization, metaphorization, paradox, which deform and question the literal character of every necessity. Necessity, therefore, exists not under the form of an underlying principle, of a ground, but as an effort of literalization.[39]

What seems to be on the edge and peripheral to subjectivity in effect constitutes it.

What is present, what can be empirically determined, is not

necessarily the sum total of elements constituting an identity or social formation. Symbolisation and metaphor suggest that what is not present may also constitute identity. The negative of silence marks the frontier of an identity. Just as MAS struggled with that gap between feeling and available vocabularies, this break in reflexivity which is an absence that remains unaddressed by language, has a determining effect upon identity. 'Synonymy, metonymy, metaphor are not forms of thought that add a second sense to a primary constitutive literality of social relations; instead they are part of the primary terrain itself in which the social is constituted.'[40] The combination of psychoanalysis and a functional marxism or sociology tends to emphasise the necessary over the contingent, the empirical over the abstract. In consequence the psyche and social are welded together and their separate relative autonomies are lost in the functionalist description. But theories of language offer a more sophisticated and complex analysis of the relation between the psyche and the social. They address the central dynamic in the formation of cultural and gendered subjectivity, the relation of speech and language acquisition to a sphere of life that does not belong to speech. It makes it possible to address the way individual subjectivity is constructed around a relation between an inner psychic realm and an external world of identity and identifications.

PSYCHOANALYSIS AND DIFFERENCE

The 1980s saw a proliferation of interest in psychoanalysis. But this was not the object relations theory employed by *The Sexuality of Men*. Interest in Althusser and structuralism introduced a primarily academic audience to the work of Jacques Lacan. Lacan's work is a complex amalgamation of ideas and theories that defy a position. His initial impetus for research and writing was a belief that the international psychoanalytic establishment was moving away from Freud's earlier writings. These had emphasised the primacy of language, the unconscious and the oedipus complex. The increasing influence of Kleinian and object relations metapsychologies were displacing all three. Lacan's 'return to Freud' was his attempt to reverse this state of affairs. In his groundbreaking address to the Rome Congress of the International Psychoanalytic Association in 1953 he stated, 'Whether it sees itself as an instrument of healing, of training, or of exploration in depth, psychoanalysis has only a single medium: the patient's speech.'[41] It is speech which is intersubjective by its nature, for it has no meaning without a reply.

Lacan sought a synthesis of Freud and structural linguistics in his description of the formation of the psyche. The imaginary realm of fantasies is the subject's identification with other human images and the world it shares with them. It constitutes Lacan's description of the pre-oedipal realm. In the oedipus complex the infant's subjectivity is constituted in the structure of language and culture's exchange of symbolic meaning. He called this structure which lies in wait for the infant the 'Symbolic'. It is only through the 'Symbolic' realm of language and meaning that the subject can represent desires and feelings.[42] In Britain his work enabled a conjunction of semiology, discourse theory and psychoanalysis which has been given a shorthand title of sexual difference theory.[43] Interest in Lacan lay in his emphasis upon the cultural construction of subjectivity and gender. It seemed to avoid Freud's own ambivalence on the determining role of biology in subjective formation. What was more, his work seemed to rectify the ambivalent place of the unconscious in object relations and Kleinian theory and the tendency to define the maturational process in moral and social terms. Lacanian psychoanalyis provided a framework for addressing the role of language in psychic formation, sexuality and gender identity. This sophisticated and complex set of theories complemented the cultural sensibilities of the 1980s and offered a seductive alternative to the moralism and essentialism that had pervaded sexual political analysis in the 1970s.

But the problem of structuralism with its insistence that the subject is structured in language was resonant in Lacan's own theories. The emergence of sexual difference theory in response to the kind of impasse faced by MAS, tended to describe a subject which had been dissolved into the ethereal world of representation. 'Gender is (a) representation' wrote Teresa de Lauretis. She went on to state: 'The representation of gender is its construction.'[44] Her assertion mirrors Lacan's own insistence that the symbolic order of society constitutes the individual in his or her entirety. The level of abstraction and the sophistication of Lacanian wordplay obscured the consequences of this death of the subject. While MAS had turned to psychoanalytic concepts to make sense of its practices in therapy and consciousness-raising groups, sexual difference theory had no such reference point. The dizzy world of theoretical analysis was an end in itself. There was no praxis that could secure theoretical abstraction to human activity.

Consequently, what little work appeared on masculinity tended to abstract the actual conditions of men's lives and relations with women. Mary Kelly, in her review of the 'Sexual Difference' exhibition at the ICA in 1985, addresses this problem.

> It is said that there is an attempt in certain work (Victor Burgin, Jeff Wall) to create a literal symmetry with the feminine term, suggesting for instance that if 'the woman' doesn't exist, than neither does 'the man', refusing the universal fact and identifying with the fictitious other.[45]

In an essay 'Man Desire Image' (Burgin 1984) Victor Burgin rejects the idea of an essential man, whose meaning and determination might exist outside language. He argues that gender is a social fiction, constructed through representation, albeit one that does have social effect. With this degree of abstraction the body may be assigned its meaning, but its somatic reality disappears from the equation. There is no praxis to ground sexual difference theory, so in rejecting the idea of a fixed identity, the question of who one is and what one does with this fictitious self remains a mystery.

Burgin quotes Lacan's enigmatic reference to 'he who finds himself male without knowing what to do about it' in an attempt to place himself in this abstract textual description of masculinity. But the dilemma is insoluble in this context. Without the subject there can be no reflexivity and no sense of historicity or biography. As Robert Young has written, 'A person in history is a biography . . . I do not mean this in order to promote a possessive individualism but to place history inside the subject rather than dissolving the subject into history.'[46] Lacanian psychoanalysis in dissolving the subject into the synchronic realm of the Symbolic removes its historical formation. In all the sophisticated attempts to outmanoeuvre the humanism and functionalism that precipitated the demise of 1970s sexual politics, Burgin is caught within the same pessimistic scenario as the men's movement. In his case he no longer even has the mythology of experience with which to sustain himself.

There has been little work on masculinity and male heterosexuality within a Lacanian framework. (For exceptions see Easthope

1986; Heath 1987; Neale 1983.) As Steve Neale has argued, sexual difference theory has left heterosexual masculinity undiscussed; '(it) has been identified as a structuring norm in relation both to images of women and gay men. It has to that extent been profoundly problematised, rendered visible. But it has rarely been discussed and analysed as such.'[47] The assumption that male heterosexuality is the structuring norm of sexual difference problematises men's use of it. Freud began to develop a theory of object relations after his essay on Narcissism (Freud 1914c), but Lacan takes the concept of narcissism as the incontestable theory of human nature. There is no interrelationship between self and objects in the maturational process, only an acquisitive subject seeking objects for his or her pleasure. The complex relationship between mind and body, culture and nature are subsumed beneath Lacan's universal structure of language. As Jane Flax comments: 'Like any narcissist's universe Lacan's writings often seem to be a series of self-referential and opaque images.'[48]

Rather than providing a deconstructive psychoanalysis of gender relations, much of Lacan's work can be read as a phenomenology of what it is like to live within a narcisissistic masculine world. There is of, course, value in this. Lacan has provided a highly sophisticated account of sexual desire and his description of the psychical processes of gender identification has been a valuable foil for feminist theorists in their task of undoing phallocentric definitions of femininity. However, there needs to be caution in his value for an analysis of masculinity. Peter Middleton writes:

> Feminism offers a misleading ease in its use of psychoanalysis. Because . . . (it) is able to work oppositionally through the already constituted marginality of women to this discipline. . . . Feminism is able to use psychoanalysis from points of both internal and external opposition. . . . The asymmetries of power and knowledge make it impossible to simply extend or reverse that critical strategy to consider men and masculinity, without reinstating the very authoritarianism that feminism has challenged.[49]

For Lacan, sexual difference is determined by the subject's relation to the transcendental signifier, the phallus, which structures gendered meaning. This, he insists, is not the penis but a symbol of plenitude and completeness. The subject's entry into language through the oedipus complex creates the unconconscious and splits the individual. The phallus represents the desire for a wholeness once again. There is a misconception that the masculine gender embodies the phallus and is therefore the signifier of meaning. This would complete the circle of the narcissist's universe. But Lacan does not say this and he leaves sufficient gaps and questions unanswered to make his work, despite its faults, a useful tool in a reflexive analysis of male subjecivity.

Sexual difference theory reduced the individual to a cipher of an already pre-ordained order, the unconscious a product of something outside of subjectivity. To assume Lacan provides analytic insights as opposed to phenomenological descriptions at this point is to take a leap of faith. It is necessary to accept that because Freudian psychoanalysis is a 'talking cure' the unconscious must be structured like a language. If this were true, there can be no place within subjectivity where desire for change can come from. As long as psychoanalysis is employed to analyse film texts and to explore the meanings of representation, it can evade these implications. But an analysis of subjectivity brings it into contact with the historical and practical articulation of identity, and it can only reduce it to a representational fiction. In such a context no-one can ever know their own selves to speak their stories or even control their own lives sufficiently to make new ones.

We are back to the same problem we encountered in Chodorow's synthesis of object relations and classical sociology. Her description of the relation between inner and outer realms of subjectivity undermined rather than explained its constitution. In Lacanian-influenced sexual difference theory the psyche is not a conduit for the production and maintenance of functional gender personalities, but one that is indissolubly part of a structured totality of linguistic and symbolic relations. The result is inertia, immobility and political pessimism. My own interest in sexual difference theory was its sophistication. Its concern with image and its objective, rational intellectualism was well suited for the 1980s, debunking the almost fetish-like belief in the subjective that had characterized the men's movement. It opened up a new way of talking about sexuality and gender which was free of a narrow prescriptive language. It offered the prospects of rethinking a theoretical and descriptive framework of masculinity which could encompass both its psychodynamic formation and its cultural differences.

The experience of intellectual political work in the 1980s was a rejection and dismissal of what had preceded it in the1970s. This generation gap was as much one of sensibility as age and it was aggravated and massaged in numerous intellectual and political disagreements. The priorities, concerns and languages of those involved in the feminist and socialist movements of the 1970s were dismissed by the brash new cultural politics as *au fait*. In turn 1970s activists were increasingly intolerant of the new interests in consumption, pleasure, media and textual analysis. There was little interaction bar the shouting. The result was a polarisation in the field of sexual politics marked out by two sets of priorities and sensibilities, with little cross-fertilisation (there were exceptions, see, for example, the work of Richard Dyer 1985). Each camp hung on to its identity through its rejection of the other. As someone who spanned both generations I played my part in this drama by dismissing my previous history of involvement in men's sexual politics and embracing the brave new world of theoretical abstraction. In the event, sexual difference theory and post-structuralism proved more seductive than useful and there seemed nowhere else to turn. Reflexivity seemed impossible within a Lacanian-inspired analysis of masculinity and equally doomed in the kind of personalised anecdotal descriptions of men's movement sexual politics.

Perhaps it is only in retrospect that it is possible to go back and take what was good from both decades. The 1980s was an almost cathartic reaction against the moral rectitude of 1970s revolutionary politics. As the decade progressed, I for one, had no desire to return to the time when consumption was a decadence and personal privation was confused with anti-sexism. It was as though the spending sprees of the 1980s were the expression of a middle class at last released from its obligations to political morality. Difference came to town and with it new political awareness. But pleasure came as well.

The first stage of the 1980s political process was to construct a consumptionist, left-wing life style out of libertarian subjectivism. Our emphasis on the quality of relationships, the nature of domestic lives, how children were moulded by capitalist patriarchy – combined, in groups like *Red Therapy* (which spawned commercial radical therapy practices) with a new attention to psychoanalysis – made it possible to justify an escape into living well, while remaining on the left.[50]

The purpose of revisiting MAS in the 1970s was to investigate how this specific class fraction of men attempted to address a failure in the reflexive capacities of their masculine identities. Since those days when life was organised around the pre-figuration of revolutionary politics a lot of myths and a great many romantic notions of change have been punctured. If the 1980s was a time of *rapprochement* with the social order, it was also one of reassessment. I want to hold on to the reflexivity of MAS and bring to it a critical psychoanalysis that will avoid some of the pitfalls of the last two decades.

4

SILENCE, LANGUAGE AND PSYCHOANALYSIS

INTRODUCTION

The failures of sexual difference and MAS theory, drawn as they are from two sometimes antagonistic positions in psychoanalytic thought, demand another attempt at a metaphorical description of the relationship between the inner realm of the psyche and the outer realm of the social. One which can provide a framework for a reflexive analysis of male subjectivity. Such a metaphor has to describe a transitional membrane or border through which speech addresses what does not belong to speech. It must also be able to describe these two realms of inner psyche and the external world as having a mutually determining relationship in which neither can be wholly reduced to the other. This suggests a partial fixing of the subject, a contingent closure within subjectivity that constructs the separation and joining of inner and outer. In other words, this is the place within which we spend our lives, where we must struggle with the dual demands of our emotional lives and our experiences in the outside world.

Rather than accept the structuralist and post-structuralist accounts of the subject constituted in language, we can argue that language is constituted upon the partial interiority of the subject. The subject cannot be reduced to an essence of his or herself, nor can language be reduced to an objective and external totality, through which the subject endeavours to mediate his or her existence. It is Laclau and Mouffe who can offer a description of this partial and contingent relationship between the subject and language.

The irresoluble interiority/exteriority tension is the condition of any social practice: necessity only exists as a partial limitation of the field of contingency. It is in this terrain, where neither a total interiority nor a total exteriority is possible, that the social is constituted. . . . In order to be totally external to each other, the entities would have to be *totally* internal with regard to themselves: that is, to have a fully constituted identity which is not subverted by the exterior. But this is precisely what we have just rejected. *This field of identities which never manages to be fully fixed is the field of overdetermination.*[1]

While they insist upon the impossibility of fixing meaning and identity, they are also opposed to their absolute non-fixity. The place of identity and meaning in the speaking subject, is on this threshold between inner and outer. It is a place which is overdetermined, an articulation of different elements into a subject identity.

This partial interiority of the subject refutes the Lacanian and structuralist assumption that a linguistic order descends upon an infant, structuring the totality of his or her existence. Language is produced out of the infant's learned use of words which give meaning to the bodily sensations and non-verbal forms of communication which exist in its partial interiority. Such language acquisition is an interactive practice involving the individual, objects and words. It is the philosopher, L. Wittgenstein, whose materialist theory of language games offers us such a description. (For another interpretation of Wittgenstein's relationship to masculinity and language, see Middleton 1986.)

WITTGENSTEIN AND LANGUAGE

In Wittgenstein's first major work *The Tractatus Logico-Philosophicus* (Wittgenstein 1961) he was interested in identifying the limits of thought. I have already mentioned his belief, at the beginning of this work, that the things that really mattered to him were those which could not be spoken of. For Wittgenstein thought can only exist within language. Therefore an investigation of it, constitutes an investigation of the latter. In the *Tractatus* he assumes that language has a single underlying essence whose logical structure could be described. He also argues that the world has its own separate structure and that the relationship between language and the material world can be analysed. In his later work *Philosophical*

Investigations (Wittgenstein 1988), Wittgenstein rejects many of his earlier arguments. Instead of the existence of a denotative link between words and objects; i.e. a name means an object, he argues against any single logic of language. Instead of having a single essence, it is made up of a vast collection of different practices, each with its own logic. Meaning is not derived from its denotative link with an object, but is the consequence of an individual's use of words, in the multiplicity of practices which make up language. This relationship between the subject, the material world and words constitutes a 'language game'.

The use of a word or expression is determined by a rule and this rule is itself determined by a culture's collective use of it; they are not imposed by some transcendental signified or a coercive standard from outside. Rules are produced from within rule-following practices and, Wittgenstein argues, children are trained to follow them. He gives an example of how meanings of words are determined by the use of objects in language games.

> A is building with building stones: there are blocks, pillars, slabs and beams. B has to pass the stones, and that in the order in which A needs them. For this purpose they use a language consisting of the words 'block', 'pillar', 'slab', 'beam'. A calls them out; – B brings the stones which he has learnt to bring at such-and-such a call. – Conceive this as a complete primitive language.[2]

Language games are not predetermined structures, they are contingent and culturally determined practices. Nevertheless they do represent the indissoluble totality of language and the actions and objects connected with it. Wittgenstein wrote that the idea of a language game, 'is meant to bring into prominence the fact that the *speaking* of language is part of an activity, or a form of life.'[3] It constitutes the meaning of subjectivity, through the articulation of inner sense and external word. Language is material in effect and in its formation, for it is a product of social relations based upon the individual's learnt linguistic usage of the objects constituting those relations.

Wittgenstein addresses the relationship of the individual's interior world of feeling to its expression in language. He argues that the word comes to replace the primitive feeling, so giving individual, idiosyncratic experience meaning to the wider linguistic community.

> A child has hurt himself and he cries; and then adults talk to
> him and teach him exclamations and, later, sentences. They
> teach the child new pain-behaviour.
> 'So you are saying that the word "pain" really means crying?'
> – On the contrary: the verbal expression of pain replaces
> crying and does not describe it.[4]

Underlying this statement is Wittgenstein's belief that there is no
such thing as a language invented by and only intelligible to one
individual. Language to have meaning must be a public and
collectively defined activity. The word 'pain' is not an outward
manifestion of some inner feeling, it is a part of a pain behaviour
which has been learnt and is cognitive and social in character.
There can be no intelligible life-world, no 'private language' that
is removed from language games.

In arguing that words come to represent feelings in order to
communicate them to others, Wittgenstein assumes that all
meaning is manifest in consciousness and that feelings are wholly
derived and constituted in language games ('We *see* emotions' he
asserts (Wittgenstein 1981, 220–5)). Inner states do not have a
separate world. One can literally look and see what kind of state
another individual is in. There is nothing hidden. For Wittgenstein, thought is simply speech we may decide not to utter.
Language is a vehicle for thought and it cannot be detached from
speaking. Thoughts and words are indissoluble. Therefore what
one thinks about oneself is determined by available vocabularies.
Wittgenstein gives the example of William James, who in order to
show that thought is possible without speech, quotes the recollec-
tion of a 'deaf-mute'. This man insisted that, in his youth and
before he could speak, he had had thoughts about God and the
world. Wittgenstein finds the claim to these wordless thoughts
inexplicable; 'Do I want to say the writer's memory deceives him?
– I don't even know if I should say *that* . . . I do not know what
conclusions one can draw from them about the past of the man
who recounts them.'[5] For Wittgenstein, silences, too, are determined by the social sphere. If an individual wants to say something
or to think anything, he or she must have learnt a language first.

If we want to think about this conscious silence, Wittgenstein
suggests we grasp at the image of speaking, a mental representation; 'the mental picture is the picture which is described
when someone describes what he imagines.'[6] But Wittgenstein is

troubled by his own insistence on the consciousness of meaning. He describes a man who is ambivalent about whether or not he is in pain, and who says, 'I do not know if what I have got is a pain or something else.'[7] To help him, Wittgenstein suggests sticking him with a pin and telling him that this is what pain means. He writes:

> If he now said, for example: 'Oh, I know what "pain" means; what I don't know is whether *this*, that I have now, is pain' – we should merely shake our heads and be forced to regard his words as a queer reaction which we have no idea what to do with.[8]

Wittgenstein places his language games exclusively in the realm of consciousness; in observable objects and quantifiable reactions, those phenomena which testify to the responsiveness of the mind to external objects. Psychological terms are determined by public criteria. What is considered 'inner' has a rule following that makes it an observable phenomenon and does not set it outside or in opposition to language games. His opposition to the idea of a private language is quite in keeping with this positivism. He is right that private languages would be nonsensical to a wider community, but that doesn't mean to say they cannot exist. It is psychoanalysis that can address this troubled field of the unspoken and the disjunctions between what an individual may feel yet be unable to speak or communicate to others and so not understand. It is these, 'sounds which no one else understands but which I *"appear to understand"*'[9] which are the object of psychoanalytic inquiry.

Wittgenstein's troubled relation to what exists on the edge or outside of language games reflects his earlier concern in the *Tractatus*, with what cannot be put into thought or language. The materialism of his philosophy of language is based on a positivistic interpretation of the elements that constitute language games. The word as present and complete, the object as a fully known phenonemon and the individual as a being fully conscious of him or herself and others of him or her. What he cannot come to terms with in such a system of linguistic communication is the negative; the absence or opposite of something actual or positive.

For Wittgenstein the objects of language games, the building block in his example, cannot be broken down or analysed into something more fundamental than themselves. This reflects his belief that language and meaning has no *a priori* existence. In the *Tractatus* objects are constituents of states of affairs. The states of affairs which exist determine which states of affairs do not exist. He was then willing to acknowledge that the meaning of language is partially determined by what does not exist. When he came to write the *Philosophical Investigations* (1988), his urgency to escape the religious-like quality he attached to this non-existent state of affairs – 'everything of value' – imbued his objects with a positivism that denied the concept of the negative.

Underlying Wittgenstein's positivism is his description of the relationship between word and object. Attributing meaning to the object is achieved through 'naming' it. He points to an object and utters 'this', 'this', in order to demonstrate the '*queer* connection' of a word with an object.[10] But he is unwilling to pursue the idea that states of affairs may consist of negatives, which cannot be named. 'Philosophical problems' he writes, 'arise when language goes on holiday.'[11] The meaning of a word is defined by its use in language. His solution to problems concerning the origin of meaning lies in the philosopher's capacity to fully understand and grasp the working of language. But he does not investigate how socially defined rules of word-use may determine what is positive and what is negative and that this dialectic has a determining influence on the linguistic descriptions of subjectivity. The existence of the negative characterises a relationship, rather than an object. What psychoanalysis is interested in, what it seeks a public language to express, is what happens to the subject in the negative, when an individual is unable to name something of him or herself; when language goes on holiday.

PSYCHOANALYSIS, ABSENCE AND SYMBOLISM

Psychoanalysis challenges the positivism which suggests that we always know what we are about to speak and that what we speak is always what we mean. Similarly, it rejects the idea that individuals learn language in the kind of crude behaviourist way suggested by Wittgenstein. Rather, language is acquired through an interaction between instinctual impulses and the social realm of language games. Psychoanalysis challenges the idea that psychological terms always have a public criterion which replaces a feeling originating from within with a word originating from outside. It also rejects the idea that what is inner constitutes an essential nature. What it does describe, is the complex relationship between inner and outer in subjectivity, between feeling and language.

It would be impossible to conceive of instinctual impulses except through language. But they do imply a mental space quite different from the mental space involved in language. It is a space which is not defined by the rational naming of objects but through the pleasure principle in which the organism finds value and meaning in activities and objects that bring well-being. An individual's subjectivity is constituted within these two spheres of inner and outer. It can only have meaning in the individual's capacity to link the two together. But this does not mean that they become congruent, or that the inner is a simple reflection of external criteria. The relationship between them is more complex.

In Chapter 2 I discussed Melanie Klein's theory of projection, whereby the infant will expel internal persecutory elements which create tension and anxiety. This process of expulsion cannot be sustained without external reality being missed. Klein described how this defensive mechanism operating in the paranoid-schizoid position is complemented by introjection. Food, holding and warmth, must be introjected from outside or the infant will be cut off from its life source. The processes of introjection and projection with the mother's body constitute a preverbal form of communication which enables maturational development towards the depressive position and the formation of the ego. They are the precursors to the development of a distinction between what is inner and what is outer, but their operation denies this differentiation. Their operation blurs the boundary dividing subject from object, fusing the infant with the mother.

Now the acquistion of language requires the absence of that object which has made this pre-verbal communication possible. In other words for the child to develop a thought, the mother must be experienced as separate and distinct. I can make this clearer by giving the example that Freud used in his essay 'Beyond the Pleasure Principle' (Freud 1920g). Freud was puzzled by a game that his one-and-a-half-year-old grandson was playing. The little boy would fling a small object and then proceed to hunt for it, giving vent to a long drawn out 'o-o-o-o'. Both Freud and his daughter agreed that the child was using the German word *'fort'* ('gone').

One day I made an observation which confirmed my view.

The child had a wooden reel with a piece of string tied round
it. . . . What he did was to hold the reel by the string and very
skillfully throw it over the edge of his curtained cot, so that
it disappeared into it, at the same time uttering his expressive
'o-o-o-o'. He then pulled the reel out of the cot again and
hailed its re-appearance with a joyful 'da' ['there']. This,
then, was the complete game – disappearance and return.[12]

Freud interpreted this game as a symbolic acting out of the child
being left by his mother and then her subsequent returning. He
had originally held to the idea that human instinctual life was
solely governed by the pleasure principle. But here he could
observe a small child's repetition of a distressing experience that
could not be a source of pleasure. Freud reached no conclusions
as to the meaning of the child's play. He was using the anecdote in
a preliminary discussion on the place of repetition in his discovery
of a death instinct. While he made a number of observations he
did not pursue the symbolic function of the child's game. He could
only affirm that the child's active acting out of a situation, in which
he had been passive, afforded a yield of pleasure and the dimin-
ishing of anxiety.

What Freud's example of '*Fort-Da*' did reveal was how the
child's use of language was derived from its symbolic acting out of
its mother's absence. Only in her absence was he able to recognise
her actual existence as a separate person. His game was both an
attempt to contain his anxiety at her absence and a way of giving
it meaning. In her theory of the depressive position, Melanie Klein
describes how the introjection of the whole object overcomes
projection and affords the infant its differentiation from the
maternal body. This process of separation and the making of a
distinction between what is inner and what is outer is central to her
work. Because she was working with children who often had little
grasp of language, Klein used games and objects to analyse this
process. Klein argued that separation and individuation is made
meaningful through the formation of symbols. It is the foundation
on which the subject's relationship to the outside world is built and
the means by which instinctual life finds a mental representation
in the psyche and so a connection to words and language (Klein
1946). Freud himself did not pursue this line of thinking, confining his discussion to symbols in dreams. So I want to concentrate
upon Kleinian and object relations theorists, who because of their

interest in the pre-verbal, pre-oedipal phase of life, developed theories of symbol formation.

From the earliest stages of his or her development, the infant begins to search for symbols in order to find relief from painful experiences. Klein viewed symbol formation as a primarily defensive mechanism against anxiety. The conflicts with primal objects (e.g. the mother's body) in fantasy promote a search for new, conflict-free relationships with substitute objects. The conflicts, however, tend to follow this displacement and so the search continues for yet another substitute (see Klein 1930). Symbol formation is precipitated by persecutory fantasies associated with the maternal body. Through the displacing effect of symbol formation the infant ego begins the process of overcoming introjection and projection which fuse it with the maternal body. This enables a relationship to the external world to develop. In this process of displacement the object is constantly deferred, creating a mental space of emptiness, out of its absence. It is in this process of displacement and deferral that the symbol is formed, providing a link between an instinctual life that has been fused with the mother and its means for a self-determined representation through language. The maternal primary object constitutes the negative, for symbol formation is constituted out of the infant's attempt to master the anxiety created by her absence.

To digress briefly, Klein's description of symbolisation places the figure of the mother at the centre of subject formation. In her theory of symbol formation it is the mother/child dyad which is the site for the pre-cursorial mental processes that will constitute thought and language. In Freudian metapsychology this dyad is repressed and consigned to the unconscious in the oedipus complex. The acquisition of language transforms the pre-oedipal structures of pre-verbal communication. This is a point emphasised by Jacques Lacan (Lacan (1949) 1980). Both he and Freud in their different ways seek to divest the role of the maternal figure in the formation of cultural and gendered subjectivity by privileging the father as the conveyor of cultural meaning and language.

Klein challenges the idea that it is the figure of the father who initiates individuation, so instigating the formation of the super-ego which defines the separation of outer from inner. She asserts that the super-ego is present before the oedipus complex, built up from identifications dating from different periods. Klein's super-ego is not paternal in character, nor simply the prohibitive voice of conscience over instinctual life. It is rather contradictory, being excessively severe and over-indulgent, invested with both maternal and paternal mental representations (Klein 1928). In the light of Klein's work the signification and representation that form subjectivity cannot be determined solely by the oedipus complex and the figure of the father. The figure of the mother plays a determining role in language acquisition and gender identification.

The psychoanalyst Christopher Bollas has developed a more sophisticated metaphor for the mother as the infant's object. He describes her as a 'transformational object' (Bollas 1987). There is a tendency in Klein's thinking to describe the object as a static and unchanging presence. Bollas suggests that the mother is experienced as a process of transformation. Symbol formation and the acquisition of language, learning to handle and differentiate between objects and to remember objects that are not present, are all transformative achievements, for they result in changes to the infant's ego and internal world. The figure of the mother comes to be signified with this process of cumulative internal and external transformations. Her presence facilitates pre-verbal communication and her absence enables the establishment of representation and language.

In his essay on 'Negation' (1925h) Freud gives voice to the ambivalence, in which what is longed for, must necessarily be absent in order to ensure one's knowledge of both one's own and its existence; a conflict which can give rise to speaking the opposite of what one may mean. Perhaps it is no surprise that he chooses the figure of the mother in his example;

> 'You ask who this person in the dream can be. It's *not* my mother'. We amend this to: 'So it *is* his mother'. In our interpretation, we take the liberty of disregarding the negation and of picking out the subject-matter alone of the association. It is as though the patient had said: 'It's true that my mother came into my mind as I thought of this person, but I don't feel inclined to let the association count.'[13]

Both Klein's object and (to a lesser extent) Bollas's 'transformational object' assume its positivity. Its presentation is confirmation of the reality of what is being presented. But Freud's comment alludes to its ambivalence. He asserts that the distinction between subjective and objective does not exist from the first, but has to be discerned by reality-testing. An object can only come into being through thinking. This enables the reproduction of an object which has already been perceived without it having to be present. But this reproduction of a perception as a presentation is not always a faithful one. Such distortions can only be ascertained by reality-testing whose precondition is that objects which once brought real satisfaction have been lost. In his essay Freud argues that this judgement between what is subjective and what is objective depends upon this absence. For without it, without the negative, thinking cannot be free of instinctual life and its governance by the pleasure principle. Hence the subject will not be able to discern presence from absence, inner from outer, positive and negative.

PREDICAMENTS, THINKING AND 'K'

Christopher Bollas has defined the failure of linguistic representation to 'speak' for the subject as 'the unthought known' (Bollas 1987). He decribes this as the inability to process a relation or object through the mental representations of language. 'While we do know something of the character of the object that affects us, we may not have thought it yet.'[14] This suggests a pre-verbal failure of communication that is structured into language through the failure of the negative. A failure which is precipitated by a breakdown in the process of differentiation and separation between the infant and the mother. I want to term this disruption of pre-verbal communication a predicament. The silence I am addressing in this work is constituted by predicaments.

A predicament can be said to exist where excessive anxiety has broken the displacing and deferring effect of symbol formation. Hanna Segal has identified two forms of symbolisation (Segal 1991). In symbolic representation a true symbol is substituted in place of the original. In symbolic equation the symbol becomes the original and becomes imbued with the same conflicts and projections. Part of the ego remains undifferentiated from the object. Movement away from symbolic equations to symbolic representations takes place with the depressive position and the increasing awareness of the difference between internal and external worlds. Failure to achieve fully the depressive position results in a confusion between self and object and the failure of the negative. Segal gives an example of one man she saw in analysis who since his illness had stopped playing the violin; 'when asked why, [he] answered with violence, "Do you expect me to masturbate in public?"'[15]

In searching for an explanation for this fusion of self and object, Segal turned to the defensive mechanism of projection in the paranoid-schizoid position and Klein's idea of projective identification. While projection implies the expulsion of persecutory feelings and anxiety onto any particular object, projective identification demands a receptacle which will allow itself to be more or less passively penetrated by the projected parts. Klein argued that this form of projection derived from the infant's attempt to control the mother. Segal holds to this view: 'The aim of primitive projective identification is to deny a psychic reality by getting rid of a part of oneself and simultaneously possessing and controlling the object.'[16] Symbol formation marks the gradual decline of this form of projection and the separateness of the subject and the object becomes more fully maintained.

Wilfred Bion is perhaps the most important of the post-Kleinian thinkers. One of his major contributions to psychoanalytic thought was his re-assessment of this concept of projective identification. He claimed that it was more than a simple defensive mechanism but the first mode of communication, preceding symbol formation. The infant splits off anxiety-arousing feelings, perceptions and sensations and projects them into the mother's body. The logic of this action is not to control the mother but to get her to contain intolerable feelings and so render them into liveable experiences. This containing function is central to Bion's work. He named it the mother's 'reverie', which is her capacity to think about her infant, to pay attention and to try and understand.

Bion gave this activity the notation 'K'. The letter stands for thinking in the sense of the act of trying to know. The mother's capacity to know, transforms a dangerous psychic reality into a tolerable experience. In turn the infant introjects the mother's 'K' and identifies with its mother's capacity to survive and contain the anxiety. This non-verbal communication is the pre-condition for the infant's capacity to survive the mother's absence and so to constitute mental representation and thought. 'K' is a form of processing instinctual life, which precedes knowledge of the physical world. It forms the basis for the development of symbolism, mental representation and verbal thought.

A failure of 'K' means that the infant is abandoned with the experience of danger. The fear, for example, that it is dying. Because its immature ego is unable to contain the enormity of this feeling it remains unprocessed. Symbol formation cannot occur and consequently the experience cannot be thought about and understood.

> Normal development follows if the relationship between infant and breast permits the infant to project a feeling, say, that it is dying into the mother and to reintroject it after its sojourn in the breast has made it tolerable to the infant psyche. If the projection is not accepted by the mother the infant feels that its feeling that it is dying is stripped of such meaning as it has. It therefore reintrojects, not a fear of dying made tolerable, but a nameless dread.[17]

In such circumstances symbol formation is concretised, producing an equation which denies the separateness of subject and object. The principle of the negative fails because the infant cannot tolerate and so recognise the mother's absence. The mother's presence as a container is a prerequisite to the infant's capacity to deal with her absence, and so operate reality-testing. It is only when the infant can recognize the absence of the object that she or he can either symbolize or think. As Bion wrote, 'No breast – therefore a thought.'[18]

Hanna Segal has written on this process of containment and the way in which it effects the development of verbal communication.

> Verbalization can be looked at from the angle of the relation between the container and the contained. Unlike other forms of symbolism, speech has to be learned, though the baby begins by making onomatopoeic sounds. These sounds have to be taken up by the environment to be converted into speech and later on words have to be learned from the environment. The infant has had an experience and mother provides the word or phrase which circumscribes this experience. It contains, encompasses and expresses the meaning. It provides a container for it. The infant can then internalize this word or phrase containing the meaning.[19]

It is a description which fits with Wittgenstein's own description of rule learning. Segal's description like his, however, omits the negative and the actual struggle around presence/absence.

Bion describes a man with a stutter as symptomatic of the failure of the containment of infantile dread.

> The words that should have represented the meaning the man wanted to express were fragmented by the emotional forces to which he wished to give verbal expression; the verbal formulation could not 'contain' his emotions, which broke through and dispersed it as enemy forces might break through the forces that strove to contain them.[20]

The failure of containment and the subsequent failure of symbol formation, creates disjunctions and disruptions in the relationship between instinctual life and language. This is the unthought known and it is primarily caused by the perception of the infant that separation from the mother threatens an intolerable catastrophe. As a result part of the ego remains fused with the maternal representation producing a symbolic equation. In this way what is known, the nameless dread of loss and abandonment, does not find its way into linguistic representation. It is a silence that is filled with experiences which cannot be mentally processed because they feel too dangerous. Far from being empty this is a silence crowded by the infant's fantasy of a mother who feels psychically dead. An 'absent' mother who must be revived and given sustenance in order to safeguard the infant's own ego.

THE THIRD SPACE

The psychoanalyst and writer André Green provides a rich source of ideas in his synthesis of French- and Lacanian-inspired theory with the British object relations school (see Green 1986). In an essay entitled 'The Analyst, Symbolization and Absence', he seeks to place object relations and symbol formation within a spatial and temporal context.

> It is no longer enough . . . to study object relations. One has to question oneself about the space in which these relations develop, its limits and its breaks as well as the temporal development in which they evolve, with its continuities and discontinuities.[21]

Psychoanalysis can disprove the positivist notions of language acquisition and language games in the negative term of the mother's absence, which forms the ontological source of thought.

But the spatial and temporal relation of speech to what does not belong to speech, of presence to absence, inner to outer and positive to negative still lacks a description. Objects themselves are necessarily ordered within relations of time and space, a process that constructs a relationship between the mental space of language and contingency and the mental space of instinctual affect and the continuity of the pleasure principle. Such a space must be the place within which the subject experiences life. A place that marks both the union and separation of these two mental spaces.

It is D.W. Winnicott, perhaps the most important practitioner and theorist of the British object relations school, who offers a metaphor for this paradoxical separation and joining of inner and outer. Unlike Klein, who concentrated her work upon the internal object and its vicissitudes, Winnicott was more interested in the interplay of the external and internal. His idea of a transitional or intermediate third space between inner and outer, provides an invaluable framework for analysing the relationship between symbolisation, language and pre-oedipal experience.

Klein's belief that instinctual life precedes object relations in determining maturational development downplayed the importance of the external actual object of the mother in her theory. Consequently, her work lacks the idea of an exchange and interplay between internal psychic life and actual objects. For Klein development of the ego is ensured through its introjection of objects which come to structure and integrate it as a more or less stable agency. At the same time, external objects are constructed through projections into the external world, derived partly from unconscious fantasy and partly from previously introjected objects. These are then re-introjected. Both the ego and its external objects are constructed out of this integration of self and the external world. Winnicott's emphasis is on the 'facilitating environment', 'primary maternal concern' and 'holding', echoing Bion's notion of a container. It places a new emphasis upon the function and role of the actual mother in facilitating the infant's maturation and ego development. 'I once said "There is no such thing as an infant"', wrote Winnicott, 'meaning, of course, that wherever one finds an infant one finds maternal care, and without maternal care there would be no infant.'[22] From Winnicott's point of view, Klein's theory of the depressive position (which he renames the 'Stage of Concern') fails to include the mother's role, who, over a long period of time, provides a holding environment within which the infant can work through the consequences of instinctual experience.

In his essay 'The Use of an Object', Winnicott develops Klein's theory of the depressive position (Winnicott 1988). In the depressive position the infant becomes aware that the hatred and aggression projected into the maternal object is potentially harmful to its own internalised good object. Because it forms the framework for the ego's development and ensures its sense of integration, reparative work is necessary. For Winnicott this requires action in the actual world; a concern for the mother. A secure sense of this internal object will enable the infant to live fully its instinctual life, without fear of destroying the internal object or the ego. But to achieve this security requires a subtle shift in the infant's relationship to the actual object. The infant needs to prove that the mother's containing function can survive its projections of rage, anxiety and destruction. Her capacity to do so will ensure that the infant's internal object can survive and contain the full range of his or her instinctual life. To be able to use the actual object means to live without fear of the ego disintegrating in a state of intolerable anxiety. Winnicott describes this process, in this imagined dialogue.

> The subject says to the object: 'I destroyed you', and the object is there to receive the communication. From now on the subject says: 'Hullo object!' 'I destroyed you.' 'I love you.' 'You have value for me because of your survival of my destruction of you.' 'While I am loving you I am all the time destroying you in (unconscious) *fantasy*.' Here fantasy begins for the individual. The subject can now *use* the object that has survived.[23]

In order to become an entity that can live for itself and attain a separation from the maternal object, the infant must be able to place the object outside of its omnipotent control. That is, to perceive the object as an external phenomenon, not as a projective entity. The concept of usage defines the growing differentiation between what is objectively perceived and what is subjectively conceived of. In other words it creates the conditions for a border between what is internal to the infant and what is external to it.

Winnicott argues that it is play which enables the infant to establish a relationship between inner and outer. Its function is similar to that of Klein's symbol formation. It is concerned with the child gathering objects from the external world, to use them in the service of some aspect of internal reality. In Winnicott's observations of babies he noted the way they became attached to an object, such as an old nappy for sucking, a soft toy or their thumb. He introduced the term 'transitional object' to describe their function as an intermediary form which both separated and united instinctual affect and external object. Winnicott argues that Klein's theory of symbol formation assumes the infant can perceive the distinction between inner objects and external objects. A transitional object lies at the root of symbol formation for it marks the infant's journey from purely subjective to objectivity.

In identifying transitional objects Winnicott needed to describe where they are experienced. Similarly the process of evolving from relating to use of an object implies a transitional phase which is neither wholly internal nor simply external.

> Of every individual who has reached to the stage of being a unit with a limiting membrane and an outside and an inside, it can be said that there is an *inner reality* to that individual. . . . This helps, but is it enough?
> My claim is that if there is a need for this double statement, there is also a need for a triple one: the third part of the life of a human being, a part that we cannot ignore, is an intermediate area of *experiencing*, to which inner reality and external life both contribute. It is an area. . . . that shall exist as a resting-place for the individual engaged in the perpetual human task of keeping inner and outer reality separate yet interrelated.[24]

A transitional object symbolises the breast or the object of the first relationship, the first not-me possession. However, its value is dependent upon the aliveness of the internal object. It is a product of both inner and outer, marking out the intermediary space of experience. Like the transitional object, play, '*is in fact neither a matter of inner psychic reality nor a matter of external reality.*'[25]

Play, Winnicott says, occurs in the potential space between the individual and the environment. It is a space which initially both joined and separated the mother and infant. At first the infant has no sense of its psychological separateness from or interchange with the mother. 'There is no interchange between the mother and the infant. Psychologically the infant takes from the breast that is part of the infant, and the mother gives milk to an infant that is part of herself.'[26] The employment of transitional objects begins the process of separation through the formation of an intermediary space between mother and baby.

> It is . . . the place in space and time where and when the mother is in transition from being (in the baby's mind) merged in with the infant and alternatively being experienced as an object to be perceived rather than conceived of.[27]

Winnicott's transitional object symbolises the joining of two separate things, the baby and the mother, *at the point in time and space of the initiation of their state of separateness*.[28]

Winnicott's concept of a third space is a border that mediates the spatial and atemporal sphere of instinctual affects and the historical and contingent relations of cultural life. It is the place where the individual experiences life. Within it, the relationships between positive and negative, inside–outside, subjective–objective, alive–not-alive are produced. It is the place of symbol formation and as such it is the place where the subject and language meet. 'Language, in my view', writes André Green, 'is the heir to the first transitional objects.'[29] The third space provides the contextualising link between affect and words. André Green writes:

> Freud's brilliant manouevre was in not hesitating to slide the discussion of language (which has its own logic) into that of the one he calls *the language of the oldest – the oral–instinctual impulses*. Do instinctual impulses then, have their own language? Or is this merely a metaphor? No, it is a necessity. It is impossible to deal with instinctual impulses except through language since . . . psychoanalysis is restricted to verbal communication. It can conceive of instinct only through language.[30]

Instinctual impulses, occupying one type of mental space must connect with word and language occupying a quite different mental space. It is in the writing of Freud that this relationship becomes clearer.

THE SILENCE OF PREDICAMENTS

In his essay, 'Instincts and their Vicissitudes', Freud defines an instinct as a 'concept on the frontier between the mental and the somatic, as the psychical representative of the stimuli originating from within the organism and reaching the mind, as a measure of the demand made upon the mind for work in consequence of its connection with the body.'[31] The instinct is a psychical representative of stimuli originating from within the organism (soma). This can only be felt and understood as a pressure upon the mind to produce symbolisation; ideational representatives of the instincts in the psyche. As Kleinians and Freud himself have sought to understand, such an event is only possible in the context of the mother's absence, creating the demand for a representation of an objectively perceived reality.

The third space is a metaphor which describes a border. There are a number of different types of border, there are lines and surfaces, with or without circulation through the frontier, or there is an osmotic membrane which allows movement from one side to another, but regulates its extent. If there is trouble inside it can expel the offending elements. If there is an excess wanting to enter it can bar it. A border implies the protection of one's self from crossing over it or from being crossed over and into. Such events do not imply the loss of a border, but of the self becoming a moving border and no longer distinguishing between space and time, inner and outer, subject and object. The border defines what is me from what is not-me and suggests two types of anxiety; separation anxiety and intrusion anxiety. In the former, a fear of abandonment and premature loss of the object heralds the death of the internal good object and ego-collapse. In the latter the intrusion of persecutory elements cluttering up the third space destroys the autonomy and agency of the ego. The central features of anxiety are too much absence and too much presence.

Both these types of anxiety presage the collapse of transitional phenomena (both the third space and transitional objects). As the development of these is the pre-condition of symbol formation and hence the capacity to represent one's instinctual life, such anxieties threaten psychosis and the capacity to live. For Winnicott the crucial factor in maturation is the availability and technique of the actual mother. For in enabling the aliveness, in the infant's mind, of the good internal object, her work ensures the development of the third space.

It is perhaps worth while trying to formulate this in a way that gives the time factor due weight. The feeling of the mother's existence lasts x minutes. If the mother is away more than x minutes, then the imago fades, and along with this the baby's capacity to use the symbol of the union ceases. The baby is distressed, but this distress is soon *mended* because the mother returns in $x+y$ minutes. In $x+y$ minutes the baby has not become altered. But in $x+y+z$ minutes the baby has become *traumatized*. In $x+y+z$ minutes the mother's return does not mend the baby's altered state. Trauma implies that the baby has experienced a break in life's continuity, so that primitive defences now become organized to defend against a repetition of 'unthinkable anxiety' or a return of the acute confusional state that belongs to disintegration of the nascent ego structure.[32]

Winnicott describes the experience of $x+y+z$ as 'primitive agonies', a state that mirrors Bion's 'nameless dread'. In his essay 'Fear of Breakdown' (Winnicott 1977), he describes how a patient's fear of a nervous breakdown in analysis is a manifestation of an event that has already occurred. Defensive mechanisms seek to protect the nascent ego structure against these primitive agonies, which themselves are unthinkable. When analysis contributes to the lessening of their power, what they have repressed and hidden becomes manifest.

Winnicott gives a number of examples of these primitive agonies. 'A return to an unintegrated state', whose defence is the experience of ego disintegration and 'Loss of capacity to relate to objects', where autism and the collapse of the differentiation between self and object serves as a defence are two examples.[33] They are psychical experiences that prove too monstrous for the infant's immature ego to contain and process. 'Madness' writes Winnicott, 'simply means a break-up of whatever may exist at the time of a *personal continuity of existence*.'[34] After each experience of $x+y+z$ the baby has to make a new start permanently deprived of the means to make sense of its continuity with its personal beginning. In other words gaps and absences are structured into the psychic formation through the failure of symbol formation, making primitive agonies incommunicable through language.

Because primitive agonies have no mental representation within the psyche, they do not constitute memories. They cannot get into the past tense until the ego is capable of gathering the trauma into its present time experience and containing it. An individual is forever searching in the future for this detail which has not been experienced and is yet to be thought and spoken of. The primitive agonies of $x+y+z$ resulting in psychotic defence mechanisms are extremes that can result in mental illness. My interest is not in the extremes, but what these extremes can tell us about the lesser traumas that constitute most people's lives. Winnicott's formulation of a 'good enough mother' implies a general capacity to manage and contain the needs and emotions of an infant. But no human being can manage this all the time and every infant will experience traumas that border on $x+y+z$. The experience of being nurtured by a single individual inevitably results in stress and distortion of an ideal developmental process. The mother will become preoccupied and concerned with something other than the needs of her infant. While she may be physically present, her mind may be elsewhere, caught up in a depression or fearful of the infant's needs and feelings. She may be sad or struggling to survive daily life. The infant will inevitably experience such preoccupations as premature absences that it feels unable to cope with.

In such moments the infant is forced to take over functions from the mother in actuality or begin as though to do so. Such borderline traumas carry with them the anxieties which threaten the destruction of the infant's ego. They also initiate a premature ego development which attempts to compensate for the failure of maternal containment (see James 1988). The threat of object loss leads to a precocity or pseudo grown-upness. The infant has to defend its own immature boundaries against the catastrophe of the loss of the object or of the impingement of the mother's mood, at a stage in its development when it is ill-equipped to do so. Precocity is designed to anticipate events that will precipitate the infant into a state of dread. Similarly, the infant adapts itself to comply with the moods and needs of the mother. Both enable evasive action to be taken. But they impair the capacity to live according to one's own needs and wishes, because aspects of instinctual life seem to threaten the well-being of the mother and without her presence the infant's ego will break down.

The failure to develop a border and a clear separation between self and object undermines the third space making it vulnerable to invasion or collapse. The capacity to be alone with oneself in the presence of another (see Winnicott 1958) fails to develop because a part of the infant's ego remains bound to the object of the mother, continually seeking to revive and encourage her, soothe her moods and enliven her existence. For it is upon her well-being that the survival of the internal object (and in turn, the infant's own ego) depends. What becomes established in this area of non-differentiation are symbolic equations which fuse subject and object. A part of the infant's ego is bound to an object which feels provisional and on the edge of falling to pieces. This failure of individuation and separation undermines the infant's capacity to be. A state that Winnicott describes as:

> [The ability] to become unintegrated, to flounder, to be in a state in which there is no orientation, to be able to exist for a time without being either a reactor to an external impingement or an active person with a direction of interest or movement. The stage is set for an id experience. In the course of time there arrives a sensation or an impulse. In this setting the sensation or impulse will feel real and be a truly personal experience.[35]

Trauma and the subsequent relative failure of transitional phenomena mean that this state can never be satisfactorily reached and that the life of the individual is tied up by the task of continually adapting to the needs of the internal object and the fantasy of a mother that threatens to die. Instead of being, there is doing, in order to evade the object's loss and a terrifying emptiness.

The infant's premature disillusionment in the containing function of the mother leads to the failure of 'K'. There is no explication of what has happened. There is only silence which surrounds something of a severity which is destined to structure an individual's subjective life. But such borderline conditions do not manifest psychotic breakdown or autism, where the subject is consumed in a world cut off from reality. A false persona is built out of the original compliance with the mother. It is a 'false self' (see Bollas 1987, 1989; Green, 'The Borderline Concept' 1986; Winnicott 1960) in the service of her moods and needs and does not reflect the subject's real experiences. This false self can be so powerfully organised that everything of value to an individual, what constitutes his or her primary creativity and desire for life is hidden. Even the individual remains unaware of what might have been or of what has been lost or is missing. Winnicott provides an example of such a man:

> He came to analysis saying that he could not talk freely, he

108

had no small talk or imaginative or play capacity, and that he could not make a spontaneous gesture or get excited . . .
Gradually it became clear that he was listening to conversations that were going on within, and reporting any parts of these conversations that he thought might interest me. In time, it could be said that he brought himself to analysis and talked about himself, as a mother or father might bring a child to me and talk about him. In these early phases (lasting six months) I had no chance of direct conversation with the child (himself).[36]

Such acting is a consequence of a confusion between thoughts, representations and affects.

It is now possible to begin gathering in the various strands of theory to present an analysis of what a predicament is and how it determines subjectivity. The confusion of mental spaces is caused by the disjunction between instinctual representations and ideational representations of external objects in the breakdown of symbol formation. Some event, object or relation remains unthought, causing the border between what is inner and what is outer to fluctuate, confusing the different mental spaces. In a psychotic defence there may be a complete breakdown in the relationship of inner to outer. But in borderline traumas the confusion amounts to an ambivalence. It can be expressed by asking the question 'Is the object dead (lost) or alive (found)?' or 'Am I dead or alive?' – to which [the] answer [is]: 'Neither Yes nor No.'[37] If there is an excess of presence (intrusion) or an excess of absence (loss) the capacity to mentally process instinctual life, to symbolise it and put it into words, is impaired. As Christopher Bollas writes: 'The object can cast its shadow without a child being able to process this relation through mental representations or language.'[38] What is lost is the capacity to put words to instinctual experiences; the capacity to feel.

Until the grasp of language, the infant's meaning resides in the mind and body of the mother. With the word the infant acquires a new transformational object enabling the establishment of subjectivity and participation in language games. But if there has been a relative failure of individuation through the dread of the loss of the object, then the mother's absence does not provide for a positive condition for establishing representation. Symbolisation fails and what has not been symbolised – elements of the experience of separation – become determining events in the secondary process of language acquisition. The symbolisation initiated by the mother's absence – 'No breast – therefore a thought', is split. The infant is stimulated to respond to her absence. But the instinctual representation of the mother's absence (the negative) is not translated into the positive terms of an ideational representation. It remains suppressed by primitive defence mechanisms, as a catastrophe. The absence of the object, instead of initiating a positive term in representation remains a negative term excluded from representation.

Alongside what the ego contains in terms of positive cathexis is what the ego has not got. The object which is perceived as absent and longed for is structured into subjectivity as a kind of statement; 'all I have got is what I have not got.'[39] The negative assumes a formative role in the development of subjectivity, affecting the linguistic representation of instinctual life and the subject's capacity for feeling. Failure of feeling occurs in an ambivalence; a positive representation 'Yes' is founded upon the 'No' of the subject's denial of the mother's absence. The principle of the negative fails in the failure to affirm her absence. The affirmation of this linguistic representation is confused with the 'yes' of the subject's instinctual life creating a failure of reality testing and a confusion of what is inner and outer. This ambivalence threatens the stability of the border. The third space becomes submerged in the subject's fusion with the internal object or else it is invaded by persecutory elements.

This confusion and ambivalence is manifest in the establishment of an adaptive, compliant and false self. The disjunction between instinctual life and its mental representations has a determining effect upon the idiom of subjectivity and its self-descriptions. Language games are not based on the simple affirmation and representation of positive objects that are present and quantifiable. It is structured also through denial and ambivalence – 'My mother has gone, but I can never leave her, she is still here.' The negative of the primary processes of the unconscious, instead of being the precursor of signification, takes on a positive role in the secondary processes of language acquisition. It becomes an organising principle structuring signification in the disjunction between instinctual life and thought. This I would claim is representative of a predicament, which through the disruption of the representation of instinctual life undermines the subject's capacity to speak of it. That is, it curtails the individual's capacity to feel the full range of instinctual life. Its significance in masculine identities lies in the oedipus complex, when its effect as a negative in the secondary process of language acquisition and identity formation is associated retrospectively with the mother and the feminine term.

THE OEDIPUS COMPLEX AND PREDICAMENTS IN MASCULINITY

Winnicott, like other object relations theorists and Klein, was concerned with the maturational process of differentiation and individuation. Sexuality and gender were not their primary considerations. But for Freud the masculine and feminine sexual dispositions were central to subject formation in the oedipus complex. It is André Green, a psychoanalyst spanning both Lacanian and object relations schools, who offers an insight into the possible relationship of symbolisation and the third space to gender and sexuality. In an interview he sought to relate it to Freud's notion of conflict.

> I believe that whenever there is antagonism, with the domination of one term over another, an alternative and oscillating domination, the excluded term tends to return, to reoccupy the space; consequently, it is possible, as in any area of movement, to imagine a no-man's-land, where the metaphor would assume a meeting in the potential reunion of what has been separated.[40]

His statement is rather vague and ambiguous but it offers an important clue to the relationship of pre-oedipal predicaments to the psychodynamic formation of gender identity. To make sense of this relationship, it is necessary to turn to Freud's description of the oedipus complex and his theory of the acquisition of gender and sexuality. At the same time I want to address the Kleinian revision of his classic model and its implications for an analysis of the formation of masculinity. In doing so I intend to concentrate on the male trajectory, rather than the female.

In the early history of the oedipus complex a little boy develops an identification with his father. He would like to be like him and take his place in the world. At the same time he develops, what Freud terms, 'a true object cathexis' towards his mother. Such an attachment is an 'anaclitic type', an object love which, in its over-valuation of the object, is characteristic of the male towards 'the woman who feeds him'.[41] Freud argues that such overvaluation is a compulsion born of the male infant's projection and hence depletion of his ego. He does not attribute this intensity of attach-ment to the female child. The boy exhibits two psychologically distinct ties. An identification with his father who serves as a model and this attachment to his mother. The former exists in the realm of the external world as a third term. The latter structures his internal object world. In Freudian psychoanalysis this split be-tween inner and outer is resolved through the oedipus complex and the establishing of the super-ego.

The little boy begins to perceive his father as standing in the way of his attachment to his mother. He begins to see him as a rival for his mother's love and develops a hostile attitude towards him. His identification with him is ambivalent, an expression of concern mixed with a longing for his removal. The small boy is forced to renounce his attachment to his mother through fear of castration by his father. Freud does not dwell on the nature or depth of the relationship of the small boy to his mother. But he alludes to the struggle that goes on in this conflict when he writes: 'the complex is not simply repressed it is smashed to pieces by the shock of threatened castration.'[42] There are two possible consequences to this conflict. The boy can maintain an identification with his mother or else he renounces his right to his possession of his mother and strengthens his identification with his father. 'We are accustomed' writes Freud, 'to regard the latter outcome as the more normal.'[43] That is a straightforward development of a he-terosexual position in which the boy takes the masculine position and adopts a female sexual object choice.

Freud's position was, however, more sophisticated than this and he argues that the boy can adopt a 'feminine' attitude towards his father; 'a boy also wants to take his mother's place as the love object of his father.'[44] The oedipus complex is inverted and the boy retains an identification with the mother through the vestiges of his continuing attachment. The father is taken as the object choice of his sexual instincts. In his description of the oedipus complex Freud reveals the intense battle between instinctual life and cultural meaning, as society seeks to enforce its cultural norms of gender relations and heterosexuality upon an instinctual life governed by the pleasure principle. In the process the pre-oedipal, mother–infant relationship and the small boy's incestuous longing for the mother are repressed by the threat of castration and come to form the unconscious. The father initiates the boy's separation from his mother and so the formation of his subjectivity. As the third term of the oedipus complex, he is the conveyor of language, meaning and culture.

This description of Freud's theory of the oedipus complex, despite its acknowledgement of contradiction suggests that it is an expression of the power of the father in miniature. The mother is consigned to a realm beyond meaning and language, where she is to play no part in the formation of a cultural and gendered subjectivity. It is an account which reduces individuation and acculturation to the internalisation of the structures of patriarchy. This is the kind of interpretation made of it by Juliet Mitchell.

> It seems to me that in Freud's psychoanalytic schema . . . we have at least the beginnings of an analysis of the way in which patriarchal society bequeaths its structures to each of us . . . gives us, that is, the cultural air we breathe, the ideas of the world in which we are born and which, unless patriarchy is demolished, we will pass on to our children and our children's children.[45]

Her analysis, inspired by the structuralist heritage of Lacan, implies that male subjectivity is analogous to a positive set of external social relations. The complex interplay of personal and power relations within families plays no part in the formation of the infant's gender identity and sexuality. And nor do the relative strengths of the feminine and masculine sexual dispositions in the psyche of the boy affect his position within and relation to patriarchal meanings and structures. Mitchell argues that, 'present or absent' 'the father' always has his place – in our culture he is present even in his absence.[46]

In structuralist terms such an argument is a definition of the subject's symbolic positioning by the laws governing cultural and linguistic exchange. Whatever an individual does with his masculine identity, representation will always position him in a way outside his control and agency. This description of the oedipus complex suggests it is no more than a function for normalising dominant social relationships. The contingencies, conflicts and instabilities of subject formation are downplayed. This analysis lies in the assumption that the subject is constituted within language.

As a result, the father as signifier of language and culture is given primacy and the mother is dismissed in the wholesale transformation of pre-oedipal, pre-verbal life which takes place with his advent. The determining effect of object relations and the depressive position have no part to play in this paradigm.

Jon Schiller has argued that Freud's discovery and depiction of the oedipus complex was only made possible when, 'in Hegel's phrase, "a shape of life (had) grown old"'[47] and that contemporary structures of family life have partially superseded his analysis. Schiller summarises this change in the way its psychological paradigm is internalised in the infant. 'Stated as a spatial metaphor, the psychic area occupied by maternal representations has expanded and the domain of the internalized paternal authority correspondingly diminished.'[48] Schiller argues that the maternal imago in the pre-oedipal structuring of the psyche is a far more powerful determining factor within the oedipus complex than Freud's writing would suggest. It is Klein's reworking of the oedipus complex and her emphasis upon the negative term in the complex that suggests a closer analogy to contemporary family life.

Klein's work with very young children enabled her to analyse the ambivalence of their identifications. She challenged the assumption that the motive of the child through the oedipus complex is a positive identification with the parent of the opposite sex. Klein emphasised the infant's dread of the maternal figure. A dread that is caused by the infant's sadistic hatred, projected into her and consequently, the perception of her as a persecutor that has a life or death control over the infant. For Klein the male child is trapped: 'This dread of the mother is so overwhelming because there is combined with it an intense dread of castration by the father.'[49]

But Schiller argues that, on balance, the father can be represented as a benign saviour who will rescue the infant from the vestiges of this persecutory world of dependency. So the paternal term is not simply a positive signifier of patriarchal relations but a masculine defence against the maternal term. As Jane Flax writes on Freud's evasion of the pre-oedipal, 'From a feminist point of view, . . . Even more problematic is his desire to repeat rather than work through the father's wish: to protect themselves and their sons against the eruption of maternal secrets into consciousness'.[50] And Schiller notes too:

by participating in his father's paternal authority, the son will be able to defend himself against women. A transvaluation of psychical values has thus been effected: the unconscious dread of women has given way to the conscious domination of them.[51]

Schiller's argument rests on the belief that the increased power of the maternal feminine disposition within the oedipus complex is a historical development. André Green attributes its contemporary significance to another factor.

> Over the years I have undertaken an exegesis of Freud and for years and years I tried above all to understand what he meant, then I realised that in modern clinical psychoanalysis what Freud said did not accord with what one saw in the analyses of difficult patients, whereas it worked perfectly in cases of hysterical or obsessional neurosis. It was necessary, therefore to work out a theory of these new facts in an epistimology that belonged to our time.[52]

The typical patient in Freud's time was the hysteric. For Green it is the borderline case.

The pressing issues of the borderline do not reside in the sphere of the oedipus complex, but in the pre-oedipal. They may become manifest in neurotic symptoms, but their causes lie elsewhere in the experience of primary fusion and the blurring of the limits of self. The fear of (sexual) penetration is now predetermined by the fear of intrusion, the threat of castration predetermined by the primal terrors of loss and abandonment by the maternal object. Rather than sexuality, the central concern is for symbolisation and the need for the subject's structural integration with the object. Green doesn't commit himself to any historical explanation for this change but suggests it is a change in the analyst; 'A fundamental change in contemporary analysis comes from what the analyst hears – and perhaps cannot help but hear – which has until now been inaudible.' And again; 'For, all things considered, there is change only to the extent that the analyst is able to understand such change and report it.'[53] The small amount of historical work now available on masculinity would support his caution in assuming any linear temporal shifts in the psychodynamics of patriarchal relations and the constitution of masculinity.[54] As Flax points out,

Freud's neglect was not due to the non-presence of the maternal imago, but to his own fear of it (Flax 1990; see Freud 1931b).

It is now possible to return to Green's statement that two conflicting terms exist in the third space and to explain how the third space and predicaments within it, play a determining role in the development of a masculine gender identity. In Freudian metapsychology the dominant term, dictating the acquisition of language and structuring subjectivity is the paternal one superseding the maternal term. But in the light of the theories of the borderline and Klein's work on the central place of the maternal object within the psyche, we can revise this classical descripton of the oedipal triangle.

THE FATHER AND MOTHER IN MASCULINITY

In Chapter 2 I discussed the work of Nancy Chodorow without making any concluding remarks and leaving the text open. I now want to turn back to it. Chodorow's thesis was an attempt to depict the significance of the mother–son relationship in the making of masculinity. She argued that an increasingly father-absent, mother-involved family produces a masculine personality suitable for participation in capitalist relations of production. This, however, assumes that the mother–son relationship produces a specific social idiom of masculinity that is congruent with the needs of society. It is a functionalism which reduces masculine identities to a singular norm. While I am in agreement with much of what Chodorow has to say about the psychodynamics of family life, I want to avoid the consequences of its synthesis with classical sociology. My investigation began with a specific class fraction of men, their identification with women's liberation and their preoccupation with the relationship of feeling to language. The mistake of Chodorow was her failure to be more specific about what class and ethnicity of masculinity she was referring to. MAS in its attempt to generalise too broadly from what was a reflexive consideration of its own constituent masculinities, fell into the same trap. As a result it reduced its own specificity to a common denominator, losing crucial insights into its own significance on the way.

I propose that the father-absent, mother-involved family produces an oedipus complex which structures pre-oedipal predicaments into the formation of gendered subjectivity. Predicaments achieve a determining effect through the disjunction between instinctual life and use of language. This affects the infants' idiom of language, determining their use of words and self-descriptions. Predicaments, in determining the mental representation of instincts, play a crucial role in structuring the subjective capacity to feel. These predicaments are not determined by any one cause. The implication in Chodorow is that they may be the product of the mother, 'experiencing her son as a definite other – an opposite-gendered and -sexed other'[55] and in consequence creating a premature separation and the infant's fear of abandonment. There is a great deal to be said for this argument. But not all mothers will follow social norms and gender stereotyping. In place of trying to single out one cause, I suggest that predicaments are overdetermined and their significant effect within male subjectivity is due to the strength of the maternal object and feminine disposition within the oedipus complex. It is the oedipus complex which retrospectively structures predicaments as a feminine term in masculinity. Predicaments become established as a maternal supplement. It is the relative strength of the paternal, masculine disposition in its capacity to repress the maternal supplement which will determine the degree to which predicaments originating in the pre-oedipal will structure a boy's idiom of masculinity.

In this revised description of the oedipus complex, the infant's perception of the third term of the father evolves as a partial product of the mother–child dyad and not as a purely external phenomenon. The figures of the mother and father are present in the oedipal triangle. But what differentiates them is not only their sexual dispositions and their function, but, in the Kleinian model, their criteria as 'good and 'bad' objects. Infantile projections of good and bad objects are infused in the oedipal triangle, suggesting a relative failure of the depressive position. With the onset of the oedipus complex and the recognition of a third term that exists outside the mother–child dyad, the infant transfers its search for the good transformational object into an identification with the father. The bad, persecutory object becomes associated with what is to be left behind – the maternal term. The significance of this process for masculinity lies in the boy's identification with the father and his experience of the castration complex which places the maternal object as the antithesis of his emerging gendered subjectivity. While it threatens his gender identity as a supplement to it, it also threatens his sense of self. Masculine identity becomes a defence not only against the disruptive presence of the feminine term in the oedipus complex, but also against the dread of maternal predicaments originating in the pre-oedipal.

André Green has termed this oedipal triangle in which one parent is bad and the other idealised, as bi-triangulation (Green 'The Borderline Concept' 1986). Green is concerned with a psychopathology, while I am concerned with the structuring of gendered subjectivity. But his insight into the way the infant's pre-oedipal relationship with the maternal object determines his or her perception of the father figure has a lot in common with Melanie Klein's description of the father originating as a part object from within the maternal body (see Chapter 6 for a discussion of this). This implies that the small boy's identification with his father is derived initially from his projective relationship with his mother. The oedipal triangle consisting of two symmetrically opposed objects of masculine and feminine has its origins in the one entity of the maternal object. The father figure is initially fashioned in the idealised image of the good mother. But the boy's transference of the good transformational object into him is something of a mixed blessing. The threat of castration denies the boy's return to the mother for reparation and completion of the depressive position. The dilemma of his masculinity becomes more evident as the idealisation of the father gives way to the reality of his actual unattainability.

Because the bad object cannot be thought, it remains within the ego, its eternal presence making it impossible to introject good objects. There is a continual quest for some 'helpful' object which will provide sustenance for the maternal object, making his mother whole and well and enabling the boy to be released from his grip on her. The oedipus complex produces the father as the object to fulfil this role. Yet the boy is unable to properly introject him. His imago hovers on the boundary, neither fully in nor out. This ambivalent presence reinforces the confusion that what is psychically significant to the boy, the maternal object, his need for its wholeness and the achievement of his separateness, is denied value or meaning in the language games that constitute his emerging masculine subjectivity. The ineffectivity of the internalised representation of the father makes his masculine position seem puny and unremarkable in the face of the maternal supplement and the son's struggle to achieve the depressive position. The father appears inaccessible, ineffectual and out of reach.

The figure of the father is split by the boy's projection. On the one hand he is an actual individual and symbol who constitutes a third term in the oedipal triangle, that is a term which exists outside the mother–son relationship. One the other hand he is a projective entity, derived out of that relationship. The infant seeks two functions from his presence. First, to contain the boy's anxiety at his separation from his mother and enable him to achieve the depressive position. Second, to contain the good elements of the maternal object and transform them into an idiom of masculinity. What is yearned for is his capacity as a container to transform the emptiness that is anticipated by the threatened loss of the maternal object. This yearning and hope provides a powerful motive for his son's identification. And because he initially embodied the positive elements of the mother–son object relationship, the masculine term comes to be associated through the oedipus complex with the establishment of thought and language. The association is more a cultural than a psychical one, sustained by the boy's perception of the status and authority of the masculine term in the outside world. The failure of the father, however, to relieve the boy of his predicaments, serves only to reinforce the disjunction between instinctual life and language along gendered lines. For the son, language assumes an untrustworthy vehicle for his emotion and feelings.

The relative strength of predicaments will affect the degree to which the boy is driven into a heterosexual, father-identified position in an attempt to escape their hold over him. Such a position, tending to rigidity, is continually undermined by the boy's need to sustain and revive the maternal object. His need to do this, reinforces his perception of it as malevolent and manipulative, creating a complementary bid to destroy it and protect himself from its power over his life. Because such action is doomed to fail, the vicious circle of attack and succumbing fuels the boy's misogynistic rage at his mother. On the surface there appears to be a close identification with women and a rejection of the paternal position. This, however, is a part consequence of the infant compliance to the maternal object. Below the surface of such a mother-identified masculinity there is an intense struggle between the ego and the occupying maternal object. A struggle in which the figure of the father is continually drawn in and then expelled.

While his presence offers the seductive hope of resolution, his ineffectivity fuels intense disappointment and anger.

The boy utilises his intellect to compensate for the failure of the father and his feeling of inferiority to his mother. Klein has termed this the 'epistemophilic impulse'. It 'enables a boy to effect a displacement on to the intellectual plane; his sense of being at a disadvantage is then concealed and over-compensated by the superiority he deduces from his possession of a penis.'[56] Masculinity is imbued with a rationalism which distances the boy from the troubling dilemmas of his pre-oedipal relationship with his mother. But the intellect cannot sustain itself cut off from emotional life. Masculinity in consequence cannot find a place to rest. It becomes an identity in oscillation between two poles. In flight from the maternal object it seeks its authority and meaning in the realm of the intellect and rationality. But the abandonment of the mental space of instinctual life, only heralds the predicaments and the threatened loss of the maternal object. Back it swings, desperately seeking a return to the maternal object in order to sustain and support it from disintegration. The oedipus complex can find no clear resolution under such conditions.

I want to go back to the first chapter and the brief sketch I gave of the cultural and historical location of MAS. I argued that men's search for a reflexive comprehension of their masculine identities led a minority of them to therapy. It was in this practice that the centrality of the mother in the making of masculinity was recognised and appreciated. For men involved in MAS, their experience of family life in the decades after the war was the predominance of the mother both in an exclusive relationship of dependency and care and later in her power in and management of affective relations within the family. In contrast the father was relatively absent, both literally and emotionally. In this context the actual figure of the father cannot live up to the son's projection into him of the good elements of the maternal object. Neither his masculinity nor his social function is conducive to him containing the idealised projections of his son. His relatively removed role in the life of his son, ensures that what the boy introjects of him does not have the potency of the maternal transformational object. The masculine disposition within the boy's psyche, in consequence, has only a limited autonomy from the maternal object. The failure of the inter-communicative logic between the father and son means that there is no resolution to the boy's predicaments. The father seems beyond reach and he doesn't feel real. In a similar sense, language and intellectual life suffer the same lack of substance.

The centrality of the maternal object relationship in the formation of masculine identity disproves the idea that patriarchal structures are positive meanings imparted through language. The inconclusiveness of the depressive position ensures that the continuing presence of predicaments within male subjectivity structure a negative term into language games. The significance of the father within patriarchal cultural exchange is the boy's identification with him as the resolution of his predicaments. Through the promise of this resolution, he will free the son from his mother, and provide a measure for reality-testing. The degree to which he succeeds or fails is a consequence of the historically and culturally determined relations between men and women. The boy's relationship with patriarchal cultural meanings derives out of the antagonism between the masculine and feminine dispositions within his subjectivity.

The continuity of patriarchal structures of meaning are not located in a transhistorical signifier, such as Lacan's phallus, nor upon their functional necessity in the service of capitalist relations (as in Chodorow). They are overdetermined and the result of the articulation of equivalences. These emerge out of the antagonism and contradictions of the son's identification with the paternal term. Culturally, the connotations of the pre-oedipal predicaments as feminine, contrast with the positive material objects and meanings of male authority, reinforcing the defensive posture of masculinity against the maternal supplement. Similarly, predicaments become equivalences of identity; similar erotic and aggressive feelings, similar frustrations; fears and anxieties structure collective identifications and preoccupations. It is these which constituted the silence and the failure of reflexivity in MAS's attempt to comprehend its constituent masculinities, creating a structure of feeling.

The psychodynamics of masculinity are marked by the disjunction between feeling and language resulting from the antagonism between the maternal supplement and the paternal realm of language. The authority of the paternal realm is imparted through the maintenance of the positivity of terms within language games and the repression of the negative. What cannot be contained within their practices is connoted as the irrationality of predicaments, the feminine term, heralding a loss of self and a

threat to masculine identity. Male authority is articulated in antagonism with the maternal supplement. This overdetermined
articulation of equivalences produces a cultural narrative, a fiction
of male superiority and potency. I want to call the articulation of
this rationalist, representational and linguistic practice, the paternal narrative. Like Lacan's phallus, it signifies the structuring of
sexual and gender difference, but unlike it, it describes a historical
and cultural practice of language and meaning.

I want to go on and explore the way in which the maternal
supplement affects and subverts this paternal narrative and how
this disturbance within individual male subjectivity finds its way
into representation. The structuring of masculinity within this
cultural construction of patriarchy excludes from it the possibilities of reparation. The boy is caught between the threat of
castration and the failure of the father. His subjectivity trapped in
an oscillation between the pre-oedipal, pre-verbal world and the
oedipal world of language. At one pole is a nostalgia for the
transformational object of the mother that feels tenuous or lost. At
the other pole is the denial of inner trauma of loss and a flight into
the external world; a manic quest for omnipotence and the desire
to out-father the father. It is this former pole of identification and
the nostalgia for the mother that I want to investigate in the next
chapter. The latter I will leave for Chapters 6 and 7.

5

NOSTALGIA

If one had to choose a single characteristic to differentiate between present-day analyses and analyses as one imagines them to have been in the past, it would surely be found among the problems of mourning.[1]

It may be that men always feel as if they have 'lost something' whenever they speak of woman or women.[2]

MOURNING AND LOSS

The MAS project of reflexivity had been an attempt to address the crisis of historicity amongst a specific class fraction of men. The turn to therapy revealed the indeterminacy of the oedipus complex and the disruptive presence of the maternal supplement. It challenged the presumption that individual consciousness had its own linear history, albeit much of it unreachable through its foundation upon the unconscious. In this model of human development historicity was seen in the context of a progressive life course, subject to derailment, but nevertheless always onward bound. Predicaments and the failure of reflexivity to speak of the gaps and absences within men's consciousness of their own pasts, suggested another story. The turn to object relations theory and the realm of the pre-oedipal was an attempt to address it.

Psychoanalysis can shed light on this changing story of subjectivity. The oedipus complex and sexuality no longer play the sole determining roles in subject formation and identity. These have been partially displaced by a preoccupation with the self and its relationship to the external world. These are the concerns of the depressive position and the fear of object loss. This is a fundamental moment in the structuring of the human psyche, when splitting and projection are overcome and a new relation to reality is introduced. The depressive position is the inception of subjective historicity. For the first time the infant begins to perceive him or herself as a separate being. But a relative failure of the experience of individuation and separation results in the ego's endeavour to retain the primary object and relive, repetitiously, its loss. A part of the ego remains fused with the object, so depleting it. This site of predicament creates a feeling of emptiness. If the internal object of the mother feels unalive and fading, the subject's ego is continually drawn back into its universe in order to sustain and nourish it. As a result there is a failure of symbol formation in the experience of separatedness. Loss and separation cannot be fully thought and represented in language and remain dreaded disturbances.

The infant learns to manage the absences of the real mother through the aliveness of the internal object. But if this feels under threat then the infant mourns for this dying object inside. In her essay 'The Psychogenesis of Manic-depressive States', Melanie Klein writes: 'The processes which subsequently become defined as "loss of the loved object" are determined by the subject's sense of failure . . . to secure his *good, internalized object*, i.e. to possess himself of it.'[3] The satisfactory outcome of the depressive position is the introjection of the whole good object and its establishment within the ego where it will serve as the framing structure which sustains the ego in the face of the actual mother's absence. For Klein, mourning is a natural part of human development. In the process the infant frees its libido from the lost object and through symbol formation establishes a relationship with a growing number of external objects.

In his essay 'Mourning and Melancholia' Freud addresses the failure of this symbol formation. The loss of the object does not result in displacement of libido on to another object, but its withdrawal into the ego. Here it serves to create an identification of the ego with the abandoned object. 'Thus' writes Freud, 'the shadow of the object fell upon the ego.'[4] In this way an object loss is translated into an ego loss. Instead of being a phase that is worked through, mourning becomes a permanent affliction which the subject attempts to resolve through a search for the transformational object of the mother or her symbolic equivalent. It is a search for something in the future which resides in the past. The subject's historicity is no longer linear, but defined by a constant return to an unresolved predicament in an attempt to repair it. As Winnicott has written, 'nostalgia. . . . belongs to the precarious hold that a person may have on the inner representation of a lost object.'[5]

This predicament exists as a spatial, rather than temporal phenomenon. A pre-verbal disturbance which has been denied representation in thought and language. Each return is characterised by an inability to process it. Instead only an emptiness awaits the subject's quest and he is driven out in search of relief, as Klein has written: 'Its torturing and perilous dependence on its loved objects drives the ego to find freedom.'[6] And in that oscillation between coming and going, mourning and mania, lies the breakdown of a self-comprehending historicity. Despite the failure of its communication in language, the attempt to resolve predicaments and the experience of mourning are signified in cultural forms and representations of nostalgia.

NOSTALGIA AND DIFFERENCE

Robert Hewison points out that nostalgia, 'filters out unpleasant aspects of the past, and of our former selves, creating a self-esteem that helps us rise above the anxieties of the present.'[7] At its heart is a sense of loss. But its representation and the events and objects of its focus have no *a priori* agreement amongst people. Nostalgic celebration is constructed out of a collective experience, its meaning a contemporary, ideological interpretation of the past. Individual longing is articulated and organised by hegemonic political and cultural discourses, which seek the endorsement and legitimation of their authority. Nostalgia operates on the sites of class, sexual, ethnic and national differences. There exists a multiplicity of non-hegemonic forms of nostalgia whose elements can oppose or coincide with more dominant widespread representations. There is a specifically masculine form of nostalgia which addresses the problems of men's historicity. Problems which are products of a transitional loss of cultural authority and a psychological feeling of loss.

I want to illustrate how this masculine nostalgia operates by using the text of an advert, taken from *Elle pour Homme*, the men's supplement to the magazine *Elle* (1988). It is for Parker pens and is titled: 'Flying may have lost the elegance of the Twenties. Writing has, however, regained it.'

The moon shatters in some dark lagoon
   as the flying boat touches down.
Distracted by the faint tinkling that
   announces the arrival of your gin sling,
you idly wonder, can it really be another
   eighteen hours to Cairo.
. . . Ah the failed memories of a more
   romantic age.

Here the 1920s is represented as a time of stability, privilege and wealth, the exclusive experience of a particular gender and racial identity. Empire, travel and the absence of domesticity paint the picture of a colonial, upper-class, English masculinity. Through retrospection, Parker pens are connoted with this supremacy. The advert is addressing an educated elite of young men who no longer have an empire, nor any particular role to play. Its promise that writing will restore to its audience the lost opulence, elegance and mastery of this time is not to do with the acquisition of wealth, but with the loss of a masculine, intellectual authority. Its nostalgia is for a colonial ideal of the universal European civilising intellect which commanded the world and spoke for it.

The image of the omnipotent white man flying across the empire appears to erase the racial and sexual antagonisms of colonialism. But they exist as negatives, their absence from the narrative ensures their presence. Denial only confirms that it is these dislocating and disruptive forces which are being excluded by the nostalgic myth. The narrative is produced from the polarity between the subject identified with and the others who threaten him. It is in the relativity of his identity and in the plurality and diversity of cultural identities that his apparently effortless superiority is undermined. Nostalgia attempts to obscure difference and alleviate contemporary antagonisms and contradictions by reframing the elements that conflict in reality into a harmonious past. It acts as a metaphor, distancing its mythology from the social antagonisms at its source. Nostalgia makes life narratable, representing what is hard to speak of. As the advert demonstrates, nostalgic myth contains a psychological element which is the element articulating the sense of loss rooted in our personal lives. A masculine identification with nostalgic representations springs from men's effort to comprehend their historicity and the troubling predicaments which obscure understanding and control over it.

Nostalgic myth mediates between the past and individual consciousness. It can function by erasing a memory or an object from the past and displacing the anxiety induced by it into a more pleasurable and less threatening object or scene. The significance of the psychological element in nostalgia is not in the image that is evoked, but in the object or scene displaced from the narrative. Returning to the advert, its effectiveness works through its displacement of men's anxieties about the lack of meaning to be found in contemporary intellectual masculine identities. Nostalgia replaces the imperfect present with a perfect past whose values and meaning are condensed into the image of a pen and the tradition of script. Acquisition of the pen promises the restoration of a lost excellence and authority, writing the promise of a male cultural authority. The threatening presence of women and ethnic difference that has precipitated men's sense of loss is evaded and reframed in a manner that addresses their disruptive presence without even mentioning them.

As a mediator, nostalgic myth maintains the power relations between hegemonic identities and others. It doesn't actually represent men's sense of loss so much as evade it. In this operation it has a relation with predicaments and the failure of symbol formation. It is a signification of men's silence, displacing the absences of predicaments with a reassuring but inert mythical denial. The negative is more real than the positive. In place of the precarious hold a person may have on their internal object, nostalgia brings verve and colour. It is voluble, chattering memories that skirt around the central and unspoken dilemma of the predicament. Where predicaments have locked specific experiences of loss and separation into pre-verbal and unthought ego disturbances, nostalgia acts as a linguistic bridge, metaphorising them and so containing them within the positivity of language games. This form of idealisation enables the ego to bear the feelings of catastrophe heralded by predicaments. The function of nostalgia is to evade anxiety and the effect of predicaments within male subjectivity.

NOSTALGIA, PREDICAMENTS AND MALE SUBJECTIVITY

Symbol formation as a metaphoric use of objects is like a narrative which establishes an individual's subjectivity. Predicaments and symbolic equivalence arrest this linear narrative forming an atemporal space which exists as a concurrently reoccurring memory trace in the present. Because they do not exist within linguistic representation they remain such, like a historical scar tissue fusing inner and outer, subject and object. It is where the principle of the negative has failed due to the infant's overwhelming feelings of anxiety at the mother's absence, that an individual cathexis with nostalgic myth is most powerful.

It is Freud's essay 'Beyond the Pleasure Principle' (Freud 1920g) and his speculations upon a 'death instinct' which provide a description of the psychodynamics of nostalgia. His anecdote about his grandson's *'Fort/Da'* game revealed the existence of a desire to repeat unpleasurable experiences. Freud argues that the perpetual recurrence of the same thing in psychic life and the compulsion to repeat some pattern of behaviour is *'an urge inherent in organic life to restore an earlier state of things* which the living entity has been obliged to abandon under the pressure of external disturbing forces.'[8] Freud presumes the 'external disturbing forces' belong to the castration complex. The 'state of things' the infant must abandon is the pre-oedipal relationship with the mother. Repetition reveals a 'death instinct', a desire to return to degree zero, to a moment of non-subjectivity and fusion with the maternal body. Nostalgic myth gives a representation to this conservative instinct to return to an earlier, older state of things.

Constituted as an absence in symbol formation, predicaments form a trace. This trace relates no less to the future than to what is called the past. While Freud assumes that such a trace would be repressed into the unconscious along with the 'earlier state of things', it cannot be simply reduced to the historical past. Just as predicaments mark the confusion of inner and outer, subject and object so, too, they create an ambivalence around what is time past and what is time present. Narrative linear time becomes spatial at the site of a predicament. It is this trace of the past recurring in the present which constitutes a failure of reflexivity and historicity and gives rise to a contemporary nostalgic longing for a former time.

The trace has no presence, but is the simulacrum of a predicament that dislocates the present, displaces time and refers beyond itself. It gives rise to mimesis, metonymy and to metaphor, but it does not find its way into the positivist representations of language games. Its relation to the signification of the paternal narrative is a disruptive one. It not only undermines its fiction as Alice Jardine has argued (Jardine 1985), it also endangers its syntax and breaks its rules. Nostalgia belongs to the paternal narrative, its task to efface this effect and re-establish the primacy of the paternal linguistic order over the maternal supplement. But as the reflexive project of MAS began to show, the impasse of certain contemporary masculinities is the inadequacy of the paternal narrative and the relative failure of securing the boundaries of the male ego from the predicaments of the maternal supplement. Faced with this dilemma masculinities attempt to evade fusion with the maternal object through a compulsion to sustain control and mastery over the signifier.

This is the function of the classical male hero in narrative. His cultural authority and masculine potency is preserved through his compulsion to move in adventure, in life on the road or in war. The fantasies of his omnipotence ensure that he never stops long enough to be consumed by his predicaments. To be still and passive is to herald the image of a small boy who still belongs to his mother and cries out for her protection. Mastery is achieved by clinging to narrative and to linear time, evading those spaces which threaten fusion and the loss of self. This fear of fusion is translated into a fear of association; invariably male heroism can only ever be a solitary pursuit.

In a discussion on the discontents of modernity the broadcaster Michael Ignatieff asks the novelist Saul Bellow what he means by the term 'Moronic Inferno', which he uses to describe modern culture.

Bellow Well, it means a chaotic state which no-one has sufficient internal organisation to resist, and which is overwhelmed by all kinds of powers. . . .

Ignatieff What is this lack of centre? You seem to be implying that if somehow we could have a different kind of self, a more resolute self, we could withstand this onslaught of forces a little better. What do you mean?

Bellow Well it doesn't need to be a different kind of self. It needs to be a self, however. That is to say one witnesses the obiliteration of true forms of individuality in this scene.[9]

The solitary male hero is a nostalgic longing for this 'organised self'. Underlying this fear of anonymity and crisis of meaning lies a preoccupation with paternal authority. It is women, particularly the figure of the mother who are blamed, both literally and metaphorically, for the instability of the paternal narrative and linguistic order. In the absence of sufficient internal boundaries men must substitute them with external action and control. What is an attempt to hold on to a sense of self is translated into an attempt to master others.

Freud's super-ego and Bellow's 'organised self' both presume that the third term of the oedipal triangle is a masculine entity entirely separate from the mother–child dyad. But as I have argued this third term is a part-object originating from the infant–mother relationship. What is lost for the male infant as he identifies his good internal objects with the father of the oedipus complex is the 'good mother'. This is the mother as transformational object who has nurtured and sustained her son and given him life. Following the cultural logic of the paternal narrative the oedipus complex attempts to erase the 'good mother' and construct the maternal supplement, which comes to represent the pre-oedipal predicaments which are feared.

But it is in these spaces of the disavowal of the 'good mother' that men can discover those terms which Alice Jardine refers to as 'not attributable to Man: the spaces of the *en-soi*, Other, without history'.[10] While Bellow seeks the restitution of the paternal narrative and its syntax, Jardine wants to usurp the positivity of language games, 'To give a new language to these other spaces'. It is a project which she concedes is, 'filled with both promise and fear . . . for these spaces have hitherto remained unknown, terrifying, monstrous.'[11] To explore these spaces would suggest some sort of implosion of male subjectivity and the loss of self in fusion with the maternal object. But perhaps it is possible to retrieve the 'good mother' out of her entrapment in the maternal supplement. She offers both a basis for selfhood and an alternative to the patriarchal logic of the paternal narrative. Masculine nostalgia in its evasion of predicaments is an attempt to seek out this good maternal transformational object. But its search is continually frustrated by the logic of the paternal narrative.

Jardine's suggestion polarises the choices open to a reflexive analysis of masculinity. The first is to re-establish the paternal narrative through a reassertion of male cultural authority. Such a project would not be the simple return to an older vocabulary of male superiority. It would be one that sought a *rapprochement* with the changing cultural and gendered identities of men and women. It would seek to re-establish practices and languages asserting the primacy of heterosexuality, male authority in the public domain and a clear division between the workplace and the domestic world of children and home. Alternatively, a reflexive analysis can hold to those earlier commitments of MAS to explore the relationship of feeling to language. In challenging the positivist objects of language games and acknowledging the existence of predicaments in male subjectivity it would be possible to develop new vocabularies out of a recognition of the negative. Despite being governed by the paternal narrative, nostalgia offers a door in search of the 'good mother'. If we open it and step beyond it, we can embark upon an exploration of men's silence.

IN SEARCH OF THE LOST OBJECT

To begin I want to turn to two films by the German director Wim Wenders. Both *Alice in the Cities* (1973) and *Paris Texas* (1985) are reflexive films whose narratives follow Wenders' fascination with the road movie and a preoccupation with movement and the search for identity. They are themes played out in relationship to masculinity, to men's relationships with women and children and to the attempt at some sort of reconciliation with them. Wenders' concerns are similar to those of MAS in this country, during the 1970s. His work offers a cultural representation of men's predicaments and the place of the parental figures in masculine identities.

In *Alice in the Cities*, a German reporter Phillip Winters is pursuing an assignment in America. His task is to capture its reality. However, he is unable to write anything down. Instead he takes an endless number of polaroid snaps, recording the iconography of American popular culture. His fascination with these signs is also his deep anxiety that they are meaningless. His futile search for meaning and substance is reflected in his transient and rootless existence. What is at stake is not his sexuality, nor his concern with masculine status. It is his struggle to feel real, to know that he is actually alive in the world.

Winters encounters a little girl, Alice, who is abandoned to his care by her mother. Together they fly back to Germany and attempt to find the girl's grandmother. On the face of it the film depicts their journey through the country, charting their growing relationship as they move from one place to the next. But there is, of course, a great deal more at stake in the film. Winters' transience has been his terror of stopping still. His aloneness has been his fear of association. His search for Alice's grandmother is an allegory for his own search for a home and a place to belong. Women exist in the film as mothers, reflecting Winters' own need to find his maternal origins. Alice symbolises the child in the adult and Winters' attempt to unite her with her grandmother represents his own struggle to communicate with the motherless child within himself. This interior narrative dominates the filmic representation of men and women's relationships. The story has little to do with an oedipal drama and nothing to do with sexuality. It can best be summarised by a small scene in which Winters is telling Alice a bedtime story.

Once there was a little boy who got lost. He went for a walk in the woods with his mother one lovely summer afternoon. And as they came to a clearing the sun was shining. His mother suddenly felt tired and wanted a rest. All of a sudden the little boy heard a rustling in the bushes and he found a hedgehog. He ran after it until he came to a stream and in the stream he saw a fish. He ran along beside the stream till he saw a bridge. On the bridge was a horseman.

The horseman sat very calmly on his horse and looked off into the distance. So the boy went onto the bridge. He carefully walked around the horse and the rider slowly rode away. The boy ran after him until he was lost from sight. Then he came to the highway. A street with lots of trucks. The boy sat at the road side until a truck stopped and the driver asked if he would like a lift. The boy was delighted. He sat proudly next to the driver who let him fiddle with the radio. And the boy rode as far as the sea. And at the sea he remembered his mother again.

In his analysis of folk tales the formalist V.I. Propp described an important prototype of all narratives (Propp 1968). His concern was to discover a common form to fairy stories; the norms which govern the structure of its narrative. He divided up the content and characters of a large number of folk tales, identifying and allotting to them specific functions. For Propp narrative was a transformative process linked like a chain from one function to another. Its purpose was to represent real life experiences of change and make them narratable. Narrative is linear, it has a beginning, a middle and an end and it is initiated by rites of separation. In Winters' story it is the boy separating himself from his mother. This places him outside the synchronic order he has existed within. The middle part is marked by the character being outside the norms of everyday life. This structured exclusion places the subject in a liminal relationship to the world he or she left behind. The metaphor of 'no man's land' describes this displacement. The end of the story is the character's re-incorporation into a new synchronic order, integrating disorder back into stability. This final part is the inverse of the beginning, representing the character's new relationship to social norms through, for example, marriage or acquired wealth.

Propp cites the oedipus story as an example of this narrative. Freud's oedipus complex has a great deal in common with Propp's narrative structure. The initial phase is the pre-oedipal mother–child relationship. This is disrupted by the third term of the father which begins a transitional process in which the infant oscillates between the maternal and paternal terms. The ending corresponds to the resolution of the oedipus complex and the closure of subjectivity around the term of the father. The pre-oedipal is relegated to the mother and the past, creating a history whose temporal movement forms an individual's consciousness of his or her own past and hence his or her identity. This is the classical tale that has become a central pillar of contemporary culture's understanding of the individual's acquisition of language and gender. It is a metaphor describing the transition from nature to culture, a transformation governed by the male term in which the maternal body is synonymous with nature. Linear and temporal, the subject moves from the maternal body, the feminine term, through a stage of liminality into the signification of the paternal narrative.

At first glance Winters' tale of the little boy's journey fits this classic oedipal story. The child leaves his mother and goes off wondering alone, pursuing various objects which lead to the horseman. This figure, astride the bridge, symbolic of the phallus, signifies sexual differentiation. The boy pursues him. Once across the bridge the world around him is transformed. Gone is the pastoral idyll and in its place is the noisy, manufactured, mechanical movement of cars and lorries. Classically, the story should now find a closure embedding the child into a gendered subjectivity.

But it doesn't do this. Instead the child arrives at the sea and remembers his mother. Winnicott has remarked, 'as a student of unconscious symbolism, I *knew* (one always *knows*) that the sea is the mother, and onto the seashore the child is born . . . so now the seashore was the mother's body'.[12] The linear, temporal movement of the narrative has become circular. There is no resolution of gendered subjectivity around the term of the father and no seamless paternal narrative. Instead the recurring presence of the maternal supplement brings the subject back to that 'earlier state of things'. Winters' tale suggests something other than an oedipal drama in its breaking of narrative convention. It is a story that fits more closely to Klein's symbol formation and the drama of resolving the depressive position. The liminality of masculine identities results from the indeterminacy of the oedipus complex, a consequence of the relative failure of differentiation from the mother. In *Alice in the Cities* Wenders identifies this preoccupation with the male self. It is in his *Paris Texas* that he struggles with the predicaments.

Wenders marked his return to Germany and European cinema, after a disastrous stint in Hollywood, with the widely acclaimed film *Paris Texas*. Despite its American location and content, the film speaks for a specifically European reflexivity: a desire for a homecoming which was the preoccupation of many Germans who grew up in the post-war years under the shadow of the Nazi past. Against this national background the film tried to appraise the dilemmas of a generation in the aftermath of the political failures of 1968. Wenders does not try to play out these cultural and political themes in realist drama. He focuses on the theme of ambivalent identity and personal dislocation through the narrative of family disintegration and an attempted reconciliation on the part of the father (Travis, played by Harry Dean Stanton). Wenders' subject could be interpreted as a capitulation to the Christian Democratic era and its pro-family rhetoric. However, in bringing his own deep confusions and predicaments to the film, he undermines the idea of the family as the font of social stability and individual fulfilment. Instead he places at the centre of his narrative a man whose masculine identity is bereft of its paternal function.

The film opens with Travis walking through a Texan desert landscape. This image of a man alone in a barren and inhospitable terrain is a recurring myth in Western culture, signifying exile and soul-searching. The desert is an uncanny space, its borders marking out the margin between the inhabitable and the uninhabitable, between the intersubjectivity of culture and the muteness of nature. As a cultural metaphor the desert's lack of familiar signs and the absence of cultural iconography depict a no-man's land, disorientating the narratives and references which determine identity. It is an image of liminality which Wenders attempts to find his way out of as the film progresses.

Travis arrives at a group of buildings, entering one he collapses onto the floor. He awakens in a doctor's surgery. He refuses to speak. The doctor asks him, 'You know which side of the border you're on? You've got a name for it?' The reference is perhaps to the Mexican border, but the ambivalence remains. Later in the film, when Travis has been re-united with his son Hunter (Hunter Carson) and together they have tracked down the boy's mother Jane (Nastassia Kinski), he recounts to her, in the third person, his feelings about the degeneration of their love into hatred and violence. 'And for the first time he wished he were far away, lost in a deep vast country where nobody knew him, somewhere without language and he dreamed about this place without knowing its name.' He had run away from her – 'I ran till every sight of man had disappeared' – a description of the escape of every solitary male hero. It is this desert scene which Travis imagined and this liminal state. It is the wrong side of the border and it doesn't have a name, for it is a world of disassociation.

Travis lives within a predicament. He is caught between two terms. At one pole is the transformational world of the mother. Here lies the 'good mother' who will save and repair him. But the threat of predicament associated with the maternal object heralds the loss of self, language and identity. At the other pole is the paternal narrative which has bequeathed to him a sexuality that has poisoned his family, and a paternity which is weak and failed. His entrapment in this liminal existence is his fear that the 'good mother'/object inside him is weak and will die before he can revive and restore her. His quest for reparation has no linguistic representation within the paternal narrative. So he walks compulsively, his silence reflecting this wordless place.

The doctor phones Travis's brother Walt, who travels down from Los Angeles. When he arrives Travis has disappeared. Walt finds him walking purposefully through the desert. They drive to a motel. Again Travis disappears to continue his walking. As the journey continues Walt becomes more frustrated with Travis's silence. He becomes quite frantic to know where Travis has been for the last 4 years. It feels impossible to live with the enigma of his silence. He tells Travis that he and his wife Ann are looking after Hunter. They haven't seen Jane since she left him on their doorstep 4 years previously. Walt decides to phone Ann to let her know that he has found Travis and is coming home. He speaks to Hunter, 'Hello it's daddy, I thought you'd be in bed. Guess who I'm visiting in Texas . . . your father.' The pun offers some kind of explanation for Travis's silence in the confusion over the meaning of paternity and the absence of the father.

Travis finally volunteers to speak. He asks Walt, 'Did you ever go to Paris?' 'No.' 'Could we go there now?' A short time later he shows Walt a small battered photograph. It is a picture of a vacant lot he has bought in Paris, a tiny hamlet in the Texan desert. He informs Walt that their mother told him he was conceived here; 'I figured that's where I began . . . Travis Clay Henderson. I started out there'. While Travis's flight may have much in common with the omnipotent, solitary male hero, he is going in the opposite direction. There is no desire to find compensation in manly deeds. His manic and obsessive search is for his origins, not a headlong rush away from them. He yearns to begin again, to abandon his heterosexuality and masculinity and return to the maternal body.

Travis stays with Walt and Ann in Los Angeles and begins to try and establish a relationsip with Hunter. The child confronts him with his role as a father. One day he is sitting reading through some magazines. The maid asks him what he is doing.

'Ah, I'm looking for uhm, the father.'
'Your father?'
'No, no, just a father, any father. What does a father look like?'

In the following scene she helps him to dress and hold himself like a father. 'To be a rich father Senor Travis you must look to the sky, never to the ground.' This search for the posture and language of fatherhood is analogous to Travis stepping back into the paternal narrative and his masculine identity.

The narrative now seems set to develop into a classical oedipal drama. Order has been restored as Travis reasserts his paternal presence. He decides to leave Walt and Ann's household to look for Jane. Hunter wants to accompany him. They track Jane down to a peep joint in Houston, where she is working. Travis enters one of the booths. Through the one-way mirror is a mock-up of a hotel bedroom. Over the intercom he requests a woman with fair hair. He watches as Jane enters the room. She sits down and attempts some kind of communication with the unknown man sitting in the booth. Travis is unable to cope with her presence in this voyeuristic setting and its connotations of prostitution. He leaves without revealing his identity.

He returns to Hunter and proceeds to get drunk in a bar. Later he tells Hunter about his own mother.

'My mother was not a fancy woman . . . she never pretended to be a fancy woman.'
'Then what was she?'
'She was just plain, good, just very good. My daddy had this idea in his head, a kind of sickness, this idea about her. He looked at her but he didn't see her. He saw this idea. He told people she was from Paris. It was a big joke . . . he started believing it. Oh God! she'd get so embarrassed.'

His story is of the destruction of his mother by his father. It is the legacy of male heterosexuality that Travis has inherited, 'a kind of sickness', in which women's reality is reduced to a figment of male sexual fantasy. What disturbed Travis when he met Jane was not just the quasi-pornographic setting, but her presence as a sexual woman, when what he was looking for was a surrogate mother.

The next day Travis returns to the peep joint. This time he begins speaking to Jane, using the telephone in the booth. He relates the story of their relationship and life together. Jane recognises it and begins to cry silently. He tells her how he had to give up his work because he could not bear to be separate from her. He began to get jealous of her, after their son was born, imagining that she was going out meeting other men. Things got steadily worse until he was locking her in the trailer and tying her up at night to stop her from running away. Finally, Jane managed to escape and set fire to the trailer. He awoke, couldn't find his wife and child so ran clear and didn't stop running.

Travis tells Jane that Hunter is waiting for her in a hotel room but that he cannot stay and must leave. She stops him and speaks about her own grief. The bitter pain and longing of their relationship is played out in this peep joint, a symbol of alienated, isolating sexualities. They are divided by a mirror. The woman on show and the man invisible, their communication mediated by a telephone. Their emotion and remorse spills into the vacant space beside them. There is no contact and apparently no possibility of one. The excursion of the film into an oedipal drama of sexual relationships is brought to an abrupt halt. There can be no reunion or conjugation and no reconciliation between adult men and women.

The film's final scene is the only expression of love and intimacy. Mother and son are reunited. Holding each other, they whirl around the hotel room. On the ground below, Travis is looking up, watching them. He climbs into his van and drives away. It is the end. Yet in the logic of the paternal narrative there is no ending. Travis emerges from a state of liminality, only to return to it. Stability and order exists with the mother and child. The film's ending suggests that Wenders is confronted by something he finds impossible to resolve. The term of the father holds no meaning and the maternal is impossible to reach without a collapse into a wordless non-identity. Masculinity seems doomed to a liminal existence, without a home and without the possibility of love. The narrative of Travis symbolises the search for reparation. But instead of finding a mother, he is confronted by female sexuality.

For Wenders, the only hope of men and masculinity is the child, only he remains untainted by heterosexual desire and only he possesses the capacity to make reparation, to heal himself and experience love. The German critic Kraft Wetzel has described Wenders as a small boy who refuses to grow up, preferring the nostalgic romanticism of children to the realities of women and his own sexuality.[13] But *Paris Texas* suggests Travis as a small boy who is unable to grow up. He is the metaphor for the emotionally wounded little boy trapped in a maternal predicament that locks him into a dependency he at once longs for and singularly fights to be free of. It is the ghost of the absent father that haunts the text of *Paris Texas*. Only he can offer delivery from this predicament and his failure is a palpable presence in the film. Travis instead of fulfilling the conventional role of the father of the oedipus complex, uses his paternal role to negate it. He returns his son to his mother: 'It was me that tore you apart and I owe it to you to bring you back together.' But in this undoing of the legacy of his own father, there is no place left for Travis. Capable of neither a sexual relationship nor paternity he can only return to his self-imposed exile.

MEN'S HETEROSEXUALITY AND THE FAILURE OF LOVE

Travis's journey to Houston was never as a husband attempting to reconcile his sexual relationship with his wife. He went in search of a mother, for both the child in himself and for his son. His desire to return Hunter to Jane is born out of his own indebtedness and guilt to her, not as his wife, but as his mother, himself not as her husband, but as her son. Freud puts this scenario of reparation succinctly.

> His mother gave him life – his own life – and in exchange he gives her another life, that of a child which has the greatest resemblance to himself. The son shows his gratitude by wishing to have by his mother a son who is like himself: in other words . . . he is completely identifying with the father.[14]

Freud defines this longing as the subject's wish to be his own father. But this is just what Travis is unable to be. His efforts to repair the damaged object within and to make it whole, ties his ego to the constant need to revive the fantasy of a dying mother. Without her he cannot survive. Travis is the metaphorical mother's boy unable to enter the syntax of the paternal narrative and occupy a third position in relation to his own son. In this state of mourning what more can he do than deliver his own son back to his mother, to the place where he longs to be, but to which access is denied by his adult sexuality.

This scenario is first played out with the birth of Hunter. Travis became his own father and in the process inherited the idiom of his heterosexuality. Jane was reduced to a sexually desirable object both longed for by and longing for other men. Freud has termed this jealousy, 'the necessary conditions for loving'[15] in which a man breathes the scandal of prostitute around his lover in order to enhance his own desire for and attraction to her. Now he can guard her from the approaches of other men, acting out his infantile, oedipal jealousy of his own father's sexual desire for his mother. As Klein has remarked; 'Jealousy is based on the suspicion of and rivalry with the father, who is accused of having taken away . . . the mother.'[16] This jealousy develops into paranoia if the mechanisms of splitting and projection are unmitigated due to the relative failure of the depressive position. Men and fathers are perceived as threats, yet as competitors they provide the cement for the subject's attachment to women.

In the absence of the father, the son is unable to turn to the mother's body for compensation. Only a female sexuality which has been debased as an undifferentiated prostitute provides a safe enough source of comfort and pleasure. So is ensured the separation of the 'affective' and 'sensual' currents of male heterosexuality, identified by Freud in his essay 'On The Universal Tendency to Debasement in the Sphere Of Love' (1912d). This sharp contrast between prostitute and mother suggests that what has been split into opposite pairs in the conscious has some sort of unity in the unconscious. Ensuring the separation of the two becomes more problematic when the failure to achieve the depressive position leaves a continuing partial fusion of the ego with the internal object of the mother. Other women are split. First, as the symbolic equivalents of a good transformational object who can complete the process of differentiation and individuation. Second, as the bad maternal object (i.e. predicament) that inhabits the subject's ego continually threatening its collapse. In this guise she is the sexual temptress feeding off men's weakness. In jealousy the otherness of female sexuality becomes persecutory. The possibility of finding reparation with women seems fraught with danger and uncertainty. For Travis it revealed levels of hatred and misogyny he had thought only belonged to his father.

In *Paris Texas* Wenders confronts this splitting of male heterosexuality only to retreat back into the inner world of the child in the final scene of mother-and-son reunion. Travis the man is marooned, cut off from his internal world. His isolation and self-negation is born of the paternal narrative and its logic of defeating the maternal supplement. For Travis love remains abandoned in the maternal moment to which he can never return. There seems little possibility of it existing within male subjectivity when silence governs the unfinished yearning for the maternal body and women exist as a form of immunisation or a source of abject confusion. Reparation has no representation in a culture where the oedipal drama has determined a gendered narrative of differentiation and masculine subjectivity which seeks to erase the 'good mother'. The predicaments of male subjectivity ensure that love is always somewhere beyond and out of reach, invested in an other that is simultaneously a source of longing and dread.

Wenders portrays a world in which there is no possibility that women can offer men an alliance in which their mutual difficulties can be negotiated and resolved. Such a contact is negated by the male predicaments which split women, placing them in comparison to and competition with the internalised object of the mother. Women become men's self-fulfilling prophecy, destined always to fail them and to serve as the victims of men's disappointment and rage. Wenders' tendency is to slide into a romanticism of men grappling alone in the nostalgic embrace of heroism. But it is a sparse universe they occupy. Not only are men doomed through guilt to be alone, but also to self-hatred. The child within that yearns for the mother is the site of intense attack, denial and repression. This metaphorical figure who comes to stand for the original predicament threatens to pull apart the public persona of an authoritative masculinity with its infantile need for the maternal body. The adult assault is an insurance for men's continued participation in the paternal narrative.

Wenders offers no way out of this bleak world of mourning. But in the character of Travis he has explored it and even in his pessimism he has highlighted the enigmatic figure of the father, who haunts both *Alice in the Cities* and *Paris Texas*. It is he who holds a key to the retrospectively structured effect of the pre-oedipal mother–son relationship upon men's masculinity. The legacy left to Travis by his father is one of failed paternity and an intrinsically violent relationship to women. In his desperate bid to avoid his son suffering the same fate, Travis enables his son's reunion with his mother. But his own legacy is his capitulation as a father of any kind. The father represents his son's destiny and future and his failure to be present and to be known serves to enhance a sense of fatalism. While he may have enabled the child to retrieve the 'good mother', adult masculinity remains bereft of her, still fastened to the legacy of a failed paternity. The fate of the 'good mother' in masculinity is bound up with the son's relationship to a father. In the next chapter I want to explore the interrelationship of the mother with the third term of the father and with it the concept of 'thirdness'.

6

'THIRDNESS' AND THE FATHER'S LOVE

I have in front of me a picture by the American photographer Duane Michals. In the foreground is the head and shoulders of a teenage boy, sideways on to the camera. He is staring forward. Behind him stands his father, hands on hips, staring resolutely, if not a little truculently into the camera. The mother is next to him, but partially hidden behind the boy, a peripheral figure in this family drama. The photograph is titled 'A Letter From My Father'. Across the top and along the bottom Michals has written this imaginary letter.

> As long as I can remember, my father always said to me that one day he would write me a very special letter. But he never told me what the letter would be about. I used to try and guess what I would read in the letter, what mystery, what family secret could at last be revealed. I know what I had hoped to read in the letter. I wanted him to tell me where he had hidden his affection. But then he died and the letter never did arrive, and I never found that place where he had hidden his love.[1]

It is as though Michals has been fated by the failure of paternal love, exposed to forces which will buffet him and knock him out of control. The longing for a 'good father' who will love his son is the hope of being held by a third figure who will ensure a sense of destiny and becoming. In the absence of this love, in the forever expectation of his potential presence, it is a longing the more keenly held.

FREUD'S FATHER

In Freudian metapsychology the paternal figure is the third term that intrudes upon the mother–child dyad, initiating the oedipus complex and sexual differentiation. He is the significant term, bringing language, individuation and access to cultural intersubjectivity, a process which transforms the pre-oedipal psychic strcuture and its forms of pre-verbal communicating. It is his figure who dominates the two parental figures internalised in the super-ego. He is the source of moral authority and conscience as well as the prohibitor of incestuous desire and the guardian of the id. He marks the smashing of the oedipus complex with the threat of castration and its resolution in the agency of the super-ego. In classical Freudian psychoanalysis the father is the key to the individual acquisition of a gendered subjectivity.

There is, however, a certain inconsistency in the Freudian father. In his essay 'The Ego and the Id' (Freud 1923b) Freud substitutes the term super-ego for ego ideal. Nevertheless he retains a distinction between them. The ideal can be depicted as the loving parent (what I will term the 'good father') while the super-ego is the voice of prohibition (the castrating or 'bad father'). Implicit in Freud's inconsistent use of these terms is the presence of both these facets in the figure of the father. He is both loving and authoritative. But the figure who predominates in the text is characterised as a rational authority, a kind of intellectualised barometer for reality testing. What eludes the Freudian text is the 'good father', his love and his bodily presence.

In his analysis of the little boy Hans, Freud provides a case history depicting his theory of the oedipus complex and castration anxiety (Freud 1909b). While the subject of the analysis is Little Hans and his phobia of horses, it is Hans's father who is the presence most strongly felt in the text. Freud conducted his analysis through Hans's father and much of the case history is in the form of the father's record of conversations he had with his son and events he noted. Freud only met the boy on a couple of occasions. In the correspondence between the two men there is a collusion, centred on the exclusion of the mother. It is Hans's fear of his mother's absence that is seen as the cause of his phobia and undermining his future as a man. Freud notes the father's intolerance towards his wife's affection for their son. '[He] accuses her, not without some show of injustice, of being responsible for the outbreak of the child's neurosis, on account of her excessive display of affection for him and her too frequent readiness to take him into her bed.'[2] Nothing further is made of this observation.

The text reveals the father's attachment to his son through an analytic discourse that seeks to decipher the little boy's fantasies and behaviour. At one point Hans's father writes to Freud.

> On April 5th Hans came in to our bedroom again, and was sent back to his own bed. I said to him: 'As long as you come into our room in the mornings, your fear of horses won't get better.' He was defiant, however and replied: 'I shall come in all the same, even if I am afraid.' So he will not let himself be forbidden to visit his mother.[3]

His paternal duty is to overcome the boy's need of his mother and save him from the paralysis of maternal enchantment. His function as a father is to bring rationality, independence and order to the life of his son by breaking his attachment to his mother. He attempts to do this but not in the offer of an alternative attachment but by intervening in the mother–child relationship.

This phenomenological relationship of father and son is given legitimacy by Freud's own psychoanalytic 'structuralist' interpretation. On one of his meetings with Little Hans, he tells the boy; 'long before he was in the world I had known that a Little Hans would come who would be so fond of his mother that he would be bound to feel afraid of his father because of it'.[4] The Freudian logic of the oedipus complex gives credence to a specific practice of paternity. While the given is that the third term of the oedipus complex is masculine, Freudian psychoanalysis has also predisposed it to signify authority and detachment rather than love and the body. The privileging of rationality to the father maintains the recurring antinomies within Freudian psychoanalysis which become organised around gendered binary terms: mind and body, culture versus nature, conscious versus unconscious. Such binary terms seek to maintain the boundaries that divide men's egos from the maternal supplement.

These antinomies have been accentuated by Lacan in his attempts to restore the classical Freudian emphasis upon the father figure. In psychoanalysis Lacan is the theorist of the father. Like Freud, he believed that the pre-oedipal ties between mother and child are so strong that an external force is required to ensure their separation. His structuralist interpretation of Freud's oedipus complex downplayed the actual phenomenological father. He argued that it is the organisation of cultural and gendered meaning structured around the phallus – the 'Law' or 'The Name of the Father' – which is introduced by the father. The actual father is of secondary importance. This is something of a narcissist's universe in which relationships to objects play a minor role. Lacan's subject comes into being very much alone. While the object relations theorists have ensured a counter-balance to this economistic model of development, they have had almost nothing to say about the father. (See, for example, Phillips (1988), on Winnicott's treatment of the father, pp. 25–30.) While the father is central to Lacanian psychoanalysis he remains an abstracted force, without any real substance, a term rather than a body. Yet Lacan, by the very fact that he speaks from this narcissist's world, provides important insights and descriptions of the father's influence upon male subjectivity.

LACAN'S FATHER

For Lacan the significance of the father lies in the infant identifying him as possessing the phallus. The phallus is not a symbol of patriarchal authority, but a symbol of plenitude and completeness which the infant perceives the mother as lacking. Lacan describes the phallus as the register of desire. He recognises that the infant's perception of this register originates in the mother but moves to the third term of the father and becomes consolidated in the symbolic as the signifier of gendered meaning. The idea that the symbol of plenitude originates in the mother comes originally from Melanie Klein's re-evaluation of the father in the oedipus complex (Klein 1928). Lacan, however, is intent on reversing the implications of her work and restoring the father to his position of primacy within Freudian metapsychology.

In his essay 'The Signification of the Phallus' (Lacan (1949) 1980) Lacan develops Klein's ideas. Her study of the pre-oedipal realm of object relations led her to shift the time and place of the father in the oedipus complex. She argued that the father was first perceived by the infant as a part object inside the mother. The infant fantasised the father's penis inside her body. With reference to the boy's position, Klein describes how he moves from an oral sucking fixation upon the mother's breast to an oral sucking fixation upon the father's penis. This displaced oral desire for the father's penis replaces the breast as a symbol of plenitude. But at the same time, this desire motivates attacks on the inside of the mother's body, for he wants to take the penis by force and at the same time hurt her. His desire and aggression induces a fear of her as his rival. The internalised penis becomes a source of anxiety for in desiring it, it provokes aggression towards the mother. The threat of castration, however, impels the boy to give up his identification with his mother in, what Klein terms, his 'feminine phase' (Klein 1928, 1986, Chapter 12). If, however, his anxiety at destroying his mother is excessive and she remains a more potent and prominent figure who 'owns' the penis inside her, he will be unable to completely give up his identification with her.

The concept of the father in the mother is not rejected by Lacan, but its implications are reversed. In Kleinian metapsychology the relative inconclusiveness of the oedipus complex retains the internal object of the mother as a significant effect within both the boy's ego and super-ego, resulting in the fantasy of the phallic mother. The devourer and destroyer who threatens the loss of self. Lacan dismisses such influence. Instead, the fantasy of the father becomes the significant term within the mother. It is the mother as subject to the father which is imparted to the infant. Central to this reversal of influence is his concept of the phallus.

Lacan uses the symbol of the phallus as a metaphor for the meeting of individual desire and language. It signifies sexual difference. Males and females are positioned differently in relation to it and through this differential relationship become gendered subjects. The phallus is a symbolic and idealised substitute for the unity of mother and child which can never reoccur. It stands for the oneness or wholeness that is denied to human subjectivity in the castration complex.

In the beginning of life, according to Lacan, the infant identifies in the mother her plenitude and completeness. The infant desires to be one with this completeness. In the Lacanian sense the infant fantasises the mother as having the phallus and so wishes to be one, in order to be her/with her. But the growing disillusion with the mother's capacity for an unaltered continuous presence breaks the infant's sense of his or her mother's completeness. She comes to lack the phallus; she is not, after all, fully present in her own existence. The infant identifies what is lacking in his or her mother as a space or place outside of both of them. The phallus comes to stand for this 'something beyond' and 'something more'. Desire is the difference between the infant's longing for satisfaction and its demand for love.[5] It goes beyond the object/mother, who will forever be associated with this lack that can never be satisfied. The phallus is an elusive quality; a desire to possess one's own desire.

This economistic model leaves little room for the actual father. The third term in Lacan's oedipus complex is predominantly a structural symbolic metaphor. The inception of the oedipus complex is triggered by the mother's lack and an identification of the phallus with the father. Masculinity and femininity are differences articulated by something imagined to be absent from each. From this position of something missing, each sex can be imagined as having what the other has not. But crucially the female is structured into a subordinate relation to the phallus. While the male strives to represent the phallus, the female desires to possess it. And because the phallus is the signifier of language and meaning, Lacan effectively structures femininity and female sexuality outside language. They come to occupy the boundaries of psychoanalytic discourse and the edge of what is intelligible. He describes this displacement of female subjectivity; 'It is for that which she is not that she wishes to be desired as well as loved. But she finds the signifier of her own desire in the body of him to whom she addresses her demand for love.'[6] Lacan has taken Klein's concept of the father in the mother and decisively shifted it back into Freudian terms. By placing femininity in a subordinate relationship to the phallus and masculinity, he has maintained the antinomies of Freud's binary terms.

But the price of this manoeuvre is the downplaying of the significance of the pre-oedipal structures of the psyche and the primary fantasy of the father as being a part object in the mother. Lacan acknowledges its importance when he writes: 'The fact that the phallus is a signifier means that it is in the place of the Other that the subject has access to it.'[7] But he is not prepared to face the implications of his own statement. By placing femininity outside the realm of phallocentric discourse, he creates a mystery and enigma which obscures the reality that it is through the maternal body that desire for the phallus originates. This is partly a consequence of Lacan's view that gendered subjectivity is unidetermined by the phallus, rather than over-determined. But it is also a consequence of his belief that narcissism is an irreducible aspect of human nature and that object relations with the mother hold little significance in subject formation. Lacan's description of the phallus and its structuring of female sexuality suggest the evasion of the power and influence of the mother.

The meaning of female sexuality is determined through its lack in relation to the phallus. But it is the female body which is its original source. The significance of this contradiction is that once the small boy discovers that his father also lacks the phallus, he is confronted by a lack which cannot be filled. For the father is also unable to provide a meaning of this lack. Neither does he provide the knowledge ('K') which can contain the boy's anxiety at his loss. The father doubly lacks. Without access to the other, the boy's relation to the phallus, his destiny, is blocked. It is not femininity that is subordinate because of its lack of the phallus. Rather, it is male heterosexuality, dependent upon the female body that lacks in women's own lack. Its identification with the third term of the father serves to increase the stress of representing something it has no access to.

Male heterosexual desire thus completes a circuit. First, its trajectory is to the father and identification with the phallus. But as Freud has pointed out the boy is faced with a contradictory desire for the father as a sexual object choice. In this space of irresolution the phallus beckons from the maternal body. The third term of the father is not a purely external phenomenon. What determines the eventual identifications and attachments of the male subject is his relationship to a culturally determined experience of a 'thirdness' in his life. A 'thirdness' which is a product of the interrelationship of the two parental figures.

'THIRDNESS'

The function of 'thirdness' is the completion of a triangular structure that marks the human psyche and subjectivity. The third term is the nodal point of destiny and the urge to establish the self in the world. It marks the future and is the place through which desire moves outward. Freud in his essay 'The Uncanny' (Freud 1919h) refers to this organisation of futures.

> There are also the unfulfilled but possible futures to which we still like to cling in fantasy, all the strivings of the ego which adverse external circumstances have crushed, and all our suppressed acts of volition which nourish in us the illusion of Free Will.[8]

149

This temporalising process has its origins in a retrospective fantasy of the parents together which forms in the oedipus complex. In the 'Ego and Id', Freud describes a 'father of individual pre-history'.[9] This is the individual's first and most important identification and the origin of the super-ego. In a footnote Freud qualifies his gendered description of this identification. 'Perhaps it would be safer to say "with the parents".'[10] He excuses his ambivalence by stating that the infant is unable to distinguish between the sexes. But as likely it is his uncertainty of the relationship of the parents together, the father in the mother. While Freud's psychoanalytical logic places the father as the dominant term in their union his uncertainty reveals his actual doubt as to the exact meaning of 'thirdness' and its origins. A more instructive approach to unveiling the genesis of the third term can be found in Freud's discussion of the primal scene.

In his case study of the 'Wolf Man' (Freud 1918b) Freud analyses the dream of the young man he is treating. He deduces that his dream about wolves is the condensation and displacement of his childish terror at the sight of his parents copulating. Freud refers to this image as the primal scene. His analysis of its significance is diminished by his literal translation of the dream. That is of a memory of an actually observed actual event. Freud suggested the primal scene is the precondition for the oedipus complex. But it isn't an actual observation, nor actual intercourse that form the preconditions. It is a retrospectively constructed fantasy of the parents together, a fantasy which is a representation of the relative strengths of the masculine and feminine sexual dispositions in the oedipus complex. This forms the individual's pre-history.

Freud's uncertainty about the gendered character of this pre-history reflects its contingent nature. The shape of the third term emerges out of the fantasy of the father in the mother. How it develops in the infant psyche is determined by the psychodynamic and material relations of family life, in particular, the historical relationship of men and women as they come to be articulated in the parental relationship. If the mental representation of the father remains within the orbit of the mother's body, 'thirdness' becomes a halfway measure that is neither part of the mother nor separate from her. In this context the father's capacity to ensure a sense of future and to contain and process the infant's fear of loss and separation is greatly diminished. Such a failure is often the result of masculine identities themselves fashioned by the inability to bear the experience of separation and separatedness.

André Green has written that, 'The father is there, both in the mother and the child, from the beginning. More exactly, *between* the mother and child.'[11] In other words there is no such entity as a mother and child dyad. For between them, in the mother's unconscious there is always the father, whether he be hated, loved or banished. The primal scene is the infant's fantasm of this triad, shaped by its experience of the parental objects. The father comes to represent the absence created by the mother's preoccupation with something other than her infant. Her own fear of separation will create the pre-conditions for a disillusionment in paternity. For she gives to her son her own disillusion with her father and his failure to alleviate her predicaments.

In classical Freudian analysis the primal scene depicts the father's sexual domination over the mother. But this presumes that the father is always the psychologically dominant term. A continued disillusion with the possibility of his potential presence or the paucity of it in effect can produce a fantasy of an impotent and resourceless father unable to sexually satisfy or contain the mother's presence. The representation of the father remains within the mother. Unlike the Freudian father who may be austere and distant, even cold and withdrawn, this father remains an unknown. Out of this representation is created a yearning, not for an authoritarian father, but a loving real father capable of giving the mother pleasure. A father who can take care of the mother's needs and anxieties, who can fill her preoccupations with love rather than disillusion. Such a third term, created out of the mother–child dyad releases the infant from his or her projective identifications which hold the ego in a state of partial undifferentiation. Such a father can contain the infant's mourning and enable it to relieve its grip upon the internal object of the mother. In this function the father is a crucial factor in establishing the infant's reality testing and third space.

The third term evolves as a psychical figuration in the space of the mother's absence. If such absences are prolonged the infant attempts to invest the father with the good objects of the mother. The search for the father's 'K' is the search for a resolution to the infant's predicaments. The relative strength of his figuration is dependent upon the father's response. His experience of separatedness will determine the degree to which he enables his son's separation from his mother and his own capacity for 'K'. His fear and his own predicaments could enforce a premature separation and a powerful threat of castration and the repression of the oedipus complex. Alternatively, it could result in his non-presence, leaving his son floundering without boundaries. A balance between love and authority is a difficult task.

Central to the establishment of 'thirdness' is the capacity of the infant to develop a subjective conception of the third term into an objective perception of it. Not only as a mental representation in the psyche, but also as an actually existing external object. Love for the father is tinged with longing and fear. The introjection of the father as a separate object emerging from the part object in the mother plays a significant role in determining the strength of the third space and the individual capacity to live and create. He can be idealised as a saviour who will rescue his son from predicaments; his potential is to provide meaning to those spaces that mother and infant have been unable to process. Yet he will be despaired of for his failure to be the 'good father' and for his fallibility. For his child within himself whose father failed him and leaves him now in adulthood 'the son' of his own son's mother.

Perhaps it is this measure of hope and dread men invest in their fathers that led Freud to write that it is the death of his father that is probably the most important event any man has to face. For in his death is the demise of individual destiny and the defence against maternal predicaments. In his essay 'Civilisation and its Discontents' (Freud 1930a) Freud wrote 'I cannot think of any need in childhood as strong as the need for a father's protection.'[12] Psychoanalysis presents us with three problematics around the 'thirdness' of the father. The first is men's feelings towards their actual father in relationship to their mothers and the nature of men's individual identification with him. The second is how this phenomenological experience of him structures men's relationship to sexual desire. And the third is an amalgam of these two and it concerns the nature of paternal love.

I want to make some sense of how their interrelationship constitutes 'thirdness' as both a force of destiny and as a defence against the maternal supplement. To do this I want to use a textual analysis of a film in much the same way psychoanalysis uses case histories. The film is *The Dead Poets Society*, directed by Peter Weir (1989). The title of the film is taken from a Walt Whitman poem

Starting From Paumanok (Hall 1979), an epic narrative of self-discovery and identity.

THE GOOD FATHER

The Dead Poets Society is a small group of boys attending Helton Academy, a top American private school. Ostensibly the film is about the repressive nature of upper-class education and its function of enforcing conformity upon its young subjects. The Dead Poets Society symbolises the idea of an unfettered, naturalistic creativity. It was founded by a former pupil, now returned to the school as the new English teacher, Mr Keating (Robin Williams). It is his presence which leads the central character Neil Perry (Robert Sean Leonard) to resurrect the Society with a group of friends. They adopt its catechism, lines from a poem by Henry Thoreau, which are read out at the beginning of each meeting of the society.

> I went to the woods because I wanted to live deliberately. I wanted to live deep and suck out all the marrow of life. To put to rout all that was not life. And not when I die, discover that I had not lived.

Mr Keating's passion for this naturalistic American poetry stands in sharp contrast to the intellectual aridity of the school's traditional approach to knowledge and learning. While this juxtaposition suggests the film's exposition is on the themes of life and learning, it has a central preoccupation with masculinity. The juxtaposition is a metaphor for the antagonism between the boys' emerging sexuality and masculine identities and the hegemonic patriarchal institution of the school. The film represents this transitional moment of adolescence and the complexities of the sons' identifications with their fathers and male authority figures. It serves also to juxtapose destiny and fate, love and death.

The opening scene of the film sets the tone of the establishment. It is the beginning of the new school year and the boys and their parents are assembled in the school hall for the headmaster's address. The headmaster praises the 'light of knowledge' and a number of candles are lit and handed to selected pupils. After the address there are the rituals of departure as small boys are kissed goodbye by their mothers.

The scene moves to a study. Neil Perry arrives to discover a

153

newcomer Todd Anderson (Ethan Hawkes) as his room mate. Todd is shy and reserved, the reticent younger brother of a national merit scholar, since departed from the school. They are joined by three of Neil's friends, Steven, Knox and Charlie. They gossip about their holidays and the state of their academic achievements. There is a knock on the door and Neil's father, a sombre and dour-faced man, enters the room. He tells Neil that he has too many extra-curricular activities and that he must drop his assistant editorship of the school annual. Neil protests that it is his favourite activity. To leave would mean letting down the others involved. His father asks leave of the other boys and takes Neil outside. 'Don't dispute me in public' he orders Neil. The boy's ebullience has drained away. 'After you've finished medical school and you're on your own, you can do as you damn well please. But until then you do as I damn well tell you. Do you understand?' 'Yes sir, I'm sorry.' 'You know how much this means to your mother don't you?' 'Yes sir.' They shake hands and Neil's father leaves.

Knox and Charlie emerge from behind the doorway. Charlie asks, 'Why doesn't he let you do what you want?' They both suggest Neil tell his father off. 'That's rich! So you tell your parents off, Mr Future Lawyer and Mr Future Banker! Don't tell me how to talk to my father.' Neil turns to leave and tells them that he doesn't give a damn about any of it anyway.

The next morning the boys assemble in a classroom for their first lesson with the new English teacher, Mr Keating. He confounds them by entering the classroom whistling Beethoven's Ninth Symphony. He walks to the other end of the class and out the door. The boys are non-plussed. He then puts his head round the door and beckons them to follow him out into the hall. They gather around him. ' "O Captain! My Captain!" – where does it come from?' None of them know so he tells them it is from a poem by Walt Whitman about Abraham Lincoln. 'In this class you can either call me Mr Keating or, if you're more daring, "O Captain! My Captain!" ' He then asks a boy to read the first part of a poem; 'To the Virgins to Make Much of Time'. The other boys giggle. After the reading he asks; 'What does *Carpe diem* mean?' A boy answers, 'Seize the day!'.

Keating asks the significance of the poem. He gets no response, so he tells them. 'Because we are food for worms lads. Because, believe it or not, each and every one of us in this room is one day going to stop breathing and die.' He beckons them over to a couple of glass cabinets inside of which are old photos of school teams. He urges them to lean in close and listen to what these now-dead boys are saying. 'They're just like you. Invincible, just like you feel. Destined for great things. Eyes full of hope.' And, as they gather in close and the camera moves across the faces in the photographs, Keating whispers, 'Seize the day!', 'Make your lives extraordinary.'

The point of this description is not to analyse Keating's particular brand of transcendental humanism, but the way it is used symbolically in the film. In these photographs lie both the fate and the destiny of the boys. Keating's exhortations are not concerned with the fulfilment of their class privilege but with their capacity to live and with what makes them alive. The poem from which Keating takes his symbolic title 'O Captain! My Captain!', provides a key to both the film's narrative and his own significance in the text. Walt Whitman signifies the first stirrings of a white, native American literary culture. He was also a homosexual whose calls for sexual emancipation were adopted by the early suffragettes. He is an historical figure whose work continues to resonate, as it does in this film, with a metaphysics of presence. A desire to be fully present in one's own existence. Such a metaphysics is synonymous with the desire for the phallus. Below is the full text of the poem which Keating draws on to represent himself to the boys.

> O Captain! My Captain! Our fearful trip
>   is done,
> The ship has weather'd every rack, the
>   prize we sought is won,
> The port is near, the bells I hear, the
>   people all exulting,
> While follow eyes the steady keel, the
>   vessel grim and daring;
> But O heart! heart! heart!
> O the bleeding drops of red,
> Where on the deck my Captain lies,
> Fallen cold and dead.

O Captain! My Captain! rise up and hear
    the bells;
Rise up – for you the flag is flung – for
    you the bugle trills,
For you bouquets and ribbon'd wreaths –
    for you the shores a-crowding,
For you they call, the swaying mass, their
    eager faces turning;
Here Captain! dear Father!
This arm beneath your head!
It is some dream that on the deck,
You've fallen cold and dead.

My Captain does not answer, his lips are
    pale and still,
My father does not feel my arm, he has no
    pulse nor will,
The ship is anchor'd safe and sound, its
    voyage closed and done,
From fearful trip the victor ship comes in
    with object won;
Exult O shores, and ring O bells!
But I with mournful tread,
Walk the deck my Captain lies,
Fallen cold and dead.

The poem follows a narrative of liminality and the subject's final reincorporation into a transformed synchronic order. As the Proppian description of narrative has emphasised, there is a striking resemblance to the oedipus complex. But this poem also conjures up a boy's adolescent fantasy of adventure and rites of passage into manhood. Its final resolution is, however, a Pyrrhic one. In the process of transition something has been lost. The voyage has been completed, but the central figure who made it possible, who acted as mentor, guide and source of love for the narrator, presumably a young man, is dead.

'O Captain! My Captain!' is the symbolic 'good father', lighting the boy's rites of passage into manhood. But in the process he is killed off and with him is extinguished the future and desire. The young man has achieved his masculine status, surmounting obstacles and journeying through uncharted seas. The waving, cheering crowd, symbolising the restored patriarchal order, welcome him home. But he can find no value or meaning in its embrace. Instead he experiences it as a moment of intense loss and bereavement. Such a reading infers that the paternal narrative, in its suppression of the maternal supplement, leads to the extinguishing of the 'good father' and the possibility of attaining the phallus.

The logical end of the paternal narrative's synchronic stability is the structural absence of the maternal supplement. The positivism of language games excludes the existence of any object or state of affairs unrepresented in its practices. Such an exclusion denies the male subject access to the 'good mother'. At the same time it will also hinder contact with those 'helpful objects' transferred into the third term, which are symbolised as the 'good father'. In Lacanian terms, access to the phallus is cut off. This cutting off is a consequence of a severe castrating father. The circuit of desire is broken. There can be no hope in futures, only the past can be revered. The castrating 'bad father' inhibits pleasure and spontaneity for these herald the return of the repressed mother and the collapse of boundaries. And with the destruction of the 'good father', fate replaces destiny in the idiom of masculinity. Christopher Bollas defines this sense of fate.

> A person who is fated, who is fundamentally interred in an internal world of self and object representations that endlessly repeat the same scenarios, has very little sense of a future that is at all different from the internal environment they carry around with them. The sense of fate is a feeling of despair to influence the course of one's life.[13]

The opening sequence of the film depicts this sense of fate; not only in Neil's impotent attempt to map out his own life in opposition to his father's wishes, but in the predestination of all the boys. Their lives have been mapped out for them by their fathers. Hope, pleasure and desire are subordinate to their incorporation into the Name of the Father. If the poem symbolises the death of the 'good father' as the price of acceptance within patriarchal relations, then it is these men, the bad fathers, who have killed him. In them the 'good father' is abandoned in the urgent grip on their own ego defences. And as the castrating father predominates, so their capacity for 'K' diminishes. The sons are left in their predicaments, the fathers too fearful of the maternal to intervene. Neil's father is such a figure. A man whose need for internal order and boundaries has led to him reducing all relationships around him to detached and ritualistic enactments of duty and propriety.

When Keating asks the boys to look at the old school photographs he is not asking them to revere the past, but to listen to its legacy. It is an attempt to redirect them subjectively in time, to foster hope and destiny in place of an internalised sterility. In adopting 'O Captain! My Captain!', Keating symbolises the 'good father', the necessary 'thirdness' in the boys' lives. A prime function of this 'thirdness' is to create a sense of future where a nostalgic longing for some past state has existed. It is not that the 'good father' embodies the phallus for all time. But as the good, helpful object he is used as a screen for the son's projections of perceptions of his capacity to be, to live and to create. He carries this aliveness into the future, enabling the early formation of the path of desire; a map to the phallus. It is just this kind of map that is symbolically acted out in the first meeting of the Dead Poets Society. Neil Perry has discovered Keating's entry in an old school annual and a reference to him as the founder of the society. He persuades his friends to start a new group and they decide to hold their first meeting that night.

THE FATHER'S DEFENCE AGAINST THE THREAT OF THE MOTHER

The boys leave the school buildings in the middle of the night to find the old Indian cave in the woods, where the meeting is to be held. Neil opens with the quote from Thoreau. He then recites a horror story. An old lady is sitting in a room alone. She is making a jigsaw puzzle. While she is fitting the pieces together, she realises that it is a picture of the room she is sitting in. As she finishes, the last pieces reveal a demented mad man staring at her through the window. The last thing she ever hears is the sound of breaking glass. The boys are out in the woods, huddled together in an old cave in the middle of the night. It would be predictable that one would tell a ghost or a horror story. But there is a significance to it and to the later pieces read out by some of the other boys. In her book *Powers of Horror* (1982) Julia Kristeva analyses the idea of horror. Using psychoanalysis she explores the gap between the ego boundaries of the subject and the first object of the mother, in the process of differentiation and individuation. She is developing Freud's essay on 'The Uncanny' (Freud 1919h), a phenonemon which he describes as: 'that class of the frightening which leads back to what is known of old and long familiar.'[14] To a time, 'when the ego had not yet marked itself off sharply from the external world and from other people.'[15]

In its first weeks of life, the infant ego will struggle to develop a unity, which is frequently fragmented by anxiety and subsequent splitting and projection into the mother. What is tentatively becoming an 'I' periodically falls apart into an unintegrated state. This is the paranoid–schizoid position that precedes the depressive position and ego integration. 'Abjection' is Kristeva's term for the precarious casting out of persecutory maternal objects which impinge upon the developing infant ego. She writes that the abject confronts us, 'with our earliest attempts to release the hold of the maternal entity even before existing outside her.'[16] Abjection is a kind of close-quarters tussle, 'a violent clumsy breaking away', of a subject not yet fully a subject and an object still undefined. Abjecting marks the self-differentiating movement that will establish the ego boundaries between self and other. Because of its threatening impingement, Kristeva defines the maternal body as abject; an object which does not 'respect borders, positions, rules' and which 'disturbs identity, system and order'.[17]

The place of this abject is in the gap opened up by the mother's preoccupation with something other than her infant. The infant's experience of this gap is his or her disillusion with the mother's lack and his or her perception of the phallus as belonging in the third term of the father. In recognition of this Kristeva calls the gap an archaic paternal space, even though she assures that the mother's preoccupation need not literally be with the father. In the structuring of male subjectivity the third term determines the power of the abject. For it plays a significant role in maintaining a necessary space between the 'I' and the object of the mother in both the mother's psyche and that of the infant. If the infant is unable to create adequate object representations of the father, the predicaments which form the abject (the fear of fusion and loss of self) retain a significant effect within his subjectivity. In the face of such a threat, the castrating 'bad father' predominates in masculine identities attacking the helpful object of the 'good father' in a desperate battle to protect the male ego against the maternal abject.

Kristeva argues that many rituals in society are concerned with renewing its initial contact with the abject and then expelling it. This can be translated in psychoanalytical terms in the role and function of the father in the oedipus complex. The culturally determined strength of the paternal narrative and its antagonistic relation to the maternal supplement will affect the relative strength of the good helpful object in the third term. A masculinity whose ego boundaries are threatened by the maternal supplement will produce a more severe castrating figure. In consequence, the energetic but rather impotent grip it seeks to maintain upon its paternal authority and authorial presence diminishes the possibility of the 'good father'.

The abject's formation lies in the absence of the mother and the struggle of the infant's immature ego to deal with this loss. It is the same absence which is also the precondition for symbol formation, language and subjectivity. The abject emerges out of a maternal object which is a double; the site of the formation of subjectivity and the site of its potential collapse. In his essay 'The Uncanny', Freud (1919h) describes this double as the ambivalence between the two terms *heimlich* (homely) and its opposite meaning *unheimlich*. What is uncanny is not the opposite of what is familiar, but an ambivalence born of familiarity.

> When all is said and done, the quality of uncanniness can only come from the fact of the 'double' being a creation dating back to a very early mental stage, long since surmounted – a stage, incidentally, at which it wore a more friendly aspect. The 'double' has become a thing of terror.[18]

Kristeva's use of its term suggests an ahistorical and general phenonemon. But like predicaments, it is contingent and historical, overdetermined by patterns of childcare, ideologies of parenting and the psychodynamic structures of family relations.

The abject mother in male subjectivity is born out of the cultural and psychical disposition of 'thirdness'.

The potential gap between subject and object is the place of the double. Here the abject exists alongside the pathway to the phallus. In his essay 'The Subversion of the Subject' (Lacan 1989 (1960)) Lacan traces this pathway in his description of the movement of an object which he calls *'objet à'* (in French it stands for *objet [a]utre*, the other object). *'Objet à'* may be an orifice or a part of the mother's breast. Its effect is in unchaining desire. It represents what the mother lacks and forms an element in the chain of signification governed by the phallus. The *'objet à'* is an object neither fully contained in the body nor entirely expelled from it, a part which is detachable and capable of confronting the subject as alien and external. They are the signifying elements that lead the subject out of the mother's absence and into the realm of language and representation. But paradoxically they can only be initially reached through the mother.

It is the place of the father who determines the outcome of the paradox of the double. This chain of signification originating in the same gap as the abject requires the object representation of a third term to affect the gendered person in language. A relative failure of 'thirdness' impels the subject to adopt psychotic defences to protect the immature ego. Lacan has attributed psychosis to the condition of the foreclosure of 'the Name of the Father'; the subject's failure to reach the Other, the third term of the triangle of human subjectivity. With this failure of 'thirdness' the infant is denied access to intersubjectivity and cultural meaning. Foreclosure of the third term of the father impels a desperate search for a father figure who can reach that gap threatened by the abject.

The double within male subjectivity is the site of a struggle which gives rise to the metaphors of rites of passage, territories to be conquered and obstacles overcome. Terms which touch upon the quality and feeling of becoming a man. The horror story also signifies this combat zone. It conjures up the phallic mother whose omnipotence has rendered the father insignificant. For the survival of his patriarchal authority and his subjectivity, man must battle against her and destroy her. The horror story depicts such symbolic wars, its misogynistic use of female genitalia and bodies depict men's terror of the abject. Horror conjures up images of gaping chasms and the monstrous maw of the vagina, waiting to suck men in and destroy them (see Creed 1986). Yet the ambivalence remains in the fact that men's access to the phallus, to the 'good father' and to their futures depends upon their access to the mother's body.

The symbolic function of Neil's horror story is this close-quarters tussle with the female body. It is a ritual in which the abject of the maternal body is met with and destroyed. The ritual enables the boys to be released from the paternal narrative and make touch with the 'good father', breaking the limitations of the patriarchal order. Keating, both literally in his non-conformist free-thinking and symbolically as the 'good father', is placed outside of this order. The good helpful objects derived from the maternal pre-oedipal relationship and transferred into the third term exist as Lacan's *objet à*. They are threatened by the paternal narrative and the castrating father, but their absence is the mark of fate and the impossibility of desire. The ritual of the horror story destroys the threat of the maternal supplement and in the process reduces the power of the castrating 'bad father'. With her demise the path of the *objet à* is open to sexuality and desire.

MALE HETEROSEXUALITY AND THE DOUBLE OF THE PROSTITUTE

As if to confirm the misogynistic outcome of the horror story a second boy reads a ditty about a man named William Bloat.

> Now he had a wife, the plague of his life
> Who continually got his goat
> And one day at dawn, with his night-shirt on
> He slit her bloody throat.

The rhyme bears witness to the fate of the mother in cultural patriarchy. Because she is a foremost threat to the male ego and consequently to masculine identities, women become the focus for men's violence. Yet the omnipresent mother that is the fantastical object of attack exists in the failure of men and fathers to establish a 'thirdness'. Women are blamed for the failures of men. The predominance of the maternal object and its predicaments within the male psyche demands a continual re-enactment of abjection. Only in such a ritual can access to the phallus be found. With the ritual concluded with two murders of women, the boys' expression of misogynistic violence gives way to their representation of female sexuality.

162

Charlie asks if the others want to hear a 'real poem'. He unfolds the centre page of *Playboy* and, to their catcalls, reveals a naked woman. He then reads a short paean to his sexual potency and capacity to love. Such a celebration would have been an impossibility while the maternal object remained, threatening that sensual current of male sexuality that Freud describes in his essay 'A Special Type of Object Choice' (Freud 1910h). It is with this pornographic image of female sexuality that the boys are able to express their own heterosexual interest and desire. In this topographical search for the phallus, the boys have located it in the body of the other. But with the failure of the 'good father' in their lives, the sons turn to an object that is culturally degraded, for fear of the abject mother. In *Paris Texas*, Travis, in his search for the mother, fled from the image of his wife as a prostitute. So these boys, on the path of heterosexual desire, turn to the female body most unlike the mother. It is a body and female sexuality structured by the splitting of male heterosexuality around the double of abjection/desire.

In his analysis of the uncanny, Freud uses an anecdote about a visit he made to a town in Italy.

> I found myself in a quarter of whose character I could not long remain in doubt. Nothing but painted women were to be seen at the windows of the small houses, and I hastened to leave the narrow street at the next turning. But after having wandered about for a time without inquiring my way, I suddenly found myself back in the same street, where my presence was now beginning to excite attention. I hurried away once more, only to arrive by another *détour* at the same place yet a third time. Now, however, a feeling overcame me which I can only describe as uncanny, and I was glad enough to find myself back at the piazza I had left a short while before, without any further voyages of discovery.[19]

Freud relates other examples of geographical mishaps and describes how their uncanny quality is that they remind the subject of his or her inner compulsion to repeat unpleasurable events (see Freud's *Fort/Da* anecdote in Chapter 4). What seems only chance takes on the aspect of something fateful and inescapable. Freud makes no direct comment about the prostitutes in his anecdote, confining himself to the uncanniness of the physical location. But their presence must have added a powerful frisson of sexual anxiety to the occasion.

It is to men's heterosexuality and the uncanny that Freud returns at the end of his essay, perhaps addressing his own fears in a circumspect and covert way, for he makes no links to his own anecdote.

> It often happens that neurotic men declare that they feel there is something uncanny about the female genital organs. This *unheimlich* place, however, is the entrance to the former *Heim* [home] of all human beings, to the place where each one of us lived once upon a time and in the beginning. There is a joke saying that 'Love is home-sickness'; and, whenever a man dreams of a place or a country and says to himself, while he is still dreaming: 'this place is familiar to me, I've been here before', we may interpret the place as being his mother's genitals or her body. In this case too, then, the *unheimlich* is what was once *heimisch*, familiar; the prefix *'un'* ['un-']is the token of repression.[20]

Freud is as much conjecturing here as making a bald statement of fact, but he offers a powerful insight into the structuring of male heterosexuality in its relationship to the abject mother.

The prostitute stands at the opening of the *heimisch*, a fantasy of male heterosexual desire which overrides and subsumes the original object of the mother which is longed for. She is what the father offers his son in his weakness and fear of the maternal. The prostitute does not offer herself, for in the male fantasy of her, she is denied a subjectivity. She acts as a receptacle, a doorway that will take the son to the phallus and his own completeness. He constructs her as alluring, sexually voracious and immoral, disguising his own longing for the maternal body and his perception of the mother as omnipresent and threatening to him. The prostitute's sexuality takes on these qualities but is 'dirtied' by the accusation of her moral degeneracy and so rendered safe and harmless. In her allure she offers the son the otherness of himself, the part that has been lost and could not be found in the mother.

Unlike the mother who is too threatening a figure, the prostitute is an object that can be ruthlessly used in the thoughtless abandonment of sexual ecstasy and orgasm. For such activity is the dissolution of the relationship of self and other in the destruction of the object and the 'I'. Lacan has called this dissolving of boundaries *jouissance*. He makes a distinction between this orgasmic sensation and ordinary pleasure. It is this latter term which Freud had argued was the underlying principle of psychical development. Both in its pursuit and in the endeavour to maintain its constancy, pleasure is what governs the psychical apparatus (Freud 1920g). In contrast *jouissance* goes beyond this law of constancy, subverting the subject's ego. In his essay 'The Subversion of the Subject', Lacan (1989(1960)) argues that pleasure acts as a defence against desire. The ego clings to the pleasure principle in order to stave off going beyond a certain limit of *jouissance*. For Lacan the defining context of the subject is not presence but absence and non-being. It is against these that the ego clings and it is these that define the place of *jouissance*. Orgasm and ecstasy, like death, dissolve the subject into non-existence.

His inference that the subject's ego exists in an emptiness echoes Freud's description of an oceanic feeling. In his essay 'Civilisation and its Discontents' (Freud 1930a) he describes how the infant's ego originally fused with the external world knows no separation between inner and outer. Freud suggests this early experience is the origin of a feeling of being unbounded and limitless. In maturity the ego effects a clear demarcation between itself and the world outside, to such a degree that 'present ego-feeling is . . . only a shrunken residue of a much more inclusive – indeed, an all-embracing – feeling which corresponded to a more intimate bond between the ego and the world about it.'[21] In the sphere of love, this demarcation can be blurred and indistinct resurrecting this earlier experience.

> At the height of being in love the boundary between ego and object threatens to melt away. Against all the evidence of his senses, a man who is in love declares that 'I' and 'you' are one, and is prepared to behave as if it were a fact. . . . There are cases in which parts of a person's own body, even portions of his mental life – his perceptions, thoughts and feelings – , appear alien to him and as not belonging to his ego.[22]

Here is the subject confronted by Lacan's *objet à*, at once promising the path to the phallus and heralding the presence of the abject mother. Neither Freud with his oceanic feeling, nor Lacan with his *jouissance* are willing to give each a gendered meaning. Both are closely bound with the pre-oedipal relationship with the mother and both threaten the integrity of the male ego. Sexual orgasm confronts the male subject with his otherness, becoming momentarily what he has lost. And in that instant of becoming the phallus and finding that completeness, he ceases to exist. The body of the prostitute is men's defence against non-being. She enables the ecstasy of such a moment where the figure of mother or her symbolic equivalent would instil dread.

If both Lacan and Freud are unwilling to acknowledge the maternal object as the origins of *jouissance* and the oceanic feeling, they are both vociferous in naming the father as the protector from its threat. Freud writes in 'The Future of an Illusion':

> As we already know, the terrifying impression of helplessness in childhood aroused the need for protection – for protection through love – which was provided by the father; and the recognition that this helplessness lasts throughout life made it necessary to cling to the existence of a father.[23]

The father's failure to establish the third term in the mind of the infant equal to the maternal representation, results in his sexual legacy of the prostitute. And, as the castrating father, he seeks to impose a law governing his son's access to *jouissance*. For Lacan the oedipus complex constructs a subject barred access to the phallus. 'Castration means that *jouissance* must be refused, so that it can be reached on the inverted ladder (*l'échelle renversée*) of the Law of desire.'[24]

Lacan's father, like Freud's, is fashioned as a defence against the maternal. His is a figure whose severity is born of Lacan's rejection of object relations. The paternal filial relationship united in its defence against the mother is devoid of other qualities. This castrating father, like Neil's father, is a man destined to fate his son. Both Freud and Lacan in their descriptions of the paternal function reveal the dilemma in psychoanalysis of determining the place of the mother in the making of male subjectivity. In their descriptions of men's love and heterosexual desire she is all-present in their preoccupation with the father. Paternal love can only exist in its function of prohibitor; the man who protects his sons from themselves. Both Freud and Lacan, in their separate ways, collude with the social arrangements of cultural patriarchy, unable to move beyond the antinomy of the double of the abject mother/prostitute. In consequence, the father becomes a figuration of masculine fear rather than an enabling presence. The vocabularies of psychoanalysis, in their tentative exploration of 'thirdness' have yet to provide a theoretical description of the 'good father'. Instead, descriptions depict a term that curtails feeling, lacks a body and flees from intuition and emotion.

HOMOSEXUALITY, MASOCHISM AND THE PATERNAL PREDICAMENT

Shortly after their first meeting, Neil auditions for a role in *A Midsummer Night's Dream*, which is to be performed in the local town hall. He tells Todd: 'For the first time in my whole life I know what I want to do and I'm going to do it, whatever my father says.' Neil auditions and succeeds in getting the part of Puck. He arrives back in his study, and much to Todd's consternation, begins typing out a letter ostensibly from his father, giving his son permission to perform in the play. The consequence of this action is delayed. Returning from rehearsals one day Neil finds his father waiting for him in his room. He has found out through an acquaintance; 'You deliberately deceived me. How did you expect to get away with it?' He orders, 'Tomorrow you quit'. Neil pleads with him, tomorrow night is the first performance. His father is intransigent: 'I made a great many sacrifices to get you here Neil and you will not let me down.'

In desperation Neil seeks help from Keating; 'He doesn't know acting means everything to me. . . . He's planning the rest of my life for me and he's never asked what I want.' Keating urges Neil to tell his father his passion for acting. 'I can't', he replies. 'I can't talk to him this way.' But Keating urges him. 'I'm trapped', says the boy. 'No you're not', says the man and tells him to phone his father straightaway. The following day Neil tells Keating, 'He didn't like it one bit, but at least he's letting me stay in the play.' The uncertainty in Keating's face suggests his doubt that Neil made the phone call. In the evening Keating and Neil's friends attend the opening performance. Shortly before Neil's final speech at the play's end, his father appears at the back of the auditorium. Neil momentarily falters, but manages to retain his composure and deliver his last lines. 'If you pardon, we will mend', takes on a poignant meaning. The house rises to its feet and Neil takes the acclaim for an exemplary performance. But, back-stage, amidst the congratulations and praise, he is summoned to appear before his father. He leads Neil outside to his waiting car. When

Keating tries to congratulate Neil, his father turns on him in a fury: 'Stay away from my son!'

In his role as Puck, Neil personifies everything that his father is not; fluidity versus rigidity, movement versus stasis, desire versus the Law, feeling versus its lack and the inkling of a destiny overcoming fate. In the part of the woodland fairy Neil becomes an effeminate sexual innocent. Puck inverts Neil's masculinity and sexuality. As arbiter of marriage and initiator of sexual love Puck signifies the phallus. In a more literal sense, too, in displaying his body to the audience, Neil turns his feminised masculinity into a spectacle, revealing the complexities of his sexuality and identity. It is his moment of rebellion against the wishes of his father and his usurpation of paternal prohibition. As he discards his father's narcissistic investment in him, he leaves behind his social identity for the alien territory of otherness.

His father watching the spectacle of his son's effeminacy, no longer perceives the father's son, but Neil as his mother's daughter. In this drama of the father's gaze the catastrophe threatened by Keating's espousal of unbridled desire is realised. The 'good father' has produced something other than a man. As his son flouts his word, he flouts the threat of castration. In the role of a sexual alchemist Neil can celebrate his body and transgressive sexual desire. For a short transitory moment he can overcome the oedipal pain of the wounded son and revel in the liminal existence of sexual and gender indeterminacy. Neil's father is confronted with a son who is momentarily an other. He is the subject of the negative trace of the oedipus complex; the son's identification with his mother and homosexual erotic attachment to his father. Perhaps this fear of homosexuality helps to explain the investment of both Lacan and Freud in a castrating father figure who appears devoid of intimacy and bodily contact with his son. What is at stake is not only the destruction of the boy's attachment to his mother, a task assiduously pursued by Little Hans's father, but also the prohibition of the son's homosexual love for his father. The 'good father' not only threatens the ego boundaries of masculinities with the proximity of the maternal, he suggests no prohibition against love between men.

It is in his writings on masochism that Freud addresses the attempt to usurp the authority of the castrating father. In his first essay on the subject, 'A Child is Being Beaten' (Freud 1919e), he analyses a certain masochistic fantasy of being beaten that a number of his patients displayed. It is clear that the subjects prone to these fantasies are primarily men. Nevertheless Freud designates masochism as a feminine trait; 'the beating-fantasy corresponds with a feminine attitude – one, that is, in which the individual is lingering on the "feminine line".'[25] At stake in these fantasies is the repression of a sexual love for the father. Freud analyses their condensations and displacements to uncover this originating wishful fantasy. In his second essay on masochism, 'The Economic Problem of Masochism' (Freud 1924c) he writes: 'We know that the wish, which so frequently appears in fantasies, to be beaten by the father stands very close to the other wish, to have a passive (feminine) sexual relation to him and is only a regressive distortion of it.'[26]

This homosexual attachment to the father confronts the boy with a secondary, paternal predicament. His longing for the 'good father' is born of the desire to resolve the predicaments of the pre-oedipal relationship with his mother. But his love for his father is first, undermined by a paternal masculinity threatened by the maternal supplement, and second, by the cultural repression of such wishes in the homophobic discourse of the paternal narrative. Freud argues that the boy evades his homosexuality by 'repressing and remodelling his unconscious fantasy'. He goes on to say, 'the remarkable thing about his later conscious fantasy is that it has for its content a feminine attitude without a homosexual object choice.'[27] The figure of the prostitute is the structuring of an opening-out of the first predicament through a flight into a loveless and exploitative heterosexuality. Masochism replaces homosexual desire in the subject's attempt to evade this secondary paternal predicament outlawing homosexual love, creating in the subject an ambivalent oscillation between the two.

Kaja Silverman mentions a possible resolution to this oscillation (Silverman 1988). The only way the boy can overcome his desire for his father is to transform object libido into narcissistic libido, and in so doing attempt to become the 'good father' (or ego ideal). But as she goes on to point out it is precisely this that the castrating father/super-ego prohibits. It denies the boy access to the 'good father'. As Freud writes, it impels the ego: 'You may not be like this (like your father) – that is, you may not do all that he does.'[28] Unable to love his father and with the impossibility of maternal love, the male subject must turn to the unsignified body of the prostitute or turn upon himself; 'the masochist must do what is inexpedient, must act against his own interests, must ruin the prospects which open out to him in the real world and must, perhaps, destroy his own real existence.'[29]

Once at home his father turns on Neil. 'Why do you insist on defying us?' Neil's mother sits in an armchair on the other side of the room, an anxious but impotent observer. His father tells Neil that he is taking him away from Helton and enrolling him in a military academy. 'I've got to tell you what I feel', the boy shouts. 'What is it?' 'What?' 'Nothing!', 'Nothing?' Neil sits in a chair, crumpled and defeated. His father leaves the room. His mother walks over to her son and touches his back in a small, enfeebled attempt at reassurance and maternal love. Both his parents retire to bed, his mother weeping and his father misreading her terrible grief as confusion over her son's waywardness. Neil goes to his bedroom, removes his clothes and places Puck's crown on his head. The camera holds on his tragic figure, dwelling on the mythology of a Christ-like wounded son. He then goes downstairs and sits behind his father's desk. He opens a drawer, removes a gun and shoots himself.

FATE AND THE FAILURE OF PATERNAL LOVE

The tragedy of Neil's suicide doesn't remove his father's self-deception and he initiates a witch hunt against Keating. The boys involved in the Dead Poets Society are forced to renounce it and sign a document that places the responsibility of Neil's suicide with Mr Keating. Only in the final sequence of the film do some of the boys of his class, led by Todd, manage to demonstrate their support for him. The film closes with the defeat of the 'good father'. Its end bearing out Whitman's narrative in 'O Captain! My Captain!' Only here the young man, with the failure of paternal love, is destroyed as well.

To make sense of the relation between this failure and Neil's suicide, I want to turn to Freud's essay, 'Narcissism: An Introduction' (Freud 1914c). He discusses a crucial stage in infant psychical development which comes between auto-eroticism and object love. In narcissism the infant withdraws libido from external objects and redirects it upon its own ego. The result is a feeling of omnipotence and the perception that objects exist only for the subject's own need and use. Freud argues that this stage of development is often fixated upon and reappears in adult life as a secondary narcissism.

I want to examine a couple of statements he makes regarding the distribution of libidinal cathexes between the ego and the outer world of objects. Freud argues that there is, 'an antithesis between ego-libido and object-libido. The more one is employed, the more the other becomes depleted.'[30] The highest condition of object-cathexis is being in love when the subject appears to give up his or her own personality. At the other extreme, in which libido is withdrawn into the ego, the external world ceases to have any meaning. Not only does this create narcissistic feelings of omnipotence, it can also produce the paranoid fantasy of the world ending. These are two extreme positions which define the parameters of the distribution of libidinal cathexes.

Freud alludes to the way this distribution between inner and outer is regulated when he writes: 'A person who loves has, so to speak, forfeited a part of his narcissism, and it can only be replaced by being loved.'[31] It is this statement that challenges Lacan's assertion of the primacy of narcissism in human nature, for it clearly asserts the necessity of object relations. The taking of the subject's own body as a love object can only occur when the internal object is sufficiently secured to allow the infant the experience of separateness.

The infant's feeling of omnipotence is crucial to the development of its capacity to cope with the mother's absence. Similarly, in the indeterminate and liminal spaces of the oedipal process, when identifications and object cathexes are in a process of change and transition, the infant sustains its sense of aliveness through its narcissism. In the male infant's growing attachment to his father, libidinal energy that has sustained his ego is transferred into the paternal object relationship. The son's attachment is to the 'good father'. But if the castrating father is in the ascendant, the infant's attachment is curtailed. At the same time the threat of castration cuts the infant from his cathexis with the mother. Subsequently, he seeks to transfer this to his father, but if there is no reciprocation and a failure of 'K', the infant is caught loving a father who cannot return his love. Without the love of the 'good father' the infant's narcissistic sense of aliveness diminishes. And while the father remains detached and withdrawn, there seems little possibility of replenishing it. The paternal predicament leads to feelings of inferiority and worthlessness. This negative narcissism is the consequence of a weakened ego unable to defend against a punishing and retributive super-ego.

The failure of the 'good father' and paternal love creates a fear of ego death. The male subject is caught in a no-man's land, cut off from the mother by the threat of castration and the fear of predicaments and simultaneously unable to achieve a paternal love that is a sufficient substitute. What is left, psychically speaking, is a very narrow, often insecure place in which to live. In Neil's case his only hope of movement lies in the love of Mr Keating. But with Keating's defeat, Neil is abandoned to his fate. At the end of his essay 'The Ego and the Id' (Freud 1923b), Freud writes about this collapse of destiny and the fear of death which lies in the failure of 'thirdness'. A failure that is caused by the destruction of the 'good father' by the castrating father and the subsequent loss of the possibility of the 'good mother'.

> The fear of death in melancholia only admits of one explanation; that the ego gives itself up because it feels itself hated and persecuted by the super-ego, instead of loved. To the ego, therefore, living means the same as being loved – being loved by the super-ego, which here again appears as the representative of the id. The super-ego fulfills the same function of protecting and saving that was fulfilled in earlier days by the father and later by Providence or Destiny. But, when the ego finds itself in excessive real danger which it believes itself unable to overcome by its own strength, it is bound to draw the same conclusion. It sees itself deserted by all protecting forces and lets itself die.[32]

7

VIOLENCE AND MASCULINE IDENTITIES

VIOLENCE AND ITS CULTURAL CONTEXT IN THE 1980s

The *Dead Poets Society* was something of a romance of the wounded son. The failure of the father was enacted in the boy's self-destruction. A more prominent cultural response to transitional changes and crises in masculine identities is violence to others. The 1980s saw a surge in the popularity of films depicting representations of mass violence. Typically, their stories involved individual men pitting themselves against overwhelming hostile forces and deploying an extraordinary degree of violence and destruction to overcome them. Many of these films dealt either directly with the Vietnam War or had militaristic themes associated with them. The films produced a group of new male stars who paraded an extreme, sometimes parodic masculine prowess. (For example, Sylvester Stallone in *First Blood* (1982) and *Rambo: First Blood Part II* (1985); Arnold Schwarzenegger in *Commando* (1986); Chuck Norris in *Missing in Action*, Parts 1 and 2 (1984–85).) These action films took the male hero to historically unparalleled levels of omnipotence. According to Susan Jeffords in her essay 'Debriding Vietnam: The Resurrection of the White American Male' (Jeffords 1988) Rambo, in *Part II* 'kills eight Russians and a score of Vietnamese soldiers and bombs and shoots several hundred more; *People* magazine counts forty-four dead by Rambo's hands alone, estimating an average of one murder every 2.1 minutes.'[1] A similar body count of Arnold Schwarzenegger's *Commando* would probably outnumber this figure.

These films of destructive masculine prowess were a response to a specific set of historical circumstances. The focus on the

173

Vietnam War signified the crisis of American world hegemony and its gradual economic decline. The geo-political changes paralleled shifting gender relations and attitudes to sexuality in American society. The films were representations of the preoccupations of various ethnic and class masculinities, struggling to come to terms with these changes. As Susan Jeffords writes:

> Although these films are militaristic, showing a James Bond fascination with the spectacle of technology and a John Wayne propensity for defeating the enemy, the militarism is subordinated to the display of an unqualified masculinity which suggests that these representations must be reviewed in relation to gender and not merely an endorsement of the military or an associated adventure.[2]

Despite the American context, they found a huge world-wide audience. In Britain, reception was polarised. On the one hand, sections of the media and middle classes were outspoken in their condemnation of the levels of violence. On the other hand, the films and specifically the character of Rambo were briefly icons of popular culture. Their reception in Britain, during the 1980s, was contextualised by growing social concerns over the levels of public male violence and the decline of morality and familial discipline.

On 19 August 1987 Michael Ryan rampaged through Hungerford town in Berkshire shooting dead fifteen people. Rambo had moved from the screen into real life. The following day, in the *Daily Mail*'s lead article, the writer A.N. Wilson despaired. 'Yet another bit of the innocence of old England has been blasted out of existence.'[3] A month later, opening the Museum of the Moving Image in London, Prince Charles condemned the 'incessant menu of utterly gratuitous violence' in the media.[4] Following hard on his heels the then Home Secretary Douglas Hurd called for the 'need to renew our traditions of self-discipline and social responsibility'.[5] As the 1980s drew to a close screen images of mayhem and murder were held to be directly responsible for the growing outbreaks of violence in public life.

The 'Big Bang' in October 1986, when the City of London's financial institutions were deregulated, unleashed an acquisitive and go-getting masculinity. Epitomised by champagne bars, cell phones and mythically large salaries, it was an identity which eschewed domesticity in favour of the Bull Market and the rise and rise of share prices. This new breed of white middle-class male was a stark contrast to his forebear of the 1970s. He represented the public assertion of masculinity and class privilege with an intensity which suggested the historical proximity of a recent near collapse of the gendered class order. These young men were the products of a market capitalism and the Thatcherite ethos of individualism. They eschewed both the old Tory paternalism of social responsibility and the social collectivism of Labour. It was a social expression of male narcissism which inevitably influenced the fashion industry, blighting men's new interest in clothes and cosmetics with a masculine arrogance. Writing in the *Independent Magazine*, the right-wing commentator Alexander Chancellor noted, a little ruefully, this development as, 'one of the nastier fall-out effects of the Thatcher revolution . . . the glorification of strength and masculinity which comes as a side effect of the culture of success'.[6] Free of the 'dependency culture', this 'market man' personified an emboldened sense of manliness.

His hybrid, the more classless lager lout soon hit the headlines, as reports of young men rampaging through the market towns of leafy Tory shires reinforced the idea of endemic disorder. Crowds of drunken young men, shouting insults, smashing windows and confronting the police were events associated in the white English psyche with the inner cities and ethnic minorities. But when it was occurring in the high streets of Chard, Taunton and High Wycombe, it alerted the middle classes that something in its own house needed to be put in order. A.N. Wilson's romantic idyll of England as 'a sceptred Isle . . . this other Eden, demi-Paradise'[7] was the signifier against which the public outbreaks of violence were measured. It was a romanticism born of a white English ethnicity under threat from Europe and a changing multi-ethnic society. But it had been the jingoistic expression of this ethnicity which had heralded the violence of the decade with its response to the Falklands War.

The *Daily Mail*, in its leader comment of 16 June 1982 commented upon the new collective identity engendered by the Falklands War. 'Neither class, age nor politics created any significant divide. There has been a coming together. And there has been a dying together.' But the significant element in this coming together was the propagation of heroic manliness. 'Cut the girl talk', wrote Peter McKay in the *Daily Express* on the 30 April, 'this is war . . . right now it must be quite hard to be a feminist.' But the aggressive nationalism fostered by the government and popular press backfired as English jingoism was kept alive by young white, working-class men on the beaches of Spain and on mainland Europe. In 1985 Liverpool football fans took Heysel Stadium in Brussels by storm. Writing in the *New Statesman* Ed Vulliamy gave an eye-witness account of events:

> it was a matter for their drunken, blood-thirsty and racist English 'honour' that the terraces be cleared of 'spiks' and the Union Jack flown unchallenged. I saw one Liverpool fan with a tee-shirt: 'Keep the Falklands British' as though he and his mates were the task force.[8]

The flag waving and the patriotic fervour and the rhetoric of the task force had been expropriated for the illegitimate purposes of promoting a subordinate working-class masculinity.

Instead of class inequality and xenophobia, the media and the government turned to the family as the cause of social indiscipline, in particular to the failure of paternal authority. In an article on violence in the *Independent*, the writer Anthony Burgess argued that the permissive society had undermined the authority of the father and was failing to suppress individuals' innate violent instincts. 'The structure of the family has traditionally encouraged this [suppression of violence], and the child has always in the same tradition, learned the duty of citizenship'. But, ' . . . our parents are no longer the custodians of an acceptable order: young boys despise their fathers.'[9] The new constituency of right-wing academics were picking up on the same theme.

Patricia Morgan, in a booklet published by the Social Affairs Unit (Anderson and Dawson 1986), argued that the breakdown of law and order was a direct consequence of the failure within certain classes to ensure a high level of paternal involvement and authority in the family. She identitifies the pathologised and fatherless families as belonging to the Afro-Caribbean communities and to the lower white working-class. It is the absent father, she argues, who is responsible for his son's criminality and poor performance in school. This class and racial dimension to the problems of paternal authority fuelled the paranoid fantasy of an English ethnicity and way of life in decline. For Morgan, feminists and other detractors of the family offer only; 'rootlessness – where there are no heritage or ties and people have no place or past, but simply wander upon the face of the earth'.[10]

Far from these sentiments being prompted by a culture of

success, they are the concerns of a society in a state of transitional loss. The football hooligans with their tee-shirts proclaiming, 'England Boys We Are Here, To Shag Your Women And Drink Your Beer', were a ghastly parody of the post-imperialist fantasies generated by the Falklands War. The perception of a decline in English ethnicity and a defensive and aggressive masculinity organised in its defence characterised the discourse of national loss, during the 1980s. The preoccupation with paternal authority created a kind of desperate scrambling to re-invent the Victorian paterfamilias, a figure who could enforce oedipal and family structures, ensuring social stability through a period of demographic upheaval. It is into this cultural context of wayward sons and failed fathers that the genre of the action films were received, creating mass pleasures and identifications amongst a wide spectrum of young men and boys.

MASCULINITY, HUMILIATION AND SILENCE

I want to concentrate on two films of this genre and explore how their themes of violence and revenge provided powerful images for identification and pleasure. The two films are *First Blood* (Kotcheff 1982) and its highly successful sequel *Rambo: First Blood Part II* (Cosmatos 1985). Both films provide representations of the failure of the third term of the father and its effect on a masculine identity. They depict a man in a state of catastrophe and the male fantasies of violence which constitute his attempts to resurrect a reflexive intelligibility and a sense of personal dignity. The central figure in *First Blood* is John Rambo (Sylvester Stallone). His character develops from a morally crushed and humiliated ex-Vietnam war veteran into a caricature of the autarchic male hero pitted against a corrupted social order. While his behaviour in the film hovers on the psychopathological, the representation of one man's paranoia and narcissism personifies a more generalised and less extreme condition of a male propensity and fascination with violence. The action genre and Rambo's minimum use of words in the film also speaks about the relationship of masculine identities to language. The idea that action speaks louder than words lies in the perception of language as an alien and corrupting medium whose use signifies humiliation and the self-denial of identity. Central to both Rambo films is the performative male body, occupying the space of intersubjective communication and imposing its own logic of aggressive violence.

The film opens with a picturesque scene reminiscent of the homesteading days of the old Hollywood West. John Rambo carrying a bag and wearing an old combat jacket and boots descends a hill to a shack by a lake. An older black woman is hanging out her washing. He asks her if Delmar Berry is home. He explains that he served with him in Vietnam in the same Special Forces team. The woman is Delmar's mother and she tells him that her son has died of cancer, caused by Agent Orange. Shocked and dismayed Rambo leaves and carries on walking until he reaches the outskirts of a small town called Hope. He is spotted by the Sheriff, Will Teasle, who offers him a lift – back out of the town. In the car he tells Rambo, 'We don't want guys like you in town. Drifters!' The Sheriff drives him over a bridge and lets him out. He offers some 'friendly advice': 'take a haircut and a bath, you wouldn't get hassled so much.' On his way back he glances in his mirror to see Rambo walking back over the bridge. Executing a quick U-turn, he stops and arrests Rambo, taking from him a large and dangerous-looking knife.

The altercation between the two men depicts Rambo as an aggrieved adolescent son who smarts in sullen silence at the injustices done to him by the older man. But if the scene constructs a father-and-son conflict, Rambo's dress and his place 'on the road', align him with the Hippies and the Beats preceding them. In his bereavement for Delmar Berry and his polite and sensitive conversation with his mother, Rambo also signifies an alignment with black American ethnicity. His position as social outcast, barred from the institutions and communities of mainstream American culture speaks for both the alienation of Vietnam vets and excluded ethnic minorities. It is out of this context of subordinate ethnicity and cultural dispossession that the central element in the film, Rambo's masculinity, emerges. This becomes clearer in the next scene.

In the police station, Rambo is supervised by the Deputy Sheriff and a number of junior officers. They want to know his name for their record of arrest. Rambo refuses to speak and his silence triggers off the sadism of the Deputy Sheriff. 'Name?' 'Your name?' 'Name!' 'Hey you looking for trouble? You come to the right place! You're going to talk to me. I promise you're going to talk to me!' The Sheriff enters the room and interrupts the

Deputy's threat of violence. When he leaves Rambo is ordered to strip and enter a cubicle. The Deputy follows him in and punches him hard. A junior officer noticing the scars covering Rambo's back and chest, urges the Deputy to go easily on him. Ignoring him, the man orders the fire hose on and Rambo is sprayed with freezing cold water.

Once dried and with his trousers back on, Rambo is approached by an officer holding a cut-throat razor and a bowl of shaving cream. He struggles to get away, but the Deputy holds him in an armlock. As the razor approaches his face, there is a flashback to Rambo in Vietnam. Spread-eagled and tied up he is being cut across the chest by a Vietnamese officer with a large knife. This flashback marks the limit of his personal terror, degradation and humiliation. He kicks out at the officer holding the razor, knocks him to the ground and rams the Deputy backward against the wall. From this moment each officer is attacked and knocked down in a choreography of violence which transforms Rambo from a sullen and humiliated drifter into a fantasy of masculine omnipotence.

This is the key scene in establishing an identification with Rambo. As his body bursts out of his self-imposed silence, Rambo retrieves an identity which is slipping out of his reach. In the process it is not language and its better articulation which he grasps, but his bodily strength and fighting skill. It was the demand for his name that Rambo resisted. To have given it would have signified something more than a personal defeat in a battle of wills. As an outsider to the established order of things, Rambo would have been re-incorporated as a petty criminal, rather than a war hero. In his essay 'Private Irony and Liberal Hope', Richard Rorty argues that the purpose of cruelty is not simply to inflict physical pain, but to rob a person of their 'final vocabulary'; the words they use to define who they are. To take this away from an individual is to imply that his or her self and world are futile, obsolete and powerless.

> For the best way to cause people long-lasting pain is to humiliate them by making the things that seemed important to them look futile, obsolete, and powerless. Consider what happens when a child's precious possessions – the little things around which he weaves fantasies that make him a little different from all other children – are described as trash.[11]

The subject is confronted with language games that omit their experience and their intuitive knowledge of who they are. It is a form of collective disavowal that leaves the subject in a state of cultural exclusion, suspended in a state of liminality and non-belonging. Without an oppositional language, the only resistance to this state of affairs is silence. It has a sharp resonance with the descriptions that women and black ethnic groups have given of their exclusion and discrimination. But Rambo's response cannot be explained solely in terms of ethnicity or of class or simply powerlessness.

The violence, the spectacle of him galvanised into life and his effortless grace as he dispatches his tormentors, is a male fantasy. Its enactment resonates with men's own fantastical resolutions of past humiliations. The pleasure of identifying with Rambo as he kicks and punches his persecutors is the willing him on to succeed; to taste the complete authority of self over other men. In the violence of the male body, language and with it the power to define and humiliate, is forced to become peripheral to intersubjectivity. Momentarily, the social conventions of inter-personal communication are suspended and the ordered discourses of authority and identity are exploded. Into this space of disruption, disorientation and fear what was once trivialised and worthless becomes all-powerful.

The narrative structures of masculine identities are akin to the Proppian description of the oedipus complex. They are structured as obstacles to be overcome, territories to be won and tests to be achieved. It is an idiom which is repeatedly portrayed in romantic adventure stories and heroism. But these elements have their inverse. Failure to achieve new territories, the inability to overcome obstacles and the fear of journeying, face the subject with a humiliating defeat. In psychoanalytical terms there are the unconscious impulses and predicaments that impel identities to take on certain idioms of being. What goads the male subject forward on his oedipal quest is the dread of the abject mother. To fail to be free of need for the mother, is the male subject's first humiliation. To be caught eternally attempting to revive the fantasy of a depressed mother is to lack independence, the prerequisite of manliness. If the failure of the father and the dilemma of the paternal predicament trap the male subject in such an atemporal stasis, it is the mother's company he must keep. The father may be feared and hated but in a misogynistic culture, the contempt and humiliation remain with the mother.

In the logic of the paternal narrative, men's humiliation is the fault of women. Humiliation feminises men. And, ironically, it is to women they turn for support in their struggle to regain their masculine status and place amongst other men. It is women who bear witness to his humiliation and it is they who are deemed as robbing him of his self in their demands for his love. In this scenario, if men do not dominate women, they are compromised by them. Women become emblems of men's fear, they offer refuge from the humiliations of other men but at the same time threaten the loss of manhood. *First Blood* has no women in it, but in their absence they define the men's relationships with one another.

The figure of the mother lies at the heart of men's fascination with violence. Melanie Klein has described the infant fantasies of sadistic violence against the mother's body in the paranoid-schizoid position. If the mother is unable or unwilling to contain these projections the depressive position cannot be fully attained. The son is left with the intense anxiety of his hatred for the mother, whom he dare not let go of for fear of her destruction. These psychical projections are continuously re-enacted, looking for women to contain them. Women become the symbolic equivalent of the maternal transformational object. The paternal predicament and the taboo on homosexuality ensure that it is women and not other men who are sought for this containing function. By enforcing heterosexuality, cultural patriarchy reinforces women as surrogate mothers and with that positioning subjects them to the projections of men's repressed hatred for their mothers. The origin of this hatred is the memory of early dependency and the humiliation it creates.

THE LAST REAL MAN

Rambo escapes from the police station. Stealing a motorbike he heads for the mountains with Sheriff Teasle in hot pursuit. Joined by a helicopter and his police officers, Teasle organises a search for Rambo. The result is the accidental death of the Deputy and the wounding of all the others in a series of elaborate traps and ambushes. Rambo, away from culture and the social order has found his element. Hunted like an animal, his body speaks in the grunts and belly sounds of a wild beast as he wills its daring and endurance. Rambo's identity and his language have dissolved into the muteness of nature and the moment of action.

After this mountain pursuit in which the quarry turns hunter, there is a scene of great activity. National Guardsmen and State Police form a backcloth for a television camera. The reporter tells his audience of a lone and dangerous fugitive hiding in the mountains. In the command tent, Sheriff Teasle is regaling the head of the State Police; 'People start fucking around with the law, all hell breaks loose.' Into the tent steps an army officer who announces, 'I've come to get my boy.' This is Colonel Trautman, Rambo's commanding officer in Vietnam. He tells them:

> Accept the fact that you are dealing with an expert in guerilla warfare. With the man who's best with guns, with knives, with bare hands. A man who's been trained to ignore pain, to live off the land, to eat things that would make a billy goat puke. In Vietnam his job was to dispose of enemy personnel. To kill, period. Rambo was the best.

Trautman serves as a link, with one foot in the law and one in Rambo's own reality; he gives Rambo and his actions an intelligibility. His symbolic function as a paternal figure in the narrative is to legitimise Rambo's 'final vocabulary' in the eyes of the social order.

Trautman, however, is not the same 'good father' as Keating in *The Dead Poets Society*. This symbolic function suggests that he is a projection of Rambo's own narcissistic self. The film begins with Rambo excluded from the social order by the language games of law and convention. Defined as a drifter his silence is a defence against the threat this law poses to his historicity. A consequence of his violence is to reconstruct the language games to represent his own reality. In this reversal, turning what was peripheral into the central element, the figure of Trautman comes to be Rambo's representative in the paternal narrative. Sheriff Teasle and his sadistic Deputy Sheriff, as representatives of the Law, become the hateful, wrongdoing and deluded paternal figures. In order to hold on to his sense of self, Rambo's perception of the world has undergone a split. It is he, not the Law, who is now at the centre; everyone else has become his persecutors. To make sense of this I want to turn to Freud's essay 'Narcissism: An Introduction' (Freud 1914c).

In this essay Freud describes how the repression instituted by the threat of castration marks the transfer of narcissistic love onto the super-ego. The good father is a projection, not only of the good maternal objects, but of an ideal which is the substitute for the lost narcissism of infancy in which the child was his or her own ideal. Thirdness contains this other element of projection;

> The ideal ego is now the target of the self-love which was enjoyed in childhood by the actual ego. The subject's narcissism makes its appearance displaced on to this new ideal ego, which, like the infantile ego, finds itself possessed of every perfection that is of value.[12]

The omnipotence of narcissism is the illusion that the infant has no need of the mother. It is a denial of internal reality, but it is this fantasy of completeness which is projected onto the figure of the father. In the context of the representation of Rambo's power, Trautman, at this point, has no place as a separate entity. Thirdness has been extinguished in the persecutory assault of the Sheriff and Trautman exists as an extension of Rambo's narcissistic delusions.

Trautman agrees to speak to Rambo over a transmitter. He uses their old war-time signal: 'Cover leader to Raven'. He names all the members who were in Rambo's Special Forces team. There is silence and then, over the air, 'They're all gone sir. Baker team, they're all dead sir. I'm the last one, sir.' Rambo is hiding in a cave in a state of primordial savagery, cut off from social norms, but constructing another set of social references from his past: 'I'm the last one, sir.' It is at this point, after the earlier identification with Rambo's revenge against his tormentors, that a shift begins. Identification with him demands not only a reversal of the language games constructing order and convention, it now involves entering a new reconstructed reality.

In one of his case histories Freud used the autobiography of a former Judge named Schreber, to analyse his illness of paranoia (Freud 1911c). Freud notes that paranoia in men can begin through 'social humiliation and slights'.[13] At the climax of Dr Schreber's illness, he became convinced of the immanence of a great world catastrophe and described himself as, 'the only real man left alive'. Freud's description of this 'end of the world' fantasy is the state of infantile primary narcissism.

> The patient has withdrawn from the people in his environment and from the external world generally the libidinal cathexis which he has hitherto directed on to them. . . . The

end of the world is the projection of this internal catastrophe; his subjective world has come to an end since his withdrawal of love from it.[14]

Emotional attachments to external objects are redirected onto the subject's ego so enhancing a feeling of aggrandisement. A narcissistic state may begin as the ego defends itself against external persecutory objects. But its persistence lies in the presence of internal persecutory objects which are reactivated by the external threat. The ego attempts to deal with these by projecting them onto objects outside, so enhancing the feeling that the world outside is persecutory. This projection undermines the subject's ability to distinguish what is inner and what is outer, what is subject and what is object. However, the subject is not cut off from external reality but rather seeks to redefine it in order to alleviate the terror and anxiety created by the internal persecutory objects.

Thirdness will alleviate these projections. It provides a term for testing reality, as well as being the location of language and identity. But in Rambo's mind, the good father and thirdness have been foreclosed and with them the possibility of negotiating an identity in relation to the reality of others. What is at stake in these representations of masculine autarchy and violence is the threat of homosexuality. For men, narcissistic love of their own bodies and love for the father are almost assimilated in the ego ideal, the figure of the good father. Homosexual longing is closely linked to an intimate, loving father and consequently to other such men. The taboo of the castrating father against homosexuality, forms the pre-conditions for a masculinity tending towards a defensive aggressiveness and paranoia. As Freud writes: 'what lies at the core of the conflict in cases of paranoia among males is a homosexual wishful fantasy of loving a man'.[15]

This wish for paternal love is projected out into other men who, in turn become persecutors. According to Freud the proposition, 'I (a man) love him (a man)' undergoes a series of transformations in the psyche to become, 'I do not love him – I hate him, because HE PERSECUTES ME.'[16] The ego is forced to reject a paternal love because of the injunction of the castrating father against homosexual love. The alternative courses open to the subject is first, a masochistic heterosexuality in which the body can be punished as proof of the subject's disavowal of homosexual love. And second, a masculinity which expresses the sadistic enactment of killing the good father in an attempt to purge homosexual longing. Rambo displays both facets of the paternal predicament in the spectacle of his wounded body and his implicitly homophobic persona.

Freud describes paranoia as a problem solely related to the father. This description is a consequence of his portrayal of a third term whose origins are entirely separate from the mother–child dyad. The description of thirdness offered in these pages suggests that what is related to a paternal predicament must also have a relationship to maternal predicaments, for the figures of the parents can never be entirely separated. Freud's analysis of projection in paranoia corresponds to Melanie Klein's own theory of the paranoid-schizoid position. In her essay 'Notes on Some Schizoid Mechanisms' (Klein 1946) she adds an appendix on Freud's analysis of the Schreber case. She argues that Freud's emphasis is upon the disturbance of object libido and relations to the external world. In contrast Klein posits the primary cause of paranoia in the splitness of the ego itself. 'The mechanism of one part of the ego annihilating other parts which, I suggest, underlies "world catastrophe" fantasy implies a preponderance of the destructive impulse over the libido.'[17] It is the failure to introject the whole object and achieve the depressive position which results in the continuation of splitting and projection and the subject's susceptibility to paranoia in adult life.

The failure of thirdness has a mutually determining relationship with maternal predicaments. Paranoia is related to psychotic illness, rather than the neurotic illnesses which have their origins in the oedipus complex and post-oedipal period. The subject experiences his or her ego as being in pieces and a perception of reality as full of holes. As a defensive mechanism against the dread of predicaments, the connections between fantasy and reality are broken. This is achieved by attacking the links between object impressions which form a mental representation or symbol which is assimilated in the psyche as thought (see 'Attacks on Linking', Bion (1990)). The attack is directed at the emotions which constitute links because they feel too powerful for the immature ego to contain. The purpose is to destroy consciousness of reality even if reality itself cannot be destroyed. The result leads to a feeling of a disintegrated world and the subject surrounded by objects whose relationships with one another are impregnated with violence and cruelty. Language collapses into its constituent parts as the subject is no longer able to contain his or her feelings within its representational function.

Rambo's slip from exhilarating retribution into paranoia marks the failure of thirdness. His silence is the failure of language and it is his body and its violence which fills the gap in signification. As the paternal figure, it is Trautman's function to end this predicament by bringing language to Rambo's silence. At the film's ending, after Rambo has destroyed half of the town of Hope, Trautman confronts him in the now-derelict police station. He is no longer simply a projection of Rambo's narcissism, but a figure of authority. He orders Rambo to stop: 'This mission is over!' Confronted with this injunction Rambo collapses in tears and for the first time articulates his pain and confusion. The more he speaks the more child-like he becomes, until he is clinging to Trautman's hand overcome with grief and fear. Language brings feelings and these are a stark contrast to the omnipotent warrior fantasy Rambo had become.

The film ends with Rambo handcuffed, being led out of the police station to a waiting car. His re-arrest marks his second reincorporation into the order of things. This time he is not the drifter and bum but an enigmatic warrior and a heroic misfit. The anomaly of the ending is this spectacle of an omnipotent masculinity defeated. The contradictory mix of warrior and victim reveals the fragmented state of his masculine identity. It is the film's sequel, *Part II*, that his struggle to emerge out of this parlous state is played out. While *First Blood* tracked one man's descent into a form of psychosis and violence, *Rambo: First Blood Part II* is a fantasy of pure masculine omnipotence. The gritty realism of the first film is replaced with a cinematic spectacle of grand-scale destruction and violence.

THE PERFORMATIVE BODY

The sequel marks Rambo's return from catastrophe to the real world. But it is one populated by enemies and persecutors who continually threaten his own existence and that of his country. The plot of the film is simple and merely serves to convey the fantasies of grandiosity and paranoia as Rambo acts out the crisis of his own intelligibility and historicity against a backcloth of America's humiliation in Vietnam. Trautman has been ordered to persuade Rambo, now serving a lengthy prison sentence with hard labour, to undertake a mission into post-war Vietnam. Reluctantly Rambo agrees. He meets the politician organising the project who tells him his task is to seek out and photograph missing American prisoners of war. Rambo parachutes into the country and makes a rendezvous with Co Bao, a dissident Vietnamese woman who acts as his guide. Together they travel up-river in a pirate boat. They find the prison camp and manage to rescue one of the prisoners. Rambo and the POW leave Co Bao and make their way to the 'extraction' point, where they will be airlifted out by helicopter. However, when the politician hears the pilot exclaim over the radio that Rambo has with him a POW, he orders the helicopter's immediate return. For the sake of political expediency Rambo is abandoned.

Rambo is captured and tortured by Russian 'advisers'. But with the help of Co Bao, he succeeds in escaping and rescuing the remaining POWs. They fly to freedom in a captured helicopter. The political discourse of the film is a right-wing product of its time. Its racist depiction of the Vietnamese, its intense chauvinism and the emotive issue of missing American POWs reflect the rise of Reaganite politics. It found its legitimacy in the intensification of the Cold War. But with the enstatement of President Gorbachev in the Soviet Union, its political message of a new belligerent national pride became an anomaly. The failure of *Rambo III* sealed its fate as the detritus of a historical period now surpassed. Nevertheless, *Rambo: First Blood Part II* is a fantastic spectacle of a masculinity attempting to assert itself over its crisis of identity. And it provides an insight into a place men can turn in such a moment; their bodies. Whether wounded and suffering or forced to the limit of human endurance and destructiveness, *Rambo: First Blood Part II* is dominated by the performative body of a white man. This spectacle of the male body in action is the central signifier of the attempted recuperation of a humiliated and defeated masculine identity.

In the film's opening scene, the lens lingers upon Rambo's body as he breaks up rocks with a sledgehammer. His tense muscles strain and bulge, glistening with sweat and the reflection of the hot sun. And, as Rambo walks across to meet Colonel Trautman, it follows his passage, revealing something new and different about Rambo's body. In *First Blood* it was tough and sinewy, but now it has been contrived into a spectacle. His musculature has greatly increased, his gait is more certain, his posture upright, his chest thrown outward in an act of defiance and self-assertion. The Rambo now on display suggests recuperation and self-assurance. It is a revivified masculinity whose self-description lies in the body not in the word. It is in the surface and the tautness of the skin, the hardness of the muscles and the deportment of his body that Rambo signifies something more than the random, defensive violence of earlier times. A new coherence and purpose has been fashioned out of this catastrophe and has been located in his body.

In 'The Ego and the Id' (Freud 1923b) Freud recognises that a person's own body, above all its surface, is a place from which both internal and external perceptions spring, so contributing to the formation of the ego. 'The ego' he writes, 'is first and foremost a bodily ego; it is not merely a surface entity, but is itself the projection of a surface.'[18] The scheme of the body places the subject into a relationship with time and space, providing an essential representation of the subject's sense of self. It comes to embody an individual's self-description as well as exposing the unconscious predicaments that serve to undermine this proclamation. In a metaphoric sense, the body outlines the ego. It acts as a screen that divides inner from outer and comes to express, physiologically, the relationship between the two.

To live subjectively, the body also requires a psychic space. The psychoanalyst Esther Bick explored this relationship through her observations of infants. She argued that it was skin contact between the mother and the baby which was the most prominent element in the earliest relationship. Bick disagreed with the Kleinian idea that the infant's ego was capable of introjection and projection from the beginning of life. These are functions which require a fair degree of ego stability and cohesion. Bick argued that this primary source of stability and the formative stages of the ego's boundaries comes from outside, by the skin functioning as a boundary. Before the ego is capable of holding mental representations of objects there has to be a concept of an internal space that holds things. For Bick, feeding and the experience of the nipple in the infant's mouth closes the hole in the boundary of the body. Once this primary containing object has been introjected the infant comes to perceive the skin as a primary receptor organ that stimulates the experience of being held and contained (Bick 1968).

Bick describes occasions when the ego fails to develop satisfactorily its containing function. Without an internal psychic space, the infant cannot project into an external object which can act as a container. Without the possibility of 'K' and subsequent symbol formation and thought, the infant's personality dissolves out into a nothingness. Bick describes this as the horror of being lost in outer space; 'When a baby is born he is in the position of an astronaut shot out into outer space without a space suit. . . . The predominant terror of the baby is of falling to pieces or liquefying.'[19] She describes 'second skin' formations as a defence against the threat of this horror (Bick 1968). These are a variety of mechanisms which will hold the infant's personality together. A typical example is a muscular development which holds the body rigid and intact.

In *First Blood* a humiliating assault upon Rambo's identity shifts the relationship of the psyche soma. To ensure the ego's safety and to protect it from further assault by both internal and external persecutors, it is literally embodied in the musculature. It is his body, in acts of defensive violence, which comes to speak for this crisis and Rambo's attempts to resolve it. It is the body, rather than the word which comes to incorporate the signifier and meaning of a masculine identity. Such an ego-defensive body no longer functions as an interface between inner and outer. It is more akin to a castle wall. But it is not static. The dread engendered by the insecurity of the ego's containing function is the consequence of a passive experience of an unsuccessful containing maternal object. Passivity breeds fear. The embodied ego is dictated by a manic defence against the maternal object and a flight into fantasies of omnipotence. Above all the body is performative. It must be spectacular in that it must be seen. If it is not seen there can be no communication with others, for it has replaced the word.

If language games serve only to undermine the individual's struggle for self-comprehension and identity, the body offers the subject control and certainty. He can will it and enlarge it and goad it to ever greater feats of performance. He can show his narcissistic wounds through actual damage and bleeding. In *First Blood*, Rambo, chased by the police, stops briefly to sew up a wound in his arm. In *Part II*, he is tied to an electrical grid, crucified like Jesus Christ and tortured. Each scene illustrates a masculinity under assault, a wounded son caught between the maternal predicaments and the failure of the father. It is a body that cries out for pity, for the love and care of the mother and in the same instance rejects such a course in a demonstration of autarchic masculinity and physical prowess.

A number of psychoanalysts, working with children suffering autism, have noticed how they adopt or 'stick to', a hard object (Meltzer 1975 and Bick 1986). This serves a similar function to the rigid musculature; a compensation for the absence of spaces to project into. A significant object in the Rambo films is his knife. Despite the technological sophistication of weaponry at his disposal, Rambo manages to lose most of it in his parachute jump. After the film's fetishistic glorying in weapons technology, Rambo reverts to a bow and arrow and his knife. Both primitive weapons, they come to symbolise a naturalistic and primordial ability to kill. Most of all it is the knife which comes to signify Rambo's violence.

On the journey to the prison camp, aboard the pirate boat, Co Bao, asks Rambo what he believes in. Rambo's response is to show her his knife. An immediate explanation is that its phallic shape and frequent use stabbing his enemies, suggests a sexual hatred. But this is too simple. For the knife contains something of Rambo's identity. Before the mission begins, the camera closes in upon its steel against his skin, as he places it in its sheaf. The sexual connotations and its proximity to his skin suggest it both enhances his presence and represents some aspect of his ego. It is not only a weapon of violence. It is an object of reassurance, literally a part of his body-schema.

In her work on autism, the psychoanalyst Frances Tustin has described how autistic children hold onto a hard object. She calls them 'autistic objects' and explains that their function is to 'shut out menaces which threaten bodily attack and ultimate annihilation'.[20] Tustin argues that autism is a consequence of the failure of the containing function of the primary object. This is a result of the catastrophic experience of premature separation. André Green also alludes to these hard objects and their existence on the edge of the psyche-soma. For the subject, a part of whose ego remains undifferentiated through its fusion with the internal fantasy of a dying or bereaved mother, there is a similar lack of internal psychic space. Because the damaged maternal object occupies the ego, there is no room to introject objects. 'In all, the subject's objects remain constantly at the limit of the ego, not wholly within and not quite without.'[21]

In an interview Frances Tustin likens the state of autistic children to a primary defensive narcissism.

autistic children need to feel all-powerful because they feel so helpless, and so tenuous in their sense of identity, and are so afraid that they are going to lose their sense of existence, so they need to feel all-powerful in order to offset this very distressing feeling.[22]

There is always a risk in using examples from psychopathology to describe phenomena of everyday life. But as Marion Milner has pointed out, autism is not necessarily just a rare condition in children but an area that is possibly in everyone. These are 'areas of total primary undifferentiation', the effects of 'prematurely having to face the gap between the infant's own body and the mother's'.[23] Rambo is an exception but also a logical extreme of a masculinity caught between this maternal predicament and the foreclosure of thirdness. Just as the interrelation of the two in the structuring of male subjectivity creates a proclivity to paranoia, so it tends to produce a kernel of autism. An area within the psyche where the relationship between affect and language has broken down and feeling is lost.

VIOLENCE AND MEN'S HETEROSEXUALITY

Rambo's one-man invasion of Vietnam is a form of manic excursion into the realm of the other in order to rob it of some secret potency which will restore his defeated masculinity. Here the phallus and desire are transposed into a homophobic and paranoid attempt to destroy the other. What motivates his killing goes beyond patriotic sentiment. The extraordinary spectacle of Rambo shooting and stabbing scores of shadowy 'evil' figures conjures up the negation of desire. It is no longer plenitude and the phallus which are pursued for they lead to one thing: homosexual longing. If it was the repression of homosexual love which marked his descent into catastrophe, heterosexual love seems an equal impossibility. At the end of the film Rambo is asked by Trautman what it is he wants. He replies, 'For our country to love us in the way that we love it. That's what I want.' But belonging is what eludes Rambo. He is the misfit son trained to kill in 'her' defence and now abandoned and alone. The only way to win back her love and so to belong to her is to destroy thirdness, to reverse the order of desire and become once more of her. His is a masculine identity that in spite of its spectacle of omnipotence, continually threatens to implode, to destroy its own future by turning its back on sexual love.

Unlike *First Blood*, its sequel figures a woman. She is resourceful, tough and intelligent. It is because of her loyalty to Rambo and her saving him from torture that he reciprocates her growing love and concern for him. But the possibility of romantic or sexual love in this spectacle of the performative body is an impossible one. Narcissism precludes such a relationship. Sexual love would negate the principle of omnipotent performance. It would both refute it for its destruction of verbal communication and intersubjectivity and it would threaten to ignite further the internal persecuting objects that already menace his ego. Within minutes of their joint declaration of love, Co Bao is shot dead. Her death serves as a symbol for Rambo's suffering and aloneness. It is yet another cross that he must bear, yet of course, it is a self-fulfilling event. His masculinity could never sustain such a relationship. There is only one person who counts in this state of narcissism and that is the mother.

Narcissism occurs in the depressive position when the infant begins to perceive itself as a separate being from his or her mother. In turning libidinal energy away from external objects and onto the ego, the infant is defending against his or her fear of the mother's loss. If this place remains unresolved, if the mother is experienced as lost through her psychic absence, there is little room for introjecting new objects. Sexual love becomes a precarious and dangerous undertaking for it threatens to displace the internal object of the bereaved mother. In adult life women will exist as part of the performance, to be played to, encouraged to praise and pity this wounded son and his gallant attempts to overcome his predicament. The valiant endeavours and innumerable narrow escapes from death enact his boyish longing for his mother's presence. But at the same time, in their grandiosity, they ward off her abjection with proof of his autonomy and separateness. There was only one object love and because that remains unrequited, it precludes any other. His love is still mortgaged to the bereaved mother within. Solitude, which was so feared in infancy is now sought after. André Green has written of this fantasy of the 'dead mother':

The subject . . . becomes his own mother, but remains prisoner to her economy of survival. He thinks he has got rid of his dead mother. In fact, she only leaves him in peace in the measure that she herself is left in peace. As long as there is no candidate to the succession, she can well let her child survive, certain to be the only one to possess this inaccessible love.[24]

In his article the day after the Hungerford massacre A.N. Wilson described how cinematic images of macho violence 'teach the insignificant little man that if he dresses up in a combat jacket and pretends to be Rambo he can achieve notoriety and fame. Someone will notice him'.[25] His description of the cause and effect of violence is too simple, but he is right in a way he may not appreciate. Rambo speaks to all men and the 'insignificant little man' inside them, the wounded humiliated little boys wanting attention and crying out for revenge. And because the retributive violence in Rambo is such a common fantasy of masculinities, it was inevitable that it would move from the fantastic to the actual outside the context of war. While it was horrific and extraordinary, the shootings in Hungerford had a familiarity to them. It was a scene repeated many times over in the fantasies of masculinity, fantasies whose material came from the filmic images of male retributive violence.

After the shootings, Michael Ryan finally sought refuge in his old school. Cornered by the police he repeatedly asked after his mother, 'Is she all right?', telling the listening policeman that he hadn't meant her any harm. She had been his first victim, the second had been a woman he tried to rape. He failed in his attempt. An attempt that was a grotesque symbol of his desire to be a proper man. From then on 'the enemy' was everywhere.

Perhaps it was no coincidence that Ryan should return to a scene of his childhood and, by all accounts, the place of his repeated humiliation. The press published photographs of a Ryan as a boy, little and frightened. The newspapers were full of small-town innuendo about his life. 'Mrs Rowland said the only person she remembered Ryan with was his mother. "I never saw him with a girlfriend", she said.'[26] And a neighbour, Denis Morley, quoted in a number of papers, described him as 'a real mother's boy, a spoilt little wimp'. He could have anything he wanted, she absolutely doted on him. But despite all her affection he would go home at night and beat her very badly.'[27] A week later the *Sun* revealed Ryan's 'kinky secret'. A man purporting to be Ryan's gay lover described a 'gentle man who wouldn't hurt a fly' a man who, 'had never had a girl in his life but really wanted one'.[28] A number of psychiatrists were asked to comment and Ryan was labelled a paranoid schizophrenic. But perhaps the most insight that could be gained on the cause of his violence was this discourse of masculinity that emerged around the event.

The language games employed by reporters and reported alike contained a vocabulary of failure, of Ryan's inability to live up to the cultural and sexual expectations of masculinity. Their deprecation focused on the perceived inability of Ryan to be free of his mother. Ryan was a failure because he had not been aggressive as a boy and remained tied to his mother's apron strings. As the byline in the *Daily Express* said: 'Doting mother's lavish gifts turned Ryan into a spoilt wimp.' In this moment the aggressive masculinity of the Falklands Task Force judges one man who never made its grade. One form of violent masculinity condemns another. In this battle between masculinities, it is symbolically and literally the body of the mother who is fought over. The masculine identity that wins is the one which can show the most distance from her. This violent and desperate scrabbling for the credentials of a 'real' manhood marks the final obliteration of the good mother. And for some men it is the moment of an intense crisis of self and identity when the inherent misogyny in men's violence turns on women. Humiliated and trapped in his own need of his mother, perceiving her as a persecutor whom he could neither leave nor live with, Ryan exploded.

AFTERWORD

Sometimes I feel like a motherless child
A long, long way from home.[1]

I began with a description of *Men Against Sexism* and its formation.
I end with a double image of a mass killer – Michael Ryan firing a
Kalashnikov, parodying Rambo with his head scarf, personal
armoury and paranoid fantasies of revenge. And Michael Ryan,
aged 8, looking shy and withdrawn, splashed across the tabloids,
a juxtaposition which was some sort of attempt to dismiss the
virulence of his murderous behaviour. Perhaps it is not such a
strange and long distance to have travelled, from radical sexual
politics to this masculine violence and instability. Both share a
similar logic in the acquisition of masculine identities. MAS
emerged out of a generational conflict between masculine sensibilities. Ryan emerged out of another form of generational
conflict; a profoundly destructive relationship between his adult
masculine persona and the child that he had once been. Both
instances share this experience of a masculine identity divided by
and through time.

In the introduction to their book *Manful Assertions* John Tosh
and Mike Roper write, 'One of the most precarious movements in
the reproduction of masculinity is the transfer of power to the
succeeding generation.'[2] The transmission of masculine subjectivities from one generation to the next is not simply an external
relationship of social conditioning and role learning between
parents and their children. Nor does it constitute a process whose
passage of time is then confined to the past. Rather, it becomes an
integral part of individual subjectivity, the child of his parents
co-existing in a complex, often antagonistic relationship with the

195

adult man. This weak link of the generational exchange of masculine values and practices, the ambivalences, conflicts and contradictions of identity, finds its expression in the structuring and dividing of the male psyche.

A masculine identity becomes an exercise in regulating and attempting to suppress and contain the predicaments of the boy, his sense of loss and his longing for the love of his 'good mother'. More specifically, it is a struggle to diminish the influence of the mother and son together in the formation of male subjectivity. In this temporal and spatial relationship between the child and the man lie the transgressions of effeminacy, homosexuality and motherlove, the antitheses of hegemonic masculinities and heterosexuality. All these were present in Ryan, a fact that was trumpeted by the tabloids, who placed the cause of his violence in this covert deviancy. The irony was in their own contribution to violence by Ryan, who was spurred into action in an attempt to destroy these socially unacceptable feelings rather than to express them.

In this intra-subjective relationship between the adult man and the child he once was lie all the storms, self-hatreds and violence mustered by a masculine identity intent upon its survival in a culture which refutes the capacity of men to love each other. The project of reflexivity, of coming to know oneself and remake oneself must be one which involves love or it can come to nothing. In his essay 'Potential Space in Psychoanalysis' André Green writes: 'Meaning does not emerge complete as Aphrodite rising from the waves. It is for us to construct it. . . . Meaning is not discovered it is created.'[3] Green is referring to the analytic situation and the capacity of the transference to establish the realisation of an absent meaning within the analysand. This capacity to make subjectivity, not to uncover a repressed element, but to create something new which had previously existed only as a potential, involves the analyst as a surrogate good mother within the transference.

In other words, for a successful analysis and therapy there must exist 'K'; the process of establishing object love through the parents' capacity to know the child's anxieties and to do something about them. This process of 'K' will enable the analysand to attain and abide in the depressive position and in so doing enable his or her own capacity to give and receive love. Melanie Klein has written that amongst the fundamental and essential feelings that we call love is a subject's identification with and desire to preserve his or her whole good object. Alongside this sense of the aliveness of oneself is a sadness relating to an expectation of its impending loss. Concerning those individuals who doubt the goodness of the loved object, she quotes Freud, using his assertion that such doubt is in reality a doubt of one's own love, 'a man who doubts his own love may, or rather *must*, doubt every lesser thing'.[4]

In this practice of love lie the processes of change and transformation. Dominant masculine identities, in their intra-subjective struggle to suppress the transgressions that threaten their psychological stability have sought relief in narrowing the parameters to the legitimate practice and expression of love. In men's silence there is always the possibility of violence, infecting men's social relationships with an element of wariness. Under such conditions what men will not allow in themselves they must deny to others of their gender; the son's intimacy with his mother, his homosexuality, campness, his confidence and his strength, a father dispossessed of his own motherlove finds such human indulgence in pleasure an unbearable affront to his own lack and longing. Masculine identities in their struggle to evade the transgressions that threaten their stability, diminish and underrate the possibility of love and with it the capacity for reparation and change.

Cultural studies has paid little attention to the cultural practice and expression of this reparative love. And despite its centrality in the transference, psychoanalysis has tended to concentrate its attention on the gendered division of sexual desire. To begin to articulate a practice and vocabulary of love and a culture of reparation is a central task of sexual politics. The family has been the traditional site of this practice. Twenty years ago feminism tore apart its practices, ideologies and cultural representations in stinging criticism. But after the heady rush into alternative lifestyles, the communes and multiple relationships foundered on all those painful issues to do with an individual's sense of belonging and home. We never got around to reclaiming and promoting the diversity of family forms which subsequently emerged. In their panic the right gave birth to the notion of 'pretended families'. Lesbian parents, gay fathers, women on their own with children, extended step-families, fathers bringing up their children, as well as family groups without children whose ties are friendship and the shared affinities of a lifestyle, of feminism, gay and lesbian sexuality or sexual politics, all offer a great experiment in new familial forms within a multicultural society. They herald changing identities and possibly changing psychodynamics of gender formation.

It is within this diversity that the gendered antinomies of the mother and father can be challenged and wrestled with. Psychoanalysis emerged out of a specific set of patriarchal social relationships. Its theories have attempted to describe the psychic processes and elements of this gendered order from within the constraints of its hierarchies, imaginations and epistemologies. To go beyond these descriptions, to discover another type of father, to end the father as a figure of defence against the mother and to challenge the maternal function, it is necessary to practise new forms of relationships. In psychical terms, as Winnicott has written, *'it is not possible to be original except on a basis of tradition'*.[5] We have been formed out of social relations that belong to the past, we bring these with us into our efforts to change ourselves and move beyond them into new subjectivities. There can be no absolute change, but out of 'pretended families' will emerge new vocabularies and sensibilities of gender identity and sexualities.

NOTES

1 LEAVING HOME

1 Laurie Anderson (1982), 'O Superman', from her album *Big Science*, Warner Brothers, 1982.

2 L. Wittgenstein (1961), *Tractatus Logico-Philosophicus*, The final sentence. Routledge and Kegan Paul, London.

3 Ibid., para. 6.42.

4 Gayatri Chakravorty Spivak (1988), 'Can the Subaltern Speak?' in *Marxism and the Interpretation of Culture*, eds Cary Nelson and Lawrence Grossberg, Macmillan, London, p. 296.

5 Walter Benjamin (1973), 'Theses on the Philosophy of History' in *Illuminations*, Fontana, London, p. 257.

6 Jean-François Lyotard (1987), *The Post Modern Condition: A Report on Knowledge*, Manchester University Press, Manchester, p. xxiv.

7 For the debate on the relationship between feminism and post-modernity see Suzanne Moore (1988), 'Getting a Bit of the Other: The Pimps of Postmodernism', in *Male Order Unwrapping Masculinity*, eds Rowena Chapman and Jonathan Rutherford, Lawrence and Wishart, London. Kelly Oliver (1988), 'Nietzsche's Woman. The Poststructuralist Attempt To Do Away with Women', in *Radical Philosophy*, No. 48. Alice A. Jardine (1985), *Gynesis Configurations of Woman and Modernity*, Cornell University Press, New York. Kate Soper (1990), 'Feminism, Humanism and Postmodernism', in *Radical Philosophy*, No. 55. Craig Owens (1987), 'The Discourse of Others: Feminists and Postmodernism' in *Postmodern Culture*, ed. Hal Foster, Pluto Press, London. Barbera Creed (1987), 'From Here to Modernity – Feminism and Postmodernism' in *Screen*, Vol. 28, No. 2, Spring 1987. Jane Flax (1991), *Thinking Fragments Psychoanalysis, Feminism, & Postmodernism in the Contemporary West*, University of California Press, Berkeley.

8 See Alice Jardine (1985), op. cit. p. 93. Also Rosa Braidotti (1987), 'Envy: or With My Brains and Your Looks,' in *Men in Feminism*, eds Alice Jardine and Paul Smith, Methuen, London.

9 Pierre Bourdieu (1986), *Distinction. A Social Critique of the Judgement of Taste*, Routledge and Kegan Paul, London.

10 For an example of this class analysis see; Alvin W. Gouldner (1979), *The Future of Intellectuals and the Rise of a New Class*, Macmillan Press, London. And Erik Olin Wright (1985) *Classes*, Verso, London. For an example of its application see Fred Pfiel (1988), 'Postmodernism as a "Structure of Feeling"' in *Marxism and the Interpretation of Culture* (see note 4). Michael Rustin (1982), 'A Socialist Consideration of Kleinian Psychoanalysis', in *New Left Review*, No. 131.

11 Vic Seidler (1985), 'Fear and Intimacy' in *The Sexuality of Men*, eds Martin Humphries and Andy Metcalf, Pluto Press, London, p. 171.

12 Zygmunt Baumann (1982), *Memories of Class Prehistory and Afterlife of Class*, Routledge, London, p. 2.

13 Ibid.

14 South London Men Against Sexism (1974), 'Where do we go from here?' in *Brothers Against Sexism*, Spring, No. 3, p. 3. I took this reference from Segal (1990) and also from Cooper (1990).

15 Stoke Newington Men's Group (1975), *Men Against Sexism* Issue 4. I took this reference from Mick Cooper (1990).

16 Andy Metcalf (1985) 'Introduction', *The Sexuality of Men* (see note 11).

17 For example, see descriptions offered by Andrew Tolson (1985), Jeff Hearn (1987), and a discussion of men's groups in *Achilles Heel*, No. 2 (1979) entitled 'Personally Speaking'.

18 From 'The Men's Therapy Group', *Red Therapy* pamphlet 1978, London, p. 46.

19 Vic Seidler (*c.* 1979), 'Raging Bull' in *Achilles Heel*, No. 5, p. 8.

20 Andrew Tolson (1985), *The Limits of Masculinity*, Tavistock Publications, London, pp. 135–6.

21 Paul Atkinson (1982), 'Inner Lives. Therapy, Men and the Men's Movement', an interview with David Harding in *Revolutionary Socialism*, No. 10.

22 For example, see Paul Morrison (*c.* 1979), 'Pregnant Fatherhood Two Years On', *Achilles Heel*, No. 3. Jeff Hearn (1983) (see note 41). Jonathan Rutherford (1987). Gavin Smith (1987). Vic Seidler (1979).

23 Ray Gordon (1979), 'The Diary of a Male House Husband', in *Achilles Heel*, No. 2.

24 Raymond Williams (1977), 'Structures of Feeling' in *Marxism and Literature*, Oxford University Press, Oxford, p. 131.

25 Op cit. p. 134.

26 Ibid.

27 Op cit. p. 132.

28 Op cit. p. 131.

29 June Jordan (1985), 'Living Room' in *Notes Towards Home*, Thunders Mouth Press, USA.

30 Taken from a transcript of the Stoke Newington Men's Group (1982). Unpublished.

31 See for example: Judy Blendis (1982), 'Men's Experience of Their Own Fathers', in *Fathers. Psychological Perspectives*, eds Nigel Beail and Jacqueline McGuire, Junction Books, London. Shere Hite (1981), *The Hite Report on Male Sexuality*, Macdonald, London. Mary Ingham (1985), *Men*, Century, London.

32 Quote taken from unpublished manuscript for *Cosmopolitan, c.* 1987, Jonathan Rutherford.

33 Stoke Newington Men's Group, from transcript of a discussion on fathers. Unpublished.

34 Anna Ford (1986), *Men*, Corgi Books, London, p. 76.

35 Lynne Segal (1990), *Slow Motion Changing Masculinities Changing Men*, Virago, London, p. 20.

36 John Osborne (1979), *Look Back in Anger*, Faber, London.

37 See Lynne Segal (1990) (1988).

38 Sandra Scarr and Judy Dunn (1987), *MotherCare/OtherCare*, Pelican Books, London, p. 99.

39 See Denise Riley (1983), *War in the Nursery: Theories of the Child and Mother*, Virago, London. Also Sandra Scarr and Judy Dunn (1987), Lynne Segal (1990).

40 Paul Durcan (1990), 'The Two Little Boys at the Back of the Bus', in *Daddy, Daddy*, The Blackstaff Press, Belfast.

41 I am referring here to unspecified copies of the *Men Against Sexism Newsletter* from *circa* 1978 and copies of *Achilles Heel*. Other examples are: Jeff Hearn (1983), *Birth and Afterbirth*, Achilles Heel Publications, London. Jonathan Rutherford (1987), 'I want something we men have no language to describe', in *Women's Journal*. Gavin Smith (1987), 'The Crisis of Fatherhood', in *Free Association*, No. 9. Clive Goodwin (1987), 'Who's Looking After the Baby', *Achilles Heel*, No. 8. Dexter Tiranti (1987), 'The Absent Father Comes Home', *New Internationalist*, No. 175. Also issue No. 17 of the *Anti-Sexist Men's Newsletter*, *circa* mid-1980s, is given over to discussions about men and childcare.

42 A number of academic studies have been published as collections of essays; *The Father Figure* (1982), eds Lorna McKee and Margaret O'Brien, Tavistock, London. *Fathers. Psychological Perspectives* (1982), eds Nigel Beail and Jacqueline McGuire, Junction Books, London. *Reassessing Fatherhood* (1987), eds Charlie Lewis and Margaret O'Brien, Sage, London. Also Brian Jackson (1983), *Fatherhood*, Allen and Unwin, London. Fraser Harrison (1985), *A Father's Diary*, Fontana, London. Tony Bradman (1985), *The Essential Father*, Unwin Paperbacks, London.

43 See Judy Blendis (1982), 'Men's Experience of Their Own Fathers' in *Fathers. Psychological Perspectives* (see note 31).

44 Vic Seidler (1979), 'Men and Feminism', *Achilles Heel*, No. 2, p. 34.

45 Transcript from Stoke Newington Men's Group discussion of fathers (1982). Unpublished.

46 'Leaping into the Abyss' in *Red Therapy* (1978), London.

47 Barbera Ehrenreich and Deirdre English (1979), *For Her Own Good: 150 Years of the Experts' Advice to Women*, Doubleday/Anchor Press, New York.

48 See Denise Riley (1983).

49 See Nancy Chodorow (1978), *The Reproduction of Mothering. Psychoanalysis and the Sociology of Gender*, University of California Press, Berkeley, p. 212.

50 R.D. Laing (1967), *The Politics of Experience*, Penguin Books, Harmondsworth, p. 89.
51 Monique Plaza (1982) 'The Mother/The Same: Hatred of the Mother in Psychoanalysis', *Feminist Issues*, Spring Issue.
52 Raymond Williams (1977) (see note 24), p. 132.

2 THE THEORY AND PRACTICE OF MEN'S SEXUAL POLITICS

1 Barry Richards (1988), 'Psychoanalysis and the Left Since '68', *Radical Philosophy*, No. 48.
2 For example, see Herbert Marcuse (1970), *5ive Lectures*, trans. Jeremy J. Shapiro and Shierry M. Weber, Allen Lane/The Penguin Press, London. Erich Fromm (1971), *The Crisis of Psychoanalysis*, Jonathan Cape, London. R. D. Laing (1971), *The Politics of the Family*, Tavistock, London.
3 Vic Seidler (1985),' Fear and Intimacy' in *The Sexuality of Men*, eds Andy Metcalf and Martin Humphries, Pluto Press, London, p. 151.
4 *Red Therapy* (1978), London, p. 24.
5 Ibid.
6 For discussion of the often tense relationship between personal politics and political practice in this time and place, see V. Seidler (1989), *Rediscovering Masculinity. Reason, Language and Sexuality*, Routledge, London, pp.72–106. Max Farrar (1989), 'The Libertarian Movement of the 1970s' in *Edinburgh Review*, No. 82. Paul Atkinson (1982), 'Inner Lives. Therapy, Men and the Men's Movement' in *Revolutionary Socialism*, No. 10, Big Flame, London. Allison Fell (1984), *Every Move You Make*, Virago, London. Sheila Rowbotham (1989), *The Past is Before Us*, Penguin, London. Lynne Segal (1979), 'Daily Life' in *Revolutionary Socialism*, No. 4. Wendy Clark (1983), 'Home Thoughts From Not So Far Away' in *What Is To Be Done About The Family*, ed. Lynne Segal, Penguin, London.
7 See Louis Althusser (1971), 'Ideology and Ideological State Apparatuses' in *Lenin and Philosophy*, Monthly Review Press, London, pp. 127–86.
8 See Claude Lévi-Strauss (1983), 'The Science of the Concrete' in *The Savage Mind*, Weidenfeld and Nicolson, London.
9 Louis Althusser and Etienne Balibar (1972), *Reading Capital*, New Left Books, London.
10 See Jacques Lacan (1949), 'The Function and Field of Speech and Language in Psychoanalysis' in *Ecrits. A Selection* (1980), Tavistock/Routledge, London.
11 For two exceptions see Peter Bradbury (1985), 'Desire and Pregnancy' and Richard Dyer (1985), in *The Sexuality of Men* (see note 3).
12 Vic Seidler (1989), *Rediscovering Masculinity*, p. x (see note 6).
13 Paul Atkinson (1979), 'The Problem with Patriarchy' in *Achilles Heel*, No. 2, p. 21.

14 For a discussion on this theme of the rise of cultural studies and the crisis in the humanities see Stuart Hall (1990), 'The Emergence of Cultural Studies and the Crisis of the Humanities' in *October*, Summer issue. And Patrick Brantlinger (1990), *Crusoe's Footprints: Cultural Studies in Britain and America*, Routledge, London.

15 See Jan Bradshaw (1982), 'Now What Are They Up To? Men in the "Men's Movement"'in *On the Problem of Men*, eds Scarlet Friedman and Elizabeth Sarah, The Women's Press, London. Mick Cooper (1990) *Searching For The Anti-Sexist Man, A History of the Men's Movement*, Achilles Heel Publication, London. Kathy Myers (1983), 'Power and Patriarchy' in *New Socialist*, No. 11, May/June.

16 Andy Metcalf (1985), 'Introduction', *The Sexuality of Men*, p. 8 (see note 6).

17 For a history of the British Independent tradition within the psychoanalytic establishment see Gregorio Kohon (ed.) (1988), 'Notes on the History of the Psychoanalytic Movement in Great Britain', in *The British School of Psychoanalysis. The Independent Tradition*, Free Association Books, London.

18 See Juliet Mitchell (1974), *Psychoanalysis and Feminism*, Pelican Books, London.

19 Nancy Chodorow (1978), *The Reproduction of Mothering Psychoanalysis and the Sociology of Gender*, University of California Press, Berkeley.

20 Ronald Fairbairn (1952), *Psychoanalytic Studies of the Personality*, Tavistock, London, p. 289.

21 For a bibliographical resource see Tim Carrigan, R. W. Connell and John Lee (1985) 'Towards a new sociology of masculinity' in *Theory and Society*, No. 14. Also Iain Craib (1987), 'Masculinity and Male Dominance' in *Sociological Review*, Routledge and Kegan Paul, London.

22 Nancy Chodorow (1978), p. 54 (see note 19).

23 Talcott Parsons and R. F. Bales (1953), *Family Socialization and the Interaction Process*, Routledge and Kegan Paul, London.

24 Iain Craib (1987) (see note 21).

25 Tom Ryan (1985), 'Roots of Masculinity' in *The Sexuality of Men*, p. 15 (see note 3).

26 Ibid, p. 22.

27 Andy Moye (1985), 'Pornography' in *The Sexuality of Men*, p. 51 (see note 3).

28 Wendy Hollway (1983) 'Heterosexual Sex: Power and Desire for the Other' in *Sex and Love New Thoughts on Old Contradictions*, eds Sue Cartledge and Joanna Ryan, The Women's Press, London, p. 134.

29 S. Freud (1912d), 'On The Universal Tendency to Debasement in the Sphere Of Love' in Pelican Freud Library Vol. 7, p. 249.

30 Ibid, p. 251.

31 Jennifer Somerville (1989) 'The Sexuality of Men and the Sociology of Gender' in *Sociological Review*, Vol. 37, No. 2, p. 305.

32 Vic Seidler (1985), 'Fear and Intimacy' in *The Sexuality of Men*, p. 151 (see note 3).

33 Andy Moye op. cit., p. 69.

34 Michael Rustin (1982), 'A Socialist Consideration of Kleinian Psychoanalysis', *New Left Review*, No. 131.

35 S. Freud (1911c (1910)), 'Psychoanalytical Notes On An Autobiographical Account Of A Case Of Paranoia (Schreber)' in PFL Vol.9, p. 138.

36 Melanie Klein (1946), 'Notes on Some Schizoid Mechanisms' in *The Selected Melanie Klein*, ed. Juliet Mitchell (1986), Peregrine Books, London, p. 179.

37 Ibid, pp. 176–7.

38 Ibid, pp.97–8.

39 Melanie Klein (1940), 'Mourning and Manic Depressive States', p. 148 (see note 36).

40 S. Freud (1923), 'The Ego and the Id', PFL Vol. 11, p. 351.

41 S. Freud (1914c), 'On Narcissism: An Introduction', p. 84.

42 Richard Rorty (1989), *Contingency, Irony and Solidarity*, Cambridge University Press, Cambridge, p. 31.

43 Jane Flax (1990), *Thinking Fragments Psychoanalysis, Feminism, and Postmodernism in the Contemporary West*, University of California Press, Berkeley, p. 56.

44 S. Freud (1910c), 'Leonardo Da Vinci and a Memory of his Childhood' in PFL Vol.14, p. 231.

45 *Achilles Heel* made a re-appearance in 1989 and is now being produced by a small collective in London and Sheffield. They can be contacted at PO Box 142, Sheffield, S1 3HG.

46 Alan Neale, Malcolm Clarke and Will Locke (1983), Introduction: 'Why Men Against Sexism should be accountable to the WLM', *Anti-Sexist Men's Newsletter*, No. 18.

47 Will Locke (1983), ' "Anything you can do, we can do better" – a critique of the autonomous men's movement', op. cit.

48 An example of this 'tendency' was my enthusiasm for the Leeds Revolutionary Feminist publication *Love Thy Enemy* and its espousal of women's separatism.

49 This quote is attributed to Daniel Cohen, despite being familiar with it for many years I cannot find a reference for it.

50 The Editorial Collective (1986), 'A different kind of Page 3.' *Men's Anti-Sexist Newsletter*, No. 23.

51 Steve Mason (1986), 'Loving Me(n)', *MAS Newsletter*, No. 23.

52 Stu Cory (1986), 'Friendship', op. cit.

53 The Editorial in *Achilles Heel* (*circa* 1981), nos 6–7.

54 Jeff Hearn (1987), *The Gender of Oppression. Men, Masculinity and Marxism*, Wheatsheaf Books, Brighton.

3 DIFFERENCE COMES TO TOWN

1 Frank Mort (1986) 'Images Change', *New Socialist*, November Issue. See also Mort (1988), Suzanne Moore (1987a, 1987b, 1988), Shelagh Young (1988), Kennedy and Lyttle (1986), Mica Nava (1987).

2 Frank Mort, ibid.

3 Suzanne Moore (1987a),' New Meanings for New Markets' in *Women's Review*, No. 18, April issue.

4 Quote from J. Rutherford (1987), 'Mothercare Man', *London Daily News*, unpublished.

5 Angela Phillips (1990), 'Sins of the Fathers', *Guardian*, date not known.

6 This interest covered a wide spectrum of the media. Here are a few examples from print; Alkarim Jivani (1987), 'Men's Mags' in *Time Out*, November 4–11. Geraint Jones (1989), 'The Marshmallow Man', *Daily Mail*, 21 July. Oenone Williams (1986), 'Wise Women Marry Wimps' in *Good Housekeeping*, March issue. 'The Hunk Who Won't Drop his Trunks' in *Sun*, 3 January, 1989. Kay Batchelor (1985), 'The Male Identity Crisis', *Women's Journal*. J. Rutherford (1986) 'The Page Three connection', *Guardian* 27 March.

7 Davina Lloyd (1989), 'Whatever became of New Fathers?' *Practical Parenting*, November issue.

8 See J. Rutherford (1988) 'Who's That Man' in *Male Order Unwrapping Masculinity*, eds Rowena Chapman and Jonathan Rutherford, Lawrence and Wishart, London. Kathy Myers (1989) 'Its a Man's World', *Blitz* magazine.

9 Virginia Mathews (1987), 'Merely male in admen's markets', *Guardian* 30 Nov.

10 J. Rutherford (1987), Murray Partridge quoted in 'Images of Men', *London Daily News*, unpublished.

11 J. Rutherford (1987), interview with Kitty O'Hagen, ibid.

12 J. Rutherford (1988), interview with Linda Kelsey in 'Men Only', *New Society* 26 February.

13 J. Rutherford (1988), interview with Marcus Van Ackerman in 'Who's That Man?', op. cit.

14 J. Rutherford (1988), interview with Steve Taylor in 'Men Only' op. cit.

15 J. Rutherford (1989), '500 Men Confess' in *Cosmo Man*. Month not known.

16 Geoff Deane (1990), 'Man-Made for 30 Nothing' in *Options*, February issue.

17 Alex Morgan (1990), 'Idol Speculation', *Elle* magazine, April issue.

18 The event attracted 250 people and a fair amount of press interest with a report in *Today* and mentions in the *Observer*, *News On Sunday* and the *Sunday Mirror*. By attracting a diversity of speakers; Ken Livingstone, Lynne Segal, Brenda Polan of the *Guardian*, the film-maker Isaac Julien, Tom Crabtree of *Cosmopolitan* and men who had been involved in the original *Achilles Heel*, the event was able to present a broad and plural perspective on the issues and 'problems' of masculinity. The event revealed that after the demise of MAS in the early 1980s, there existed a continuing activity which had its roots in the sexual politics of the 1970s. There had also been the emergence of a new kind of men's sexual politics. Their differences were highlighted in the final plenary session. Kobena Mercer talking about race and black masculinity and Frank Mort talking about consumption and style brought a critical response from men who adhered to the

'men's movement'. The clash of languages and priorities revealed as much of a gulf as a shared set of interests between the two political sensibilities.

19 L. Lederer (1980), *Take Back the Night*, William Morrow.

20 John Stoltenburg (1990), *Refusing to be a Man*, Fontana, London, p. 121.

21 John Stoltenburg (1990), 'Pornography and Homophobia', unpublished address to the Opposing Pornography Conference for Men, held in Brixton, London, in September 1990.

22 John Stoltenburg (1990), *Refusing to be a Man*, pp. 128–9 (see note 20).

23 John Stoltenburg (1990), 'Pornography and Homophobia' (see note 21).

24 Peter Baker and Nicholas Martin (1990), 'You've got his body, where's his mind?' in *Cosmopolitan* magazine, March issue.

25 Peter Baker (1989), 'Real Gentle Men', *Company* magazine, December issue.

26 Michel Foucault (1984), *The History of Sexuality. An Introduction*, Peregrine Books, London, p. 59.

27 Ibid, p. 62.

28 Kobena Mercer (*circa* 1986),' Issues in Search of an Agenda. Racism and Sexual Politics', *Emergency* magazine, No. 4. See also its reprinting in Kobena Mercer and Isaac Julien (1988), 'Race, Sexual Politics and Black Masculinity: A Dossier' in *Male Order Unwrapping Masculinity* (see note 8).

29 Ibid.

30 Ibid.

31 Cynthia Cockburn (1981), 'The Material of Male Power', *Feminist Review*, Autumn issue.

32 See for example, Stuart Hall (1977), 'Rethinking the Base and Superstructure Metaphor' in *Papers on Class, Hegemony and Party*, ed. J. Bloomfield, Lawrence and Wishart, London. pp. 43–72.

33 Ernesto Laclau and Chantal Mouffe (1989), *Hegemony and Socialist Strategy*, Verso, London, p. 104.

34 Ibid, p. 105.

35 Lawrence Grossberg (1988), *It's a Sin. Postmodernism Politics and Culture*, Power Publications, Sydney, p. 37.

36 See Jacques Derrida (1981), 'Semiology and Grammatology', interview with Julia Kristeva in *Positions*, trans. Alan Bass, University of Chicago Press, US. pp.27–28.

37 Jeffrey Archer (*circa* 1987), quoted in 'People are Passionate About...' in *Cosmopolitan* magazine.

38 Jean-Paul Sartre (1985), 'The Hole' in *Existentialism and Human Emotions*, Citadel Press, New Jersey, p. 85.

39 Laclau and Mouffe (see note 33) p. 114.

40 Ibid, p. 110.

41 Jacques Lacan (1989), 'The Function and Field of Speech and Language in Psychoanalysis' in *Écrits A Selection*, Tavistock/Routledge, London.

42 For an Introduction to Lacan's thought see; Bice Bienvenuto and

Roger Kennedy (1986), *The Works of Jacques Lacan*, Free Association Books, London.

43 The discourse of sexual difference theory emerged through a number of journals. See, for example; *Screen* magazine, Vol.28, No. 1, Winter 1987. *mf journal*, The Sexuality Issue, Nos. 5–6, 1981. *Oxford Literary Review*, Sexual Difference Issue, Vol.8, Nos 1–2, 1986.

44 Teresa de Lauretis (1987), 'The Technology of Gender' in *Technologies of Gender. Essays on Theory Film and Fiction*, Indiana University Press, p. 3.

45 Mary Kelly (1987), 'On Representation Sexuality and Sameness. Reflections on the Difference Show', *Screen*, Vol.28, No. 1.

46 Robert M. Young (1989), 'Postmodernism and the Subject: Pessimism of the Will', *Free Association*, No. 16.

47 Steve Neale (1983), 'Masculinity as Spectacle', *Screen*, Vol.24, No. 6, Nov.–Dec. issue.

48 Jane Flax (1990), *Thinking Fragments Psychoanalysis, Feminism, and Postmodernism in the Contemporary West*, University of California Press, Berkeley, p. 92.

49 Peter Middleton (1989) 'Socialism Feminism and Men', *Radical Philosophy*, No. 53.

50 Max Farrar (1989), 'The Libertarian Movements of the 1970s. What can we learn', *Edinburgh Review*, No. 82.

4 SILENCE, LANGUAGE AND PSYCHOANALYSIS

1 Ernesto Laclau and Chantal Mouffe (1989), *Hegemony and Socialist Strategy*, Verso, London, p. 111.

2 Ludwig Wittgenstein (1988), *Philosophical Investigations*, Basil Blackwell, London, paragraph 2.

3 Ibid, p. 23.

4 Ibid, p. 244.

5 Ibid, p. 342.

6 Ibid, p. 367.

7 Ibid, p. 288.

8 Ibid, p. 288.

9 Ibid, p. 269.

10 Ibid, p. 38.

11 Ibid, p. 38.

12 S. Freud (1920), 'Beyond the Pleasure Principle' in Pelican Freud Library Vol.11, p. 284.

13 S. Freud (1925), 'Negation' in PFL Vol.11, p. 437.

14 Christopher Bollas (1987), *The Shadow of the Object: Psychoanalysis of the Unthought Known*, Free Association Books, London, p. 3.

15 Hanna Segal (1991), *Dream, Phantasy and Art*, Tavistock/Routledge, London, p. 35.

16 Ibid, p. 40.

17 Wilfred Bion (1990), 'A Theory of Thinking' in *Second Thoughts*, Maresfield Press, London, p. 116.

18 Wilfred Bion (1970), *Attention and Interpretation*, Tavistock Publications, London.

19 Hanna Segal (1978), 'On Symbolism', *International Journal of Psychoanalysis*, No. 59, p. 318.

20 Wilfred Bion (1970) p. 94 (see note 18).

21 André Green (1986), 'The Analyst, Symbolization and Absence in the Analytic Setting' in *On Private Madness*, Hogarth Press, London, p. 45.

22 D.W. Winnicott (1960), 'The Theory of the Parent–Infant Relationship', in *International Journal of Psychoanalysis*, 41, pp. 585–95.

23 D.W. Winnicott (1988), 'The Use of an Object' in *Playing and Reality*, Pelican, London, p. 105–6.

24 D.W. Winnicott (1988), 'Transitional Objects and Transitional Phenomena', op. cit., p. 23.

25 D.W. Winnicott (1988), 'The Location of Cultural Experience', op. cit., p. 113.

26 D.W. Winnicott (1988), 'Transitional Objects and Transitional Phenomena', op. cit., p. 14.

27 D.W. Winnicott (1988), 'The Location of Cultural Experience', op. cit., p. 115.

28 Ibid.

29 André Green (1986), 'The Analyst, Symbolization and Absence in the Analytic Setting', p. 47 (see note 21).

30 André Green (1986), 'Negation and Contradiction', p. 260 (see note 21).

31 Freud (1915c), 'Instincts and their Vicissitudes' in PFL Vol.11, p. 118.

32 D.W. Winnicott (1988), 'The Location of Cultural Experience', p. 114 (see note 22).

33 D.W. Winnicott (1988), 'Fear of Breakdown', in *The British School of Psychoanalysis. The Independent Tradition*, Free Association Books, London, p. 176.

34 D.W. Winnicott (1988), 'The Location of Cultural Experience', op. cit., p. 115 (see note 22).

35 D.W. Winnicott (1965), 'The Capacity to be Alone' in *The Maturational Process and the Facilitating Enviroment*, Hogarth Press, London.

36 D.W. Winnicott (1986), *Holding and Interpretation: Fragment of an Analysis*, Hogarth Press, London, pp.19–20.

37 André Green (1986), 'The Borderline Concept', p. 82 (see note 21).

38 Christopher Bollas (1987), p. 3 (see note 14).

39 D.W. Winnicott (1988), 'Transitional Objects and Transitional Phenomena', p. 28 (see note 22).

40 Interview with André Green in Anne Clancier and Jeannine Kalmanovitch (1987), *Winnicott and Paradox. from Birth to Creation*, Tavistock, London, pp.123–4.

41 For a discussion of object love see Freud (1914c), 'On Narcissism: An Introduction' in PFL Vol.11, pp. 81–4. And Freud (1921), 'Group Psychology and the Analysis of the Ego' in PFL Vol.12, pp.134–47.

42 S. Freud (1925j), 'Some Psychical Consequences of the Anatomical Distinction Between the Sexes' in PFL Vol.7, p. 341.

43 S. Freud (1923b), 'The Ego and the Id' in PFL Vol.11, p. 371.

44 Ibid.

45 Juliet Mitchell (1984), 'On Freud and the Distinction Between the Sexes' in *Women: The Longest Revolution Essays in Feminism, Literature and Psychoanalysis*, Virago, London, pp.231–2.

46 Ibid.

47 Jon Schiller (1981), 'The New "Family Romance"', *Triquarterly*, No. 52.

48 Ibid.

49 Melanie Klein (1928), 'The Early Stages of the Oedipus Complex' in *The Selected Melanie Klein*, ed. Juliet Mitchell (1988), Penguin, London.

50 Jane Flax (1990), pp.78–9.

51 Jon Schiller (1981) (see note 45).

52 Interview with André Green in Clancier and Kalmanovitch (1987).

53 André Green (1986), 'The Analyst Symbolization and Absence in the Analytic Setting', pp.32–3, and 33–4 (see note 21).

54 See, for example, John Tosh's discussion on the sons of Thomas Carlisle in Michael Roper and John Tosh (eds) *Manful Assertions Masculinities in Britain Since 1800* (1991), Routledge, London.

55 Nancy Chodorow (1978), *The Reproduction of Mothering Psychoanalysis and the Sociology of Gender*, University of California Press, Berkeley, p. 105.

56 Melanie Klein (1928) 'Early Stages of the Oedipus Complex', p. 75 (see note 47).

5 NOSTALGIA

1 André Green (1986), 'The Dead Mother' in *On Private Madness*, Hogarth Press, London, p. 142.

2 Alice Jardine (1985), *Gynesis Configurations of Woman in Modernity*, Cornell University Press, p. 68.

3 Melanie Klein (1935), 'The Psychogenesis of Manic Depressive States' in *The Selected Melanie Klein* (1988), ed. Juliet Mitchell, Penguin, London, p. 121.

4 S. Freud (1917e (1915)), 'Mourning and Melancholia' in PFL Vol.11, p. 258.

5 D.W. Winnicott (1988), 'Transitional Objects and Transitional Phenomena' in *Playing and Reality*, Pelican, London, p. 27.

6 Melanie Klein (1935), p. 132 (see note 3).

7 Robert Hewison (1987), *The Heritage Industry Britain in a Climate of Decline*, Methuen, London.

8 S. Freud (1920g), 'Beyond the Pleasure Principle' in PFL Vol.11, p. 308.

9 Saul Bellow (1987), 'The Moronic Inferno' in *Voices. Modernity and its Discontents*, eds B. Bourne, U. Eichler and D. Herman, Spokesman Books, London, pp. 11–12.

10 Alice Jardine (1985), *Gynesis Configurations of Woman in Modernity*, Cornell University Press, pp.72–3.

11 Ibid, p. 73.

12 D.W. Winnicott (1988), 'The Location of Cultural Experience', p. 112 (see note 5).
13 Kraft Wetzel (1989) speaking in the documentary film on Wim Wenders, *Motion Emotion*, directed by Paul Joyce, Lucida Productions.
14 S. Freud (1910h),' A Special Type of Choice of Object Made by Men' in PFL Vol.7, p. 231.
15 Ibid.
16 Melanie Klein (1956) 'A Study of Envy and Gratitude', op. cit., p. 218.

6 'THIRDNESS' AND THE FATHER'S LOVE

1 Duane Michals, taken from a private print. See also Duane Michals (1985), *Photographs/Sequences/Texts 1958–1984*, Museum of Modern Art, Oxford.
2 S. Freud (1909b), 'Analysis of a Phobia in a Five-Year-Old Boy ('Little Hans')' in PFL Vol.8, p. 190.
3 Ibid, p. 209.
4 Ibid, p. 204.
5 Jacques Lacan (1989), 'The Signification of the Phallus' in *Écrits A Selection*, Routledge, London, p. 287.
6 Ibid, p. 290.
7 Ibid, p. 288.
8 S. Freud (1919h), 'The Uncanny' in PFL Vol.14, p. 358.
9 S. Freud (1923b),' The Ego and the Id' in PFL Vol.11, p. 370.
10 Ibid, see footnote.
11 André Green (1986) 'The Dead Mother' in *On Private Madness*, Hogarth Press, London, p. 147.
12 S. Freud (1930a), 'Civilisation and its Discontents' in PFL Vol.12, p. 260.
13 Christopher Bollas (1989), *Forces of Destiny Psychoanalysis and the Human Idiom*, Free Association Books, London, p. 41.
14 S. Freud (1919h), 'The Uncanny' in PFL Vol.14, p. 340.
15 Ibid, p. 358.
16 Julia Kristeva (1982), *An Essay on Abjection*, trans. Leon S. Roudiez, Columbia University Press, New York. pp. 12–13.
17 Ibid, p. 2.
18 S. Freud (1919h), p. 358.
19 Ibid, p. 359.
20 Ibid, p. 368.
21 S. Freud (1930a), p. 255 (see note 12).
22 Ibid, p. 253.
23 S. Freud (1927c), 'The Future of an Illusion' in PFL Vol.12, p. 212.
24 Jacques Lacan (1989), 'The Subversion of the Subject and the Dialectic of Desire in the Freudian Unconscious' in *Écrits A Selection*, Routledge, London, p. 324.
25 S. Freud (1919e) 'A Child is being Beaten', in PFL Vol.10, p. 187.
26 S. Freud (1924c), 'The Economic Problem of Masochism' in PFL Vol.11, p. 424.

27 S. Freud (1919e), p. 187 (see note 25).
28 S. Freud (1923b), op. cit., p. 374.
29 S. Freud (1924c), op. cit., p. 425.
30 S. Freud (1914c),' On Narcissism: An Introduction' in PFL Vol.11, p. 68.
31 Ibid, p. 93.
32 S. Freud (1923b), op. cit., p. 400.

7 VIOLENCE AND MASCULINE IDENTITIES

1 Susan Jeffords (1988), 'Debriding Vietnam' in *Feminist Studies*, Vol.14, No. 3, p. 536.
2 Ibid, p. 534.
3 A.N. Wilson (1987), 'Yesterday, Something Uniquely English Died Too' in the *Daily Mail*, 20 August.
4 Report of Prince Charles's Speech at the opening of the Museum of the Moving Image in the *Daily Mail*, Friday 16 September, 1988.
5 Report of Douglas Hurd's Speech to Tory Party workers in Lancaster in the *Daily Mail*, 20 September 1988.
6 Alexander Chancellor (1988), 'On Blood Lust and Barbarities' in the *Independent Magazine*, 17 September.
7 A.N. Wilson op. cit. (see note 3).
8 Ed Vulliamy (1985), 'Live by Aggro, Die by Aggro' in *New Statesman*, 7 June.
9 Anthony Burgess (1988), 'Criminality by Clockwork' in the *Independent*, 27 August.
10 Patricia Morgan (1986), 'Feminist Attempts to Sack Father: A Case of Unfair Dismissal' in *Family Portraits*, eds Digby Anderson and Graham Dawson, Social Affairs Unit, London.
11 Richard Rorty (1989), 'Private Irony and Liberal Hope' in *Contingency, Irony and Solidarity*, Cambridge University Press, Cambridge, UK, p. 89.
12 S. Freud (1914c), 'On Narcissism: An Introduction' in PFL Vol.11, p. 88.
13 S. Freud (1911c), 'On the Mechanisms of Paranoia' in 'The Schreber Case' in PFL Vol.9, p. 197.
14 Ibid, pp. 208–9.
15 Ibid, p. 200.
16 Ibid, p. 201.
17 Melanie Klein (1946), 'Notes on Some Schizoid Mechanisms' in *The Selected Melanie Klein*, ed. Juliet Mitchell (1988), Penguin, London, p. 199.
18 S. Freud (1923b), 'The Ego and the Id' in PFL Vol.11, p. 364.
19 Esther Bick (1986), 'Further Considerations of the Function of the Skin in Early Object Relations', *British Journal of Psychoanalysis*, No. 2, pp. 292–9.
20 Frances Tustin (1981), *Autistic States in Children*, Routledge and Kegan Paul, London, p. 100.

21 André Green (1986) 'The Dead Mother' in *On Private Madness*, Hogarth Press, London, p. 154.
22 Frances Tustin (1989), 'Omnipotence as a Protective Reaction' a discussion with Robert Olin in *Winnicott Studies*, The Journal of the Squiggle Foundation, No. 4, p. 43.
23 Marion Milner (1989), 'Autistic Areas in All of Us?' in *Winnicott Studies*, No.4, p. 9.
24 André Green (1986), p. 156 (see note 21).
25 A. N. Wilson (1987) (see note 3).
26 *Daily Mail* 21 August 1987.
27 *Daily Telegraph* 21 August 1987.
28 *Sun* 27 August 1987.

AFTERWORD

1 Traditional song by Van Morrison (1987), 'Sometimes I feel like a motherless child', on *Poetic Champions Compose*, Essential Music.
2 Mike Roper and John Tosh eds (1991), 'Introduction' in *Manful Assertions: Masculinities in Britain Since 1800*, Routledge, London, p. 17.
3 André Green (1986), 'Potential Space in Psychoanalysis' in *On Private Madness*, Hogarth Press, London, p. 293.
4 Melanie Klein (1935), 'A Contribution to the Psychogenesis of Manic Depressive States' in *The Selected Melanie Klein*, ed. Juliet Mitchell (1988), Peregrine Books, London.
5 D.W. Winnicott (1988), 'The Location of Cultural Experience' in *Playing and Reality*, Pelican Books, London, p. 117.

BIBLIOGRAPHY

Althusser, Louis (1971), 'Ideology and Ideological State Apparatuses' in *Lenin and Philosophy*, Monthly Review Press, London.
—— (1977), 'Contradiction and Overdetermination' in *For Marx*, New Left Books, London.
Althusser, Louis and Balibar, Etienne (1972), *Reading Capital*, New Left Books, London.
Atkinson, Paul (1979), 'The Problem with Patriarchy', *Achilles Heel*, No. 2.
Baker, Peter (1990), 'Loose Talk; What Men Really Feel About Their Emotions' in *Company*, February issue.
—— (1990), 'You've Got His Body, Where's His Mind?' in *Cosmopolitan*, March issue.
Baker, Peter and Martin, Nicholas (1989), 'Real Gentle Men' in *Company*, December issue.
Balint, M. (1956), 'Pleasure, Object and Libido. Some Reflections on Fairbairn's Modifications on Psychoanalytic Theory' in *The British Journal of Medical Psychology*, Vol. 29, pp. 162–167.
Battersby, Christine (1989), *Gender and Genius. Towards a Feminist Aesthetics*, The Women's Press, London.
Bauman, Zygmunt (1982), *Memories of Class Prehistory and Afterlife of Class*, Routledge, London.
Beail, Nigel and McGuire, Jacqueline (1982), *Fathers' Psychological Perspectives*, Junction Books, London.
Behar, Henri (1990), 'Painting By Numbers' Interview with Sylvester Stallone, *Empire*, January issue.
Benjamin, Jessica (1978), 'Authority and the Family Revisited: or, A World Without Fathers?' *New German Critique*, Winter issue.
Bick, Esther (1968) 'The experience of the Skin in Early Object Relations', in Bott Spillus ed. (1988) *Melanie Klein Today: Development in Theory and Practice, Volume 1, Mainly Theory*, Hogarth Press, London.
—— (1986), 'Further Considerations of the Function of the Skin in Early Object Relations', *British Journal of Psychoanalysis*, No. 2.
Bienvenuto, Bice and Kennedy, Roger (1986), *The Works of Jacques Lacan An Introduction*, Free Association Books, London.

Bion, Wilfred (1970), *Attention and Interpretation*, Tavistock Publications, London.

—— (1986), *The Long Weekend 1897–1919*, Free Association Books, London.

—— (1990), 'Differentiation of the Psychotic from the Non-psychotic Personalities' in *Second Thoughts*, Maresfield Library, London.

—— (1990), 'Attacks on Linking', in *Second Thoughts*, Maresfield Library, London.

—— (1990), 'A Theory of Thinking', in *Second Thoughts*, Maresfield Library, London.

Bollas, Christopher (1987), *The Shadow of the Object: Psychoanalysis of the Unthought Known*, Free Association Books, London.

—— (1989), *Forces of Destiny Psychoanalysis and Human Idiom*, Free Association Books, London.

Bourdieu, Pierre (1986), *Distinction. A Social Critique of the Judgement of Taste*, Routledge and Kegan Paul, London.

Bradbury, Peter (*c.* 1980), 'Sexuality and Male Violence' in *Achilles Heel*, No. 5.

Brantlinger, Patrick (1990), *Crusoe's Footprints: Cultural Studies in Britain and America*, Routledge, London.

Bristow, Joseph (1988), 'How Men Are: Speaking of Masculinity' in *New Formations*, No. 6, Routledge, London.

Brownmiller, Susan (1976), *Against Our Will*, Penguin, London.

Burgin, Victor (1984), 'Man Desire Image' in *ICA Document on Desire*, ICA, London.

Carmichael, Nicole, 'New Decade, New Man?' in *Girl About Town*, January issue.

Carrigan, Tim, Connell, Bob and Lee, John (1985), 'Toward a New Sociology of Masculinity' in *Theory and Society* 14.

Chapman, Rowena and Rutherford, Jonathan (eds) (1988), *Male Order Unwrapping Masculinity*, Lawrence and Wishart, London.

Chodorow, Nancy (1978), *The Reproduction of Mothering Psychoanalysis and the Sociology of Gender*, University of California Press, Berkeley.

Clancier, Anne and Kalmanovitch, Jeannine (1987), *Winnicott and Paradox. From Birth to Creation*, trans. Alan Sheridan, Tavistock Publications, London.

Cockburn, Cynthia (1981), 'The Material of Male Power' in *Feminist Review*, Autumn issue.

—— (1985), *Machinery of Dominance. Women, Men and Technical Knowhow*, Pluto Press, London.

Connell, R.W. (1987), *Gender and Power*, Polity Press, Cambridge.

Cook, Jon (1988), 'Fictional Fathers' in *Sweet Dreams. Sexuality, Gender and Popular Fiction*, ed. Susannah Radstone, Lawrence and Wishart, London.

Cooper, Mick (1990), *Searching for the Anti-sexist Man, A History of the Men's Movement*, Achilles Heel Publication, London.

Craib, Iain (1987), 'Masculinity and Male Dominance' in *Sociological Review*, Routledge and Kegan Paul, London.

Creed, Barbera (1986), 'Horror and the Monstrous-Feminine – an Imaginary Abjection' in *Screen*, Vol. 27, No. 1, Jan–Feb.

Crisp, Tony (1989/90), 'On Being a Man: Modern Man in Search of a Role', *i to i*, Winter issue.

Deane, Geoff (1990), 'Man-Made for 30 Nothing' in *Options*, February issue.

Derrida, Jacques (1981), *Positions*, trans. Alan Bass, University of Chicago Press.

Dinnerstein, Dorothy (1976), *The Rocking of the Cradle and the Ruling of the World*, The Women's Press, London.

Dworkin, Andrea (1981), *Pornography Men Possessing Women*, Women's Press, London.

Dyer, Richard (1985), 'Male Sexuality in the Media' in *The Sexuality of Men*, eds Andy Metcalf and Martin Humphries, Pluto Press, London.

—— (1989), 'Don't Look Now' in *New Statesman and Society*, 8 June.

Easthope, Anthony (1986), *What a Man's Gotta Do, The Masculine Myth in Popular Culture*, Paladin, London.

Ehrenreich, Barbera and English, Deirdre (1979), *For Her Own Good: 150 Years of the Experts' Advice to Women*, Doubleday/Anchor Press, New York.

Eichenbaum, Louise and Orbach, Susie (1982), *Outside In, Inside Out*, Penguin, Harmondsworth.

—— (1984), *What Do Women Want?*, Fontana, London.

Everywoman (1988), *Pornography and Sexual Violence, Evidence of the Links*, Everywoman, London.

Fairbairn, Ronald (1952), *Psychoanalytic Studies of the Personality*, Tavistock Publications, London.

Fell, Allison (1984), *Every Move You Make*, Virago, London.

Finlay, Marike (1989), 'Post-Modernizing Psychoanalysis/Psycho-analyzing Post-Modernity', *Free Associations*, No. 16.

Flax, Jane (1990), *Thinking Fragments Psychoanalysis, Feminism and Postmodernism in the Contemporary West*, University of California Press, Berkeley.

Ford, Anna (1986), *Men*, Corgi Books, London.

Forgacs, David (ed.) (1988), *A Gramsci Reader*, Lawrence and Wishart, London.

Foster, Alistair (and Mcgrath, Roberta) (1988), *Behold the Man. The Male Nude in Photography*, Stills Gallery, Edinburgh.

Foucault, Michel (1984), *The History of Sexuality. An Introduction*, Peregrine Books, London.

Freud, Sigmund (1900a), 'The Interpretation of Dreams', Pelican Freud Library, Vol. 4.

—— (1905c), 'Jokes and their Relation to the Unconscious', PFL Vol. 6.

—— (1909b), 'Analysis of a Phobia in a Five-Year-Old Boy ('Little Hans')', PFL Vol. 8.

—— (1909c), 'Family Romances', PFL Vol. 7.

—— (1910c), 'Leonardo da Vinci and a Memory of his Childhood', PFL Vol. 14.

—— (1910h), 'A Special Type of Object Choice Made by Men', PFL Vol. 7.

—— (1911c (1910)), 'Psycho-Analytic Notes on an Autobiographical Account of a Case of Paranoia (Dementia Paranoides)', PFL Vol. 9.

—— (1912d), 'On the Universal Tendency to Debasement in the Sphere of Love', PFL Vol. 7.

—— (1914c), 'On Narcissism: An Introduction', PFL Vol. 11.

—— (1915c), 'Instincts and their Vicissitudes', PFL Vol. 11.

—— (1915e), 'The Unconscious', PFL Vol. 11.

—— (1916 (1915–17)), 'Dreams', PFL Vol. 1.

—— (1917e (1915)), 'Mourning and Melancholia', PFL Vol. 11.

—— (1918b (1914)), 'From the History of an Infantile Neurosis (The 'Wolf Man')', PFL Vol. 9.

—— (1919e), 'A Child is being Beaten', PFL Vol. 10.

—— (1919h), 'The Uncanny', PFL Vol. 14.

—— (1920g), 'Beyond the Pleasure Principle', PFL Vol. 11.

—— (1921c), 'Group Psychology and the Analysis of the Ego', PFL Vol. 12.

—— (1923b), 'The Ego and the Id', PFL Vol. 11.

—— (1924c), 'The Economic Problem of Masochism', PFL Vol. 11.

—— (1924d) 'The Dissolution of the Oedipus Complex', PFL Vol. 7.

—— (1925a), 'A Note upon the "Mystic Writing Pad" ', PFL Vol. 11.

—— (1925h), 'Negation', PFL Vol. 11.

—— (1925j), 'Some Psychical Consequences of the Anatomical Distinction between the Sexes', PFL Vol. 7.

—— (1926d (1925)), 'Inhibitions, Symptoms and Anxiety', PFL Vol. 10.

—— (1927c), 'The Future of an Illusion', PFL Vol. 12.

—— (1930a), 'Civilization and its Discontents', PFL Vol. 12.

—— (1931b), 'Female Sexuality', PFL Vol. 7.

—— (1940e (1938)), 'Splitting of the Ego in the Process of Defence', PFL Vol. 11.

Friedman, Scarlet and Sarah, Elizabeth (1982), *On the Problem of Men*, The Women's Press, London.

Fromm, Erich (1971), *The Crisis of Psychoanalysis*, Jonathan Cape, London.

Giddens, Anthony (1974), *The Class Structure of the Advanced Societies*, Hutchinson, London.

Gouldner, Alvin W. (1979), *The Future of Intellectuals and the Rise of the New Class*, Macmillan Press, London.

Grayling. A. C (1988), *Wittgenstein*, Oxford University Press, Oxford.

Green, André (1986), 'The Analyst, Symbolization and Absence in the Analytic Setting' in *On Private Madness*, Hogarth Press, London.

—— 'The Borderline Concept', in *On Private Madness*, Hogarth Press, London.

—— 'The Dead Mother', in *On Private Madness*, Hogarth Press, London.

—— 'Negation and Contradiction', in *On Private Madness*, Hogarth Press, London.

—— 'Potential Space in Psychoanalysis', in *On Private Madness*, Hogarth Press, London.

—— 'The Double and the Absent', in *On Private Madness*, Hogarth Press, London.

Griffin, Susan (1982), *Made From the Earth. Selections from her Writings*, Women's Press, London.

Gross, Elizabeth (1990), 'The Body of Signification' in *Abject Melancholia and Love.The Work of Julia Kristeva*, eds John Fletcher and Andrew Benjamin, Routledge, London.

Grossberg, Lawrence (1988), *It's a Sin. Postmodernism Politics and Culture*, Power Publications, Sydney.

Hall, Donald (1979), *A Choice of Whitman's Verse*, Faber and Faber, London.

Hall, Stuart (1977), 'Rethinking the Base and Superstructure Metaphor' in *Papers on Class Hegemony and Party*, ed. Jon Bloomfield, Lawrence and Wishart, London, pp.43–72.

—— (1990), 'The Emergence of Cultural Studies and the Crisis of the Humanities', *October*, Summer issue.

Harding, David (1982), 'Inner Lives, Therapy, Men and the Men's Movement. An Interview with Paul Atkinson', *Revolutionary Socialism*, Big Flame, No. 10.

Hearn, Jeff (1987), *The Gender of Oppression. Men, Masculinity and the Critique of Marxism*, Wheatsheaf Books, Brighton.

Heath, Stephen (1987), 'Male Feminism' in *Men in Feminism*, eds Alice Jardine and Paul Smith, Methuen, London.

Henwood, Melanie, Rimmer, Lesley and Wicks, Malcolm (1987), *Inside the Family: Changing Roles of Men and Women*, Family Policy Studies Centre, London.

Hewison, Robert (1987), *The Heritage Industry Britain in a Climate of Decline*, Methuen, London.

Hinshelwood, R.D. (1991), *A Dictionary of Kleinian Thought*, Free Association Books, London.

Hodson, Phillip (1984), *Men*, Ariel Books, London.

Hollway, Wendy (1983), 'Heterosexual Sex: Power and Desire for the Other', in *Sex and Love, New Thoughts on Old Contradictions*, eds Sue Cartledge and Joanna Ryan, Women's Press, London.

Horkheimer, Max (1936), 'Authority and the Family' in *Critical Theory* (1972), Herder and Herder, New York.

Itzin, Catherine and Sweet, Corinne (1990), 'What You Feel About Pornography', *Cosmopolitan*, March issue.

James, Martin (1988), 'Premature Ego Development: Some Observations on Disturbances in the First Three Months of Life' in *The British School of Psychoanalysis. The Independent Tradition*, ed. Gregor Kohon, Free Association Books, London.

Jardine, Alice (1985), *Gynesis Configurations of Woman in Modernity*, Cornell University Press, New York.

Jardine, Alice and Smith, Paul (1987), *Men in Feminism*, Methuen, London.

Jay, Martin (1984), *Marxism and Totality*, Polity Press, London.

Jeffords, Susan (1988), 'Debriding Vietnam: The Resurrection of the White American Male', *Feminist Studies*, Vol. 14, No. 3, Winter.

Kennedy, Britan and Lyttle, John (1986), 'Wolf in Chic Clothing', *City Limits*, 4–11 December.

Kerr, Susan (1989), 'A Dad is Born', *Practical Parenting*, November issue.

Klein, Melanie (1926), 'The Psychological Principles of Early Analysis', *International Journal of Psychoanalysis*, No. 8, pp. 25–37.
—— (1928), 'Early Stages of the Oedipus Complex' in *The Selected Melanie Klein*, ed. Juliet Mitchell, Penguin, London.
—— (1930), 'The Importance of Symbol Formation in the Development of the Ego', in *The Selected Melanie Klein*, ed. Juliet Mitchell, Penguin, London.
—— (1935), 'A Contribution to the Psychogenesis of Manic-Depressive States', in *The Selected Melanie Klein*, ed. Juliet Mitchell, Penguin, London.
—— (1940) 'Mourning and Its Relations to Manic-Depressive States', in *The Selected Melanie Klein*, ed. Juliet Mitchell, Penguin, London.
—— (1946), 'Notes on Some Schizoid Mechanisms', in *The Selected Melanie Klein*, ed. Juliet Mitchell, Penguin, London.
—— (1956), 'A Study of Envy and Gratitude' in *The Selected Melanie Klein*, ed. Juliet Mitchell, Penguin, London.
—— (1986), *The Psychoanalysis of Children*, trans. Alix Strachey, The Hogarth Press, London.
Kohon, Gregorio (ed.) (1988), *The British School of Psychoanalysis. The Independent Tradition*, Free Association Press, London.
Kristeva, Julia (1982), *An Essay on Abjection*, trans. Leon S. Roudiez, Columbia University Press, New York.
Lacan, Jacques (1949), 'The Mirror Stage as Formative of the Function of I as Revealed in Psychoanalytic Experience' in *Écrits. A Selection* (1980), Tavistock/Routledge, London.
—— (1953), 'The Function and Field of Speech and Language in Psychoanalysis' in *Écrits. A Selection* (1980), Tavistock/Routledge, London.
—— (1958), 'The Signification of the Phallus', in *Écrits. A Selection* (1980), Tavistock/Routledge, London.
—— (1989 (1960)), 'The Subversion of the Subject and the Dialectic of Desire in the Freudian Unconscious', in *Écrits. A Selection* (1980), Tavistock/Routledge, London.
Laclau, Ernesto and Mouffe, Chantal (1989), *Hegemony and Socialist Strategy*, Verso, London.
Laing, R.D. (1967), *The Politics of Experience and The Bird of Paradise*, Penguin, London.
—— (1971), *The Politics of the Family*, Tavistock, London.
Lederer, L. (1980), *Take Back the Night*, William Morrow.
Lévi-Strauss, Claude (1983), *The Savage Mind*, Weidenfeld and Nicolson, London.
Lloyd, Davinia (1989), 'Whatever Became of New Fathers?', *Practical Parenting*, November issue.
Lyotard, Jean François (1987), *The Postmodern Condition: A Report on Knowledge*, Manchester University Press, Manchester.
McKee, Lorna and O'Brien, Margaret, eds (1982), *The Father Figure*, Tavistock, London.
Marcuse, Herbert (1970), *5ive Lectures*, Allen Lane/Penguin, London.

Meltzer, Donald (1975), 'Adhesive Identification', *Contemporary Psychoanalysis II*.

Mercer, Kobena (1986), 'Review Article', *Emergency*, No.4.

Mercer, Kobena and Julien, Isaac (1988), 'Race Sexual Politics and Black Masculinity' in *Male Order Unwrapping Masculinity*, eds Rowena Chapman and Jonathan Rutherford, Lawrence and Wishart, London.

Middleton, Peter (1986), 'Wittgenstein and the Question of Masculinity', *Oxford Literary Review*, Sexual Difference Issue, Vol. 8, Nos 1–2.

—— (1989), 'Why Structure Feeling', *News From Nowhere*, No. 6.

—— (1989), 'Socialism, Feminism and Men', *Radical Philosophy*, No. 53.

Milner, Marion (1989), 'Autistic Areas in All of Us' in *Winnicott Studies* No. 4, The Squiggle Foundation, London.

Mitchell, Juliet (1974), *Psychoanalysis and Feminism*, Pelican Books, London.

—— (1984), *Women: The Longest Revolution Essays in Feminism, Literature and Psychoanalysis*, Virago, London.

—— (1988), 'The question of femininity and the theory of psychoanalysis' in *The British School of Psychoanalysis. The Independent Tradition*, ed. G. Kohon, Free Association Press, London.

Mitscherlich, Alexander (1963), *Society Without the Father: A Contribution to Social Psychology*, Schocken Books, New York.

Moore, Suzanne (1986), 'Fathers '86. Playboys or Mothercare Men?', *Women's Review*, No. 12.

—— (1987a), 'New Meanings for New Markets', *Women's Review*, Issue 18, April.

—— (1987b), 'Target Man', *New Socialist*, January issue.

—— (1988), 'Here's Looking at You Kid!' in *The Female Gaze*, eds Lorraine Gammon and Margaret Marshment, Women's Press, London.

Morgan, Alex (1990), 'Idol Speculation', *Elle*, April issue.

Morgan, Patricia (1986), 'Feminist Attempts to Sack Father: A Case of Unfair Dismissal?' in *Family Portraits*, eds Digby Anderson and Graham Dawson, The Social Affairs Unit, London.

Mort, Frank (1986), 'Images Change', *New Socialist*, No. 43.

—— (1988), 'Boys Own? Masculinity, Style and Popular Culture' in *Male Order Unwrapping Masculinity*, eds Rowena Chapman and Jonathan Rutherford, Lawrence and Wishart, London.

Mulvey, Laura (1987), 'Changes. On Myth, Narrative and Historical Experience', *History Workshop Journal*, No. 23, Spring.

Myers, Kathy (1989), 'It's a Man's World', *Blitz*, month not known.

Nava, Mica (1987), 'Consumerism and its Contradictions' in *Cultural Studies*, Vol. 1, No. 2.

Neale, Steve (1983), 'Masculinity As Spectacle', *Screen*, No. 24, Vol. 6, Nov.–Dec.

O'Shaughnessy, Edna (1988), 'W. R. Bion's Theory of Thinking and New Techniques in Child Analysis', in *Melanie Klein Today*, ed. Elizabeth Bott Spillius, Routledge, London.

Padel, John (1988), 'Ego in Current Thinking', in *The British School of Psychoanalysis. The Independent Tradition*, ed. G. Kohon, Free Association Press, London.

Parsons, Talcott and Bales, R. F (1953), *Family Socialization and the Interaction Process*, Routledge and Kegan Paul, London.

Pfiel, Fred (1988), 'Postmodernism as a "Structure of Feeling"' in *Marxism and the Interpretation of Culture*, eds Cary Nelson and Lawrence Grossberg, Methuen, London.

Phillips, Adam (1988), *Winnicott*, Fontana, London.

Plaza, Monica (1982), 'The Mother/The Same. Hatred of the Mother in Psychoanalysis', *Feminist Issues*, Spring issue, USA.

Propp, V.I. (1968), *Morphology of the Folktale*, University of Texas Press, Dallas.

Red Therapy (1978), *Red Therapy*, London.

Riley, Denise (1983), *War in the Nursery: Theories of the Child and Mother*, Virago, London.

Roberts, Yvonne (1988), 'Just When You Thought You Knew All About Men', *New Women*, August issue.

Rogerson, Gillian and Wilson, Elizabeth (eds) (1991), *Pornography and Feminism. The Case Against Censorship*, Lawrence and Wishart, London.

Roper, Michael and Tosh, John (eds) (1991), *Manful Assertions Masculinities in Britain Since 1800*, Routledge, London.

Rorty, Richard (1989), *Contingency, Irony and Solidarity*, Cambridge University Press, Cambridge.

Rowbotham, Sheila (1989), *The Past is Before Us*, Penguin, London.

Rutherford, Jonathan (1983), 'Masculinity: Fear and Wanting', *Anti-sexist Anti-Patriarchy Newsletter*, No. 16.

—— (1987) 'Why Men Divide Women into Madonnas and Whores', *Cosmopolitan*.

—— (1987a), 'Grappling with Male Violence', *Cosmopolitan*.

—— (1987b) 'I Want Something That We Men Have No Language to Describe . . .', *Women's Journal*.

—— (1988), 'Men Only', *New Society*, 26 February.

—— (1989), '500 Men Confess', *Cosmo Man*.

Scarr, Sandra and Dunn, Judy (1987), *MotherCare/OtherCare*, Pelican Books, London.

Segal, Hanna (1991), *Dream, Phantasy and Art*, Tavistock/Routledge, London.

Segal, Lynne (ed.) (1983), *What Is To Be Done about The Family?* Penguin, London.

—— (1987), *Is the Future Female? Troubled Thoughts on Contemporary Feminism*, Virago, London.

—— (1988), 'Look Back in Anger. Men in the Fifties', in *Male Order. Unwrapping Masculinity*, (eds) Rowena Chapman and Jonathan Rutherford, Lawrence and Wishart, London.

—— (1990), *Slow Motion Changing Masculinities Changing Men*, Virago, London.

Seidler, Vic (1979), 'Men and Feminism', *Achilles Heel*, No. 2.

—— (1980), 'Raging Bull', *Achilles Heel*, No. 5.

—— (1985), 'Fear and Intimacy' in *The Sexuality of Men*, (eds) Andy Metcalf and Martin Humphries, Pluto Press, London.

—— (1987), 'Reason, Desire and Male Sexuality', in *The Cultural Construction of Sexuality*, ed. Pat Caplan, Tavistock, London.

—— (1989), *Rediscovering Masculinity*, Routledge, London.

Silverman, Kaja (1988), 'Masochism and Male Subjectivity', *Camera Obscura*, No. 17.

Smith, Gavin (1987), 'The Crisis of Fatherhood', *Free Associations*, No. 9.

Somerville, Jennifer (1989), 'The Sexuality of Men and the Sociology of Gender', *Sociological Review*, Vol. 37, No. 2.

Stoltenburg, John (1990), *Refusing to be a Man*, Fontana, London.

Taylor, C. (1975), *Hegel*, Cambridge University Press, Cambridge.

Tolson, Andrew (1985), *The Limits to Masculinity*, Tavistock, London.

Williams, Raymond (1977), *Marxism and Literature*, Oxford University Press, Oxford.

—— (1979), *Politics and Letters Interviews with New Left Review*, Verso, London.

Winnicott D.W. (1958), 'The Capacity To Be Alone', in *The Maturational Processes and the Facilitating Environment: Studies in the Theory of Emotional Development* (1965), Hogarth Press, London.

—— (1960), 'Ego Distortion in Terms of True and False Self' in *The Maturational Processes and the Facilitating Environment: Studies in the Theory of Emotional Development* (1965), Hogarth Press, London.

—— (1977(1988)), 'Fear of Breakdown' in *The British School of Psychoanalysis The Independent Tradition* (1988), ed. G. Kohon, Free Association Press, London.

—— (1986), *Holding and Interpretation: Fragment of an Analysis*, Hogarth Press, London.

—— (1988), *Playing and Reality*, Pelican, London.

Wittgenstein, L. (1961), *Tractatus Logico-Philosophicus*, Routledge and Kegan Paul, London.

—— (1981), *Zettel*, eds G. Anscombe and G. von Wright, Blackwell, London.

—— (1988), *Philosophical Investigations*, Blackwell, London.

Wright, Eric Olin (1985), *Classes*, Verso, London.

Wright, Patrick (1979), *On Living in an Old Country*, Verso, London.

Young, Shelagh (1988), 'Feminism and the Politics of Power Whose Gaze is it Anyway?' in *The Female Gaze*, eds Lorraine Gammon and Margaret Marshment, The Women's Press, London.

INDEX

abjection 159–62, 180–1
absence: of father 35–7, 116, 136, 138–9, 176–7; of mother 93–7, 98–100, 105–11, 124–5, 151–2, 159–62
Achilles Heel 7, 31–2, 57, 60, 74
advertisements: men in 64, 65, 125–7
affective relations *see* feelings
Alice in the Cities (film) 131–4
Althusser, L. 29, 75
Anti-Sexist Men's Newsletter 58, 59–60
anxiety 50, 105–9; displaced by nostalgia 127; *see also* trauma
Arena 66
Atkinson, P. 10, 30
authority: of fathers 18, 35, 176–7; of men 41–2
autism 190–1

bad father 144–5, 151, 153–8, 166–7, 168–70, 171–2
Baker, P. 70–1
Balint, M. 34
Bauman, Z. 5
Bellow, S. 129–30
Benjamin, W. 2
Bick, E. 188–9
binarism 76–8
Bion, W. 98–9, 100
bi-triangulation 118
Blendis, J. 19
body, performative 186–91

Bollas, C. 96, 97, 109, 157
borders of identity 74–80, 105
boundaries: of ego 165–6, 188–91
Bowlby, J. 22
Braidotti, R. 3
Brothers Against Sexism 6
Burgess, A. 176
Burgin, V. 82

capitalism 35–6, 116
castrating father 144–5, 151, 153–8, 166–7, 168–70, 171–2
castration 112–13
categorical theory 73–4
childcare 17, 18–19, 64
Chodorow, Nancy 79, 84, 116; object relations theory 32–40
class: difference 46, 72–86, 125–7; and lack of paternal authority 176–7; of Men Against Sexism members 3–4
Cockburn, C. 74
co-counselling 59–60
Connell, R.W. 73
consciousness: in children 53; and language 90–1
consumerism 63–8
containment 188–91; of infant dread 99–100, 107
Cosmo Man 65, 67
cruelty 179
cultural capital 3–4
cultural studies 197; rise of 31
culture: exclusion from 178–80,

181–6; and male sexuality 4–5; and masculinity 63–8; and violence 173–7

Dead Poets Society (film) 152–72
Dean, G. 67
death instinct 50, 128
dependence 40–1, 42
depressive position 51, 94, 101–2, 123–5, 192
Derrida, J. 76
desire, heterosexual 43–4
difference: of men 72–86; and nostalgia 125–7; and politics 46–7; and psychoanalysis 80–6; sexual 147–9
domesticity 10–11, 15, 18–19, 64
double: of maternal object 160–7
Durcan, P. 18

ego: and boundaries 165–6, 188–91; death 172; loss 124–5; premature development of 107–8; see also infants, psychic development
Ehrenreich, B. 21–2
Eichenbaum, L. 40–1
Elle 67
Elle Pour Homme 66, 125–7
emotion see feelings
English, D. 21–2
epistemophilic impulse 120
experience: politics of 45–8

Fairbairn, R.D. 34, 42–3
Falklands War 175–6, 177
false self 108–9, 110–11
family: effect of capitalism 35, 116; and gender identity 12–24; kinds of 197–8; lack of paternal authority 176–7; see also fathers; infants; mothers
fantasies: and reality 185–6; sexual 43, 71; of violence 180, 193
fate 170–2
fathers: absence of 35–7, 116, 136, 138–9, 176–7; authority of 18, 35, 176–7; in Freud 111–16,

144–6, 149–51, 152, 166–7, 168–9; in Lacan 145–9; and language acquisition 95–6; and love 143–73; and masculinity 13–19, 21, 116–22, 136–7; and narcissism 182–5; and paranoia 184–5; and thirdness 149–53; and threat of the mother 158–62; see also infants; oedipus complex
feelings: feminine, in men 70–1; lack of 6–7, 8–11; in language games 89–90; structures of 11–26
feminism 197; and difference 74; in Men Against Sexism 4–11, 57–60; object relations theory 32–41; and pornography 68; and psychoanalysis 83
films: masculinity in 15–16; violence in 173–4, 177–92
financiers: aggression of 174–5
First Blood (film) 177–86, 189
Flax, J. 54, 83, 114, 115–16
folk tales 132–3
football violence 175, 176, 177
Ford, A. 14
Foucault, M. 72
Freud, S. 95, 96–7, 104–5, 139; and death 128, 172; fathers in 144–6, 166, 149–51, 152, 166–7, 168–9; heterosexual desire 43–4; narcissism 54–5, 182–4, 170–1; oedipus complex 111–16, 133–4; paranoia 183–6; pleasure principle 33, 93–4; and psychic development 49, 50, 124, 165, 188; theory of the unconscious 53; uncanny 159, 160, 163–4
frontiers: of identity 74–80, 105

gender difference 46, 72–86, 125–7
gender identity: and the family 12–24; in object relations theory 32–40; and oedipus complex 111–22; see also masculinity

good enough mother 22, 107
good father 144, 151, 153–8,
    166–7, 168–70, 171–2
good mother: loss of 130–1;
    search for 131–42
Green, A. 100, 190, 192–3, 196;
    on fathers 118, 151; language
    104; third space 111, 115, 116

Hearn, J. 60
Hegel, G. 46–7
hero, male 15, 129–30; violence of
    173–94
heterosexuality, male 40–5; and
    pornography 41–3, 47–8,
    68–72; splitting of 137–8,
    139–42, 162–7; and violence
    191–4; see also oedipus complex
historicity 123–5
holding environment 101–2
Hollway, W. 42, 43, 44
homosexuality 167–70, 184–5
Horkheimer, M. 35
horror 158–9, 161–2
humanities: decline of 31
humiliation 177–81, 193–4
Humphries, M. 32
Hungerford Massacre 174, 193–4,
    195–6

identity: frontiers of 74–80, 105;
    masculine see masculinity
Ignatieff, M. 129–30
impotence 44
individuation 49–53, 93–111;
    failure of 105–11
infants: absence of father 35–7,
    116, 136, 138–9, 176–7;
    absence of mother 93–7,
    98–100, 105–11, 124–5, 151–2,
    159–62; depressive position 51,
    94, 101–2, 123–5, 192; gender
    identity 12–24, 32–40, 111–22;
    individuation 49–53; language
    acquisition 93–111; mourning
    and loss 123–5; paranoid-
    schizoid position 51, 93, 98,
    159, 181, 185; psychic
    development 22–4, 81, 181,

188–91; symbol formation
    94–8; trauma 106–11; see also
    fathers; mothers; narcissism;
    oedipus complex
instincts 34, 104–5
introjection 51, 93

Jardine, A. 77, 129, 130–1
Jeffords, S. 173, 174
Jordan, J. 12
jouissance 165–7

K 98–9, 149, 151–2, 196–7; failure
    of 108–9
Kelly, M. 82
Kelsey, L. 65
Klein, Melanie 34, 120, 196–7;
    depressive position 51, 94,
    101–2, 123–5, 192; father in
    146–7; infant development 22,
    49–53, 114, 124;
    paranoid-schizoid position 51,
    93, 98, 159, 181, 185
Kristeva, J. 159–61

Lacan, J. 29, 95, 161, 162; father
    in 145–9; jouissance 165–7;
    sexual difference theory 80–6
Laclau, E. 74–6, 79, 87–8
Laing, R.D. 23
language: and feeling 9–26; and
    predicaments 97–100, 104–22;
    replaced by performative body
    177–8, 179–80, 186, 189; and
    structuralism 28–31; and
    symbolism 52, 94–100; and
    third space 100–4
language games 88–92
Lauretis, T. de 81
linguistics, structural 28–31, 75–7,
    81
Lloyd, D. 64
logocentrism 76–7
loss: and mourning 123–5;
    transitional 176–7; see also
    nostalgia
love 196–7; failure of 139–42;
    paternal 143–73
Lyotard, J.F. 3

magazines: men in 65–7
marxism 35, 45–7
Men Against Sexism (MAS) 120,
  195; background 1–11; demise
  of 61–2; and difference 72–3;
  and morality 53–60; and object
  relations theory 41–5; and
  politics of experience 45–8; and
  psychoanalysis 27–32;
  relationship with parents
  12–24; and structures of feeling
  11–26
masculinity: cultural politics of
  63–8; and difference 72–86;
  and fathers 143–72; and
  language 87–122; and nostalgia
  123–42; sexual politics of
  27–62; and violence 177–91; see
  also fathers; heterosexuality;
  homosexuality; Men Against
  Sexism
masochism 168–70
maternal deprivation 22–3; see also
  absence
media: male image in 15–16,
  64–7, 125–7; and violence
  173–92
men see fathers; heterosexuality;
  homosexuality; Men Against
  Sexism; masculinity
men's liberation: and MAS 4–11,
  57–60
Mercer, K. 72–3
Metcalf, A. 6, 32, 45
Michals, D. 143
Middleton, P. 12, 83
Mitchell, J. 113
Mitscherlich, A. 35
morality: and pornography
  68–72; and psychoanalysis
  48–57; sexual 57–60
Morgan, A. 67
Morgan, P. 176
Mort, F. 63
mothering: role of women 21–3,
  35–7
mothers: absence of 93–7, 98–100,
  105–11, 124–5, 151–2, 159–62;
  and language acquisition

93–111; loss of good 130–42;
  and male sexuality 41–5; and
  masculinity 19–24, 35–7,
  116–22, 195–6; and narcissism
  192–3; and prostitutes 137–8,
  139–42, 163–6; and thirdness
  149–53; threat of 158–62,
  180–1; and violence 193–4,
  196; see also infants; oedipus
  complex
Mouffe, C. 74–6, 79, 87–8
mourning 51, 123–5
Moye, A. 41–5, 47–8

narcissism 54–5, 83, 182–4,
  190–1; primary 170–1, 192–3
narrative structure 132–4, 180–1
nationalism: and violence 175–6,
  187
Neale, S. 83
newspapers: on violence 175–6
nostalgia 123–42; and difference
  125–7; and predicaments
  128–42

O'Hagen, K. 65
object relations theory 32–40,
  100–1; and MAS 41–5
objects: good and bad 117–18;
  loss of 123–5; notion of 34
objet à 161, 162
oedipus complex 32–3, 130,
  133–4, 144–9; classic 111–16;
  and language acquisition 95–6;
  revised 116–22
Options 67
Orbach, S. 40–1
Osborne, J. 15–16
overdeterminism 75, 88

paranoia 49, 183–6
paranoid-schizoid position 51, 93,
  98, 159, 181, 185
Paris Texas (film) 134–42
Parsons, Talbot 35, 38, 39
Partridge, M. 65
paternal narrative 122, 129–31
performative body 186–91
phallus, symbol of 83–4, 146–9

Phillips, A. 64
play 102–4
pleasure principle 33, 93–4, 165
plenitude, symbol of 146–7
politics, sexual: and Men Against
    Sexism 1–26, 45–62; and
    psychoanalysis 27–44
pornography 41–3, 47–8, 68–72
post-structuralism 30
predicaments 97–100, 104–11; of
    masculinity 111–22; and
    nostalgia 128–42; paternal
    167–70
pretended families 197, 198
primitive agonies 106–8
private and public spheres 8–12,
    14–15, 17–19
projection 50–2, 93, 98, 185
Propp, V.I. 132–3
prostitutes: women as 137–8,
    139–42, 163–6
psyche see infants, psychic
    development
psyche-soma 33–4
psychoanalysis: and difference
    80–6; and language 92–7; and
    morality 48–57; and sexual
    politics 27–62; and sociology
    37–40
psychosis 49

race: and lack of paternal
    authority 176–7; differences 46,
    72–86, 125–7, 178–80
Rambo: First Blood Part II (film)
    186–92
Rambo III 187
reality: and fantasy 185–6
Red Therapy 27, 28, 59
reflexivity 196; in MAS 4–11,
    57–60; see also masculinity
reverie 98
Romanticism 46–7, 53–4
Roper, M. 195
Rorty, R. 54, 179
Rustin, M. 48–9, 52–3
Ryan, Michael 174, 193–4, 195–6
Ryan, T. 41

Saussure, F. de 29, 75–6
Schiller, J. 114–15
Segal, H. 97–8, 99
Segal, L. 15
Seidler, V. 9, 30, 45, 56
self-disclosure 71–2
separation: failure of 105–11; of
    infants and mothers 49–53,
    93–111
sexual difference theory 81–6
sexuality: female 137–8, 147–9,
    163–6; male see heterosexuality;
    homosexuality
Sexuality of Men, The 57, 58, 73,
    79; on feelings 48; and morality
    55, 56; and psychoanalysis 45;
    themes of 32, 41
Short, Clare 68
silence 2, 90–1, 136, 179–80, 186;
    of predicaments 104–11; on
    mothers 19–21; see also
    language; predicaments
Silverman, K. 169
skin: as boundary 188–91
sociology: and object relations
    theory 34–5; and
    psychoanalysis 37–40
Somerville, J. 32, 45
Spivak, G.C. 1
splitting 50–2, 185
Spock, B. 17
Stoltenburg, J. 68–9
structuralism: in language 28–31,
    81
super-ego 95–6, 112; see also
    infants, psychic development
Symbolic 81
symbolic equation 97–8, 128
symbolic representation 97
symbols, formation of 52, 94–100

Taylor, S. 66
Thatcherism 174–5
third space 100–4; collapse of
    105–11
thirdness 149–72, 184–6
thought: and language 90; see also
    K
Tolson, A. 9–10

Tosh, J. 195
transformational object 96–7
transgressions: suppression of 197
transitional objects 103–4;
    collapse of 105–11
trauma 106–11
Tustin, F. 190–1

UK: violence in 174–7
US: violent films 173–4, 177–92
uncanny 159, 163–4
unconscious: theory of 53

Van Ackerman, M. 66
Vietnam War 173–4, 186–7
violence 197; cultural context in
    1980s 173–7; and male
    heterosexuality 191–4; and
    masculine identities 177–91;
    towards women 162–3

Weir, P.: *Dead Poets Society* 152–72
Wenders, W.: *Alice in the Cities*
    131–4; *Paris Texas* 134–42
Wetzel, K. 138
Whitman, W.: *O Captain! My
    Captain!* 154–7
Williams, R. 11–12, 25–6
Wilson, A.N. 174, 175, 193
Winnicott, D.W. 22, 134, 198;
    good enough mother 105–8;
    third space 101–4
Wittgenstein, L. 1; and language
    88–92
women: and binary difference
    77–8; as mothers or prostitutes
    137–8, 139–42, 163–6; *see also*
    mothers
women's liberation *see* feminism
Women's Therapy Centre 40